The Rise of
Nazi Germany

Other Books in the Turning Points Series:

Turning Points

IN WORLD HISTORY

The Rise of Nazi Germany

Don Nardo, *Book Editor*

David L. Bender, *Publisher*
Bruno Leone, *Executive Editor*
Bonnie Szumski, *Series Editor*

Greenhaven Press, Inc., San Diego, California

Every effort has been made to trace the owners of copyrighted material. The articles in this volume may have been edited for content, length, and/or reading level. The titles have been changed to enhance the editorial purpose.

No part of this book may be reproduced or used in any form or by any means, electrical, mechanical, or otherwise, including, but not limited to, photocopy, recording, or any information storage and retrieval system, without prior written permission from the publisher.

Library of Congress Cataloging-in-Publication Data

The rise of Nazi Germany / Don Nardo, book editor.
    p.   cm. — (Turning points in world history)
    Includes bibliographical references and index.
    ISBN 1-56510-965-1 (lib. bdg. : alk. paper). —
ISBN 1-56510-964-3 (pbk. : alk. paper)
    1. Germany—Politics and government—1933–1945. 2. National socialism. 3. Jews—Persecutions—Germany. 4. Hitler, Adolf, 1889–1945. 5. Germany—Economic conditions—1918–1933. 6. Germany—Social conditions—1918–1933. I. Nardo, Don, 1947–   . II. Series: Turning points in world history (Greenhaven Press)
DD256.5.R5276 1999
943.086—dc21   98-8404
                                                                   CIP

Cover photo: Library of Congress

©1999 by Greenhaven Press, Inc.
P.O. Box 289009, San Diego, CA 92198-9009

Printed in the U.S.A.

Contents

Chapter 1: The Causes of the Rise of Nazi Germany

in the early 1920s as runaway inflation caused money to become nearly worthless.

Chapter 2: The Birth and Early Growth of the Nazi Party

Chapter 3: Hitler Comes to Power

After the Nazi takeover, the German people no longer had access to reliable, truthful information. Under Joseph Goebbels, propaganda minister of the Third Reich, the Nazis tightly regulated mass communications, including radio, press, and films, in an attempt to control and shape people's views and ideas.

Chapter 5: Nazi Germany Threatens the World

the rest of Europe. In time, however, the Allies, led by Britain, the United States, and the Soviet Union, turned the tide against Hitler's war machine. In 1945, the führer and his universally hated regime met their doom in the blood-soaked rubble of Berlin.

Foreword

Certain past events stand out as pivotal, as having effects and outcomes that change the course of history. These events are often referred to as turning points. Historian Louis L. Snyder provides this useful definition:

> A turning point in history is an event, happening, or stage which thrusts the course of historical development into a different direction. By definition a turning point is a great event, but it is even more—a great event with the explosive impact of altering the trend of man's life on the planet.

History's turning points have taken many forms. Some were single, brief, and shattering events with immediate and obvious impact. The invasion of Britain by William the Conqueror in 1066, for example, swiftly transformed that land's political and social institutions and paved the way for the rise of the modern English nation. By contrast, other single events were deemed of minor significance when they occurred, only later recognized as turning points. The assassination of a little-known European nobleman, Archduke Franz Ferdinand, on June 28, 1914, in the Bosnian town of Sarajevo was such an event; only after it touched off a chain reaction of political-military crises that escalated into the global conflict known as World War I did the murder's true significance become evident.

Other crucial turning points occurred not in terms of a few hours, days, months, or even years, but instead as evolutionary developments spanning decades or even centuries. One of the most pivotal turning points in human history, for instance—the development of agriculture, which replaced nomadic hunter-gatherer societies with more permanent settlements—occurred over the course of many generations. Still other great turning points were neither events nor developments, but rather revolutionary new inventions and innovations that significantly altered social customs and ideas, military tactics, home life, the spread of knowledge, and the human condition in general. The developments of writing, gunpowder, the printing press, antibiotics, the electric light, atomic energy, television, and the computer, the last two of which have recently ushered in the world-altering information age, represent only some of these innovative turning points.

Each anthology in the Greenhaven Turning Points in World History series presents a group of essays chosen for their accessibility. The anthology's structure also enhances this accessibility. First, an introductory essay provides a general overview of the principal events and figures involved, placing the topic in its historical context. The essays that follow explore various aspects in more detail, some targeting political trends and consequences, others social, literary, cultural, and/or technological ramifications, and still others pivotal leaders and other influential figures. To aid the reader in choosing the material of immediate interest or need, each essay is introduced by a concise summary of the contributing writer's main themes and insights.

In addition, each volume contains extensive research tools, including a collection of excerpts from primary source documents pertaining to the historical events and figures under discussion. In the anthology on the French Revolution, for example, readers can examine the works of Rousseau, Voltaire, and other writers and thinkers whose championing of human rights helped fuel the French people's growing desire for liberty; the French *Declaration of the Rights of Man and Citizen*, presented to King Louis XVI by the French National Assembly on October 2, 1789; and eyewitness accounts of the attack on the royal palace and the horrors of the Reign of Terror. To guide students interested in pursuing further research on the subject, each volume features an extensive bibliography, which for easy access has been divided into separate sections by topic. Finally, a comprehensive index allows readers to scan and locate content efficiently. Each of the anthologies in the Greenhaven Turning Points in World History series provides students with a complete, detailed, and enlightening examination of a crucial historical watershed.

Introduction: Adolf Hitler and the Rise of Nazi Germany

For the man whom the world has come to view as history's most infamous villain, the end came at 3:30 P.M. on Monday, April 30, 1945, in a concrete bunker deep beneath the streets of Berlin, the German capital. Realizing that American and Soviet armies were fast closing in on the city, fifty-six-year-old Adolf Hitler, dictator of Germany, placed a revolver in his mouth and pulled the trigger. His body fell beside that of Eva Braun, his longtime mistress, whom he had married the day before. She had just poisoned herself, preferring death to a life without Hitler and his vision of a Nazi-dominated world.

In the following few days, German armies surrendered all over Europe, thus ending both World War II in Europe and Hitler's Third Reich, the empire he had prophesied would last a thousand years. During the reich's tumultuous twelve years of existence, he had promised to elevate Germany to eternal glory, but the Nazi reign had instead brought the nation and much of the rest of Europe untold devastation and misery. Berlin and other German cities lay in ruins and some 7 million German soldiers and civilians lay dead. Almost 6 million Jews had been exterminated in Nazi death camps during the war. And added to these gruesome figures were the deaths of other Europeans and Americans, bringing the overall toll in Europe to a staggering 40 million.

Clearly, the ordeal that Europe and the world had endured between 1939 and 1945 had been the largest single conflict, with the most far-reaching consequences, of any in history. In large degree, the war had been caused by Nazi Germany's naked aggression and expansion in the late 1930s. And Nazi Germany was largely Hitler's creation. In a sense, then, the twisted dreams of one man ended up shattering those of millions of people and forever transforming the borders, goals, and fortunes of dozens of nations. As the renowned modern historian John Toland writes:

Adolf Hitler was probably the greatest mover and shaker of the twentieth century. Certainly no other human disrupted so many lives in our times or stirred so much hatred. He also inspired widespread adoration and was the hope and ideal of millions. . . . To the few who remained his faithful followers he is a hero, a fallen Messiah; to the rest he is still a madman, a political and military bungler, an evil murderer beyond redemption whose successes were reached by criminal means.[1]

Because Hitler and his Nazi regime ended up affecting the lives and futures of so many nations and peoples, the rise of Nazi Germany to the status of Europe's dominant state by the late 1930s marks one of history's greatest turning points.

Fascinated by Germany's "Glorious" Past

The question most often asked about Hitler and Nazi Germany is: How could such an unbalanced and dangerous individual rise to a position of such tremendous power and influence in a supposedly civilized modern country? Historians agree that there is no easy answer to this question. Many and diverse factors contributed to the rise of Nazism, some of them military and political, others economic and social, and still others driven by the beliefs, whims, and activities of specific groups and individuals. An examination of Hitler's years as a student and young man reveals how such factors shaped his thinking and ultimately made his agenda appealing to large numbers of Germans.

Hitler was born on April 20, 1889, in the small Austrian town of Braunau am Inn. As he grew older, he, like many of his countrymen, came to identify strongly with Austria's German roots. In medieval and early modern times, Austria and other German regions had been united under the noble House of Habsburg as the Holy Roman Empire, one of the strongest states in Europe. In 1871, the powerful German region of Prussia established a new German union that excluded Austria; however, World War I witnessed the emergence of a German-Austrian alliance. When this alliance was defeated by France, Britain, and the United States in 1918, the victors, known as the Allies, forbade Austria from reuniting with Germany, which angered many Germans and Austrians, including Hitler. "Today it seems providential that Fate should have chosen Braunau am Inn as my birthplace," he wrote in 1923, at age thirty-four.

> For this little town lies on the boundary between two German states which we of the younger generation . . . have made it our life's work to reunite by every means at our disposal. German-Austria must return to the great German mother country. . . . One blood demands one Reich. . . . Their sword will become our plow, and from the tears of war the daily bread of future generations will grow. And so this little city on the border seems to me the symbol of a great mission.[2]

Fascinated and inspired by the glories of Germany's past, Hitler liked reading about mythical German heroes. Especially appealing to him were the tall, blond Teutonic knights and gods of old, the so-called Aryans, characters portrayed with dramatic flair in the operas of nineteenth-century German composer Richard Wagner (pronounced VOG-ner). Short, with dark hair, Hitler realized that he did not look like the ideal Aryan. Yet he fancied himself a member of that fanciful, superior race.

In school, Hitler was not a good student. He was argumentative and placed most of the blame for his poor grades on his teachers, an excuse he clung to throughout his life. "When I recall my teachers at school," he stated in 1942, "I realize that half of them were abnormal. . . . The majority of them were somewhat mentally deranged."[3] This tendency to shift the blame became one of Hitler's hallmarks. Just as it was supposedly his teachers' fault that he did poorly in school, he later held that Germany's troubles in the years before he took power were not the fault of Germans, but of "enemies" in their midst, particularly Jews and communists.

Hitler the Drifter and Soldier

When he was sixteen, Hitler dropped out of school and for three years roamed about aimlessly, occasionally trying his hand at painting. Finally deciding he needed formal art training, in 1908, at age nineteen, he journeyed to Austria's capital, Vienna, in hopes of enrolling in the prestigious Arts Academy. Because of the poor quality of his sketches, however, the school rejected his application. In the four years that followed, he barely made a living working as a laborer and painting cheap postcards. Poor and homeless, he spent much of his time reading German history and anti-Semitic literature. Thanks to constant exposure to the latter, he developed an irrational fear and intense hatred of Jews, as shown in this excerpt from his earliest known anti-Semitic writing, which characterizes Jews in racial rather than religious terms:

> Through a thousand years of inbreeding, often practiced within a very narrow circle, the Jew has in general preserved his race . . . much more rigorously than many of the peoples among whom he lives. And as a result, there is living amongst us a non-German, foreign race, unwilling and unable to sacrifice its racial characteristics. . . . [The Jew's] weapon is that public opinion which is never given utterance by the press, but is always led by it and falsified by it. . . . Everything which makes men strive for higher things, whether religion, socialism, or democracy, is for him only a means to an end, to the satisfaction of a lust for money and domination. His activities produce a racial tuberculosis among nations.[4]

Ironically, many of the shelters and soup kitchens that Hitler availed himself of in his homeless days were founded and supported by a German Jew. And the young homeless man received his only warm coat from a Jewish clothes merchant who took pity on him.

Unhappy in Vienna, Hitler moved to Munich, in southern Germany, in 1912. There, he continued to drift about, working as a carpenter and poster painter until the outbreak of World War I in 1914, at which time he enlisted in the German army infantry. In his four years in the military, he served as a message carrier and fought on the western front against the British. Temporarily blinded by poison gas during a battle, he was hospitalized for shell shock and fatigue and eventually received two medals for bravery. A comrade later described how Hitler, a loner who never asked for or went on leave, would often sit "in the corner of our mess [platoon] holding his head between his hands, in deep contemplation." Without warning, he would "leap up and, running about excitedly, say that in spite of our big guns victory would be denied us," because Germany's "invisible foes" posed a greater danger than the enemy.[5] Then he would launch into a tirade about these foes, namely the "degenerate" Jews and communists.

Germany Stabbed in the Back?

When Germany lost the war, as Hitler had worried it would, he was extremely bitter, a feeling he shared with most Germans. Humiliated, Germany was forced to sign the Treaty of Versailles in early 1919, which officially brought the conflict to a close and imposed very harsh penalties on Germany. The country had to cede some of its best industrial territories to the victors, pay huge reparations (moneys to compensate for the damages suffered by its opponents), and overall lost much power and prestige. The traumatic effect the loss of the war had on the German people cannot be overstressed. As historian Crane Brinton explains:

> For the overwhelming majority of the German people, defeat in 1918 came as a great shock. The military authorities who ran the German Empire during the last years of the war had failed to report to the public German reverses on the battlefield. No fighting had ever taken place on German soil, and the Germans had got used to thinking of their armies as in firm possession of the foreign territories they had overrun. . . . Schooled in reverence for their military forces, the Germans could not grasp the fact that their armies had lost the war.[6]

Moreover, the harsh fact that German leaders had ordered their forces to surrender because they were no longer in any shape to fight was never effectively publicized in Germany. So the legend quickly grew that civilians at home, principally liberal politicians, communists, and Jews, had somehow betrayed the nation. This so-called "stab in the back" soon became an article of faith among Germans of all walks of life, and it is therefore not surprising that so many of them later agreed with Hitler's denunciations of those who had supposedly sold the country out. "The German people wanted simple answers to their questions and simple solutions to their problems," wrote the late Princeton University scholar Erich Kahler. "Hitler gave them what they wanted. . . . He told his audiences that the Jews, the socialists, the bankers, and the Allies were responsible for Germany's woes. . . . He told the people what they wanted to hear, and he told it to them with remarkable effect."[7]

The Birth of Nazism

While the "stab in the back" was only imaginary, the Germans faced some very real and serious problems in the years immediately following the great war. In November 1918, with total defeat imminent, the leaders of the German Social Democratic Party had proclaimed the country a republic, which became known as the Weimar Republic after the town in which they drew up its constitution. William (or Wilhelm) II, the former kaiser, or emperor, soon afterward left the country and abdicated; this opened the way for Germany to join the United States, Britain, and other great and prosperous modern democracies.

But the economic hardships Germany faced in the wake of the war made prosperity, at least for the foreseeable future, an impossible dream. The heavy war reparations imposed by the Allies, combined with the country's already huge debts and the fact that its paper money was not backed by gold, caused horrendous inflation. In 1923, at the height of the economic crisis, 1 billion marks (the mark was Germany's main unit of currency) were needed to equal the buying power of just one prewar mark! Money became worth so little that it required a large potato sack crammed with paper bills to purchase a pair of shoes. Not surprisingly, millions of people lost their jobs and life savings.

It was during these desperate years, as the Weimar government earnestly struggled to keep Germany from the brink of complete ruin, that Adolf Hitler began the political activities that would eventually lead him into the corridors of ultimate power. After war's end, Hitler returned to Munich. There he attended meetings of some of the many small political groups that wanted to rid the nation of the democracy they viewed as impotent and useless. One night in 1919, at a meeting in a run-down tavern, he found himself drawn to one of these groups, the German Workers' Party. Later, he wrote how "the conviction grew in me that through just such a little movement the rise of the nation could some day be organized." After thinking it over for two days, he finally decided to join. "It was the most decisive resolve of my life. From here there was and could be no turning back. And so I registered as a member of the German Workers' Party and received a provisional membership card with the number 7."[8]

When the enthusiastic and diligent Hitler was appointed party propaganda officer, the group quickly became better organized and began drawing many new members. In April 1920, at his insistence, it changed its name to the National Socialist German Workers' Party, or NSDAP.[9] The term *Nazi* was a convenient abbreviation of the German words for National Socialist. By July 1921, when Hitler became the group's supreme leader, Nazi membership stood at about six thousand; in the next two years, aided in no small degree by the party's own right-wing newspaper, the *Munich Observer*, that number mushroomed to fifty-five thousand.

During this period, Hitler also established the *Sturmabteilung*, or "storm troopers," known more simply as the SA, basically strong-arm men who guarded him, patrolled party meetings, and carried out various acts of violence and intimidation at his orders. The storm troopers, led by Ernst Röhm, who had worked as a political adviser to local German infantry units, wore brown shirts (prompting their nickname, the "brownshirts") and carried weapons. Their armbands sported the new Nazi emblem, the swastika, a mystic symbol of ancient origin.[10] The symbol's four crooked arms supposedly indicated the four directions of the earth, implying world conquest, and also stood for the party's violent anti-Semitism. The party's flag (which eventually became Germany's flag) showed a black swastika in a white disk, the disk surrounded by a bright red background. "As

National Socialists, we see our program in our flag," Hitler later declared. "In *red* we see the social idea of the movement, in *white* the nationalistic idea, and in the *swastika* the mission of the struggle for the victory of the Aryan man . . . [which] has been and always will be anti-Semitic."[11] (The italics are Hitler's.)

Hitler's Ideas, Oratory, and First Bid for Power

Beyond this and other ambiguous references to "national struggles" against Jews, communists, and liberal democratic institutions, it is difficult to isolate and analyze Nazi doctrine, that is, its system of principles and beliefs. It is clear that from the beginning Hitler and his followers wanted to take over the national government. But aside from that tactical goal, as Kahler points out, National Socialism was based more on the use of force to get its way than on any clear-cut or original set of ideas.

> Although Nazism embodied principles that had long been at work in Western society, it certainly cannot be considered an ideological movement like socialism [or] communism. . . . Despite its ideological slogans proclaiming a new order in a new Europe, National Socialism never had the slightest awareness of its true function in human history. In and of itself it was nothing but a criminal conspiracy of national and international proportions. . . . Nazism did not hesitate to appropriate anything that could serve its purpose, perverting ideas and ideologies only to discard them when they had outlasted their usefulness. But National Socialism had no ideas or ideology of its own . . . or to put it another way, its ideological basis was pure hoax. The Nazi state did not operate on principle but on tactics. . . . The only lasting "principles" in the Nazi bag of tricks were racism, anti-Christianism, and anti-humanitarianism, all of which had permanent value as means of destroying the moral judgment of the population.[12]

Relying on this "bag of tricks," as an orator at the early Nazi Party meetings Hitler demonstrated his ability to hold an audience spellbound. Although wartime mustard gas had scarred his vocal cords, making his voice harsh and raspy, he possessed a natural charisma and emotional intensity that made people pay attention to him. Often when he spoke, he provoked extreme reactions. Sometimes, his audiences became so impassioned that fights erupted between his supporters and those who disliked his ideas. And such detractors were numerous, for his agenda and personal manner were so outrageous that at first many people laughed at him and refused to take him or the Nazis seriously. Some were sure that he was mentally unbalanced. One such observer was Friedrich Reck-Malleczewen, a well-to-do German businessman, who described meeting Hitler at the house of a friend in 1920:

A jelly-like, slag-gray face, a moon-face into which two melancholy jet-black eyes had been set like raisins. So sad, so unutterably insignificant, so basically misbegotten. . . . He had come to a house, where he had never been before, wearing gaiters [leather lower-leg coverings], a floppy, wide-brimmed hat, and carrying a riding whip. . . . Eventually, he managed to launch into a speech. He talked on and on, endlessly. He preached. He went on at us like a division Chaplain in the Army. We did not in the least contradict him, or venture to differ in any way, but he began to bellow at us. The servants thought we were being attacked, and rushed in to defend us. . . . When he had gone, we sat silently confused. . . . There was a feeling of dismay, as when on a train you suddenly find you are sharing a compartment with a psychotic. . . . It was not that an unclean body had been in the room, but something else: the unclean essence of a monstrosity.[13]

Reck-Malleczewen and others who did not take Hitler seriously were likely surprised when he made his first major bid for power late in 1923. On the night of November 8, some three thousand senior state officials and military men held a meeting at the Buergerbräukeller, a large beer hall on the southern outskirts of Munich. After Hitler's SA troops surrounded the building, he suddenly burst into the hall, jumped up on a table, and fired a pistol into the air. "The National Revolution has begun!" he shouted. Meanwhile, Röhm led other SA units in a takeover of Munich's army headquarters. But within a day their daring *putsch*, or coup, failed after senior army generals in Berlin ordered police and army personnel in the Munich area to suppress the Nazis. The authorities promptly arrested Hitler and dissolved the National Socialist Party. The führer (supreme leader), as he had come to call himself, went to trial in February 1924 and on April 1 received a sentence of five years in prison.

"My Struggle"

As it turned out, because Hitler was eligible for early parole he served only nine months of his sentence. These months constituted a pivotal period both for him and the German nation, for it was in his prison cell that he penned much of his famous volume, *Mein Kampf* ("My Struggle").[14] The book combines accounts of his life up to the time of the beer hall *putsch* with tracts outlining his political and anti-Semitic views and his own interpretations of German and world history. From a literary standpoint, the writing is unoriginal, pompous, repetitive, disorganized, and often inconsistent. Yet the volume sold many copies and became the gospel of Nazism. It also gave Hitler, whom so many people had laughed at in the past, a kind of pseudo-intellectual respectability in the eyes of the German public.

Most importantly, a number of the ideas Hitler discussed in the book appealed to millions of Germans who felt betrayed by the "stab in the back" and who were presently suffering from the economic ravages of the postwar inflation. Themes he harped on often included the Jews' "inferiority" and "dishonesty" and the "unfair" treatment of Germany by the Allies and international bankers. Particularly appealing to many Germans was Hitler's discussion of *Lebensraum*, or "living space," a theme that obsessed him for the rest of his life. In his view, Germany's future hinged on its forceful seizure of European lands, into which German settlers could expand, live comfortably, and propagate more "superior" Aryans. The most suitable territories, he said bluntly, were the Russian steppes, which must first be cleared of "inferior" peoples, among them the Slavs. "Let us be given soil we need for our livelihood," he wrote.

True, they [the displaced peoples] will not willingly do this. But then the law of self-preservation goes into effect; and what is refused to amicable methods, it is up to the fist to take. . . . If land was desired in Europe, it could be obtained, by and large, only at the expense of Russia, and this means that the new Reich must again set itself on the march along the road of the Teutonic Knights of old [who invaded Russia in the thirteenth century], to obtain by the German sword sod for the German plow and daily bread for the nation.[15]

Working Within the System

Although *Mein Kampf* touched a nerve with many Germans, its effect was far from revolutionary, and Hitler's public popularity and influence grew only gradually in the years following his release from prison. On the one hand, many Germans wanted to give the weak but still promising Weimar democracy a chance to prove itself. On the other, the Nazis' botched 1923 coup had shown Hitler that the strong-arm approach was, at least for the present, dangerous and unrealistic; to gain governmental power, he now realized, the newly reestablished National Socialists would have to work within the existing system as a legitimate political party.

At first, the Nazis fared poorly in national elections. In the 1928 election, for instance, they received less than 3 percent of the national vote. This was due largely to the fact that Weimar Germany underwent a period of increasing economic recovery in the late 1920s. However, the worldwide effects of the Great Depression initiated by the crash of the New York stock market in 1929 delivered the new German economy a sudden and catastrophic blow. Thrown back into bitterness and despair, the German people increasingly came to support right-wing parties that promised a quick fix for the nation's problems.

The results of the subsequent series of elections show how the strongest of these groups, Hitler's National Socialist Party, steadily gained appeal and electoral power. In the 1930 election for seats in the Reichstag, the German parliament, the Nazis received an impressive 18 percent of the vote, which translated into 107 seats. Two years later, the term of office of the country's weak and aged president, Paul von Hindenburg, expired, necessitating a presidential election.[16] Hitler, who emerged as Hindenburg's leading opponent, garnered 30 percent of the vote. Although Hindenburg beat him by a wide margin, no single candidate gained a clear majority, so a runoff election was held a month later; Hindenburg won again, but this time Hitler's share of the vote increased to almost 37 percent. In July 1932, Franz von Papen, the new chancellor (prime minister of the presidential cabinet, in charge of formulating national policies), called a new Reichstag election. He hoped that the Nazis would lose ground and therefore end up playing only a small role in the government. But to his surprise, the Nazis won 230 seats in the parliament, becoming the nation's largest single party. Hitler now demanded the chancellorship. Neither Hindenburg nor Papen wanted to see Hitler in that powerful office, but after much political intriguing and maneuvering by both sides, they came to believe that they could make him chancellor and then dominate and control him.

However, these politicians had sorely underestimated the Nazi leader. Immediately after Hindenburg appointed him chancellor on January 30, 1933, Hitler swiftly and ruthlessly initiated a series of moves designed to give him dictatorial powers. First, he temporarily dissolved the Reichstag and called for new elections. During the campaign, Nazi storm troopers intimidated and terrorized opposing candidates and denied them the use of radio and press. In the meantime, a communist agitator played right into Hitler's hands by setting fire to the Reichstag building. Fearing a rash of similar terrorist incidents, and urged on by Hitler, Hindenburg issued emergency decrees suspending free speech and press, which made it even easier for Nazi storm troopers to spread their own brand of terror. Although the Nazis did not achieve a majority of votes in the election, their 44 percent share was enough. When the new Reichstag convened on March 23, 1933, all non-Nazi members, under threat of retaliation by the SA, voted with the Nazis for the Enabling Act. This act suspended the Weimar constitution and conferred dictatorial powers on the government, thereby giving birth to the Third Reich.[17] Hitler's long struggle for ultimate power in Germany had at last been crowned with success.

The Nazis Transform Germany

Under the new Nazi dictatorship, Germany swiftly became a police state. The job of enforcing Nazi policies and maintaining control over the populace fell on an elite and "racially pure" force of honor guards, the SS (the *Schutzstaffel*, or "defense corps"), led by the ruthless Heinrich Himmler. Using a special branch of the SS, the Gestapo, or secret police, Himmler effectively used terror tactics to root out and often torture and kill those opposed to Nazism.

The power of the SS and its importance to Hitler inevitably put both on a collision course with Röhm's SA, which had grown extremely large and powerful. Many SA members expected to be handed prime positions of power in the reich in return for helping Hitler rise to power. When he did not so reward them, some became disgruntled, and Hitler, now seeing them as a threat to his new order, decided to eliminate them. On June 30, 1934, the führer himself led the "blood purge," the so-called Night of the Long Knives, in which as many as one thousand SA leaders, including Röhm, were arrested and executed. Years later, the warden of Munich's Stradelheim prison recalled how the once powerful Röhm met his end:

> Two SS men asked at the reception desk to be taken to Röhm. . . . [In the cell] they handed over a Browning [revolver] to Röhm, who once again asked to speak to Hitler. They ordered him to shoot himself. If he did not comply they would come back in ten minutes and kill him. . . . When the time was up, the two SS men reentered the cell, and found Röhm standing with his chest bared. Immediately one of them . . . shot him in the throat, and Röhm collapsed on the floor. Since he was still alive, he was killed with a shot point-blank through the temple.[18]

This naked display of treachery and murder was Röhm's reward for his many years of loyalty and friendship to Adolf Hitler.

Meanwhile, using similarly forceful means, the Nazis steadily transformed German society. Public demonstrations were banned. Schoolteachers had to teach Nazi principles and use history texts rewritten to conform to Hitler's distorted version of past events. At the same time, some 8 million boys and girls between the ages of ten and eighteen were ordered to join the Hitler Youth movement, which indoctrinated them with National Socialist ideals and instilled in them fanatical devotion for the "beloved führer." These young people were encouraged to spy on their own parents and report on the anti-Nazi views of their teachers and others. Both children and adults now regularly greeted each other with the Nazi salute (raising the right arm) and the expression "Heil Hitler!" (Hail Hitler!). The Reich Chamber of Culture, under propaganda minister Joseph Goebbels (pronounced GER-blz), tightly controlled and censored the press, radio, films, and other forms of communication. Goebbels also oversaw the distribution of a steady stream of anti-Semitic and anti-Christian propaganda and the burning of books deemed harmful to Nazism. Not surprisingly, some Christians and most Jews suffered discrimination, persecution, threats, and at times violent attacks.

Awaiting the Moment of Challenge

Hitler's persecution of Jews came as no surprise to most people, since years before in *Mein Kampf* he had clearly spelled out the need to "put the Jews in their place." With his achievement of total power over Germany, the rest of Europe now began to worry about other ominous statements contained in the Nazi Bible. Hitler had frankly discussed the inevitability of the *Anschluss*, the reunification of Germany and Austria; the need for German "living space" at the expense of the Russians and others; and the importance of getting revenge on France for the Versailles Treaty and other past humiliations. Many Europeans nervously asked: Would the German dictator now implement such policies and threaten his neighbors?

Their answer was not long in coming. In 1934, Germany initiated a large-scale program of military rearmament and expansion in violation of the Versailles Treaty, which had set limits on the size of its armed forces. And in 1936, Hitler and Italy's fascist (dictatorial) leader, Benito Mussolini, signed a pact, creating the so-called Berlin-Rome Axis. Some French, British, and American leaders recognized these events as the proverbial handwriting on the wall. British statesman Winston Churchill, for example, repeatedly warned that war with Germany and the Axis was inevitable if European politicians did not use diplomatic means to contain Hitler's ambitions. "Once Hitler's Germany had been allowed to rearm without active interference by the Allies," Churchill later wrote,

> a second World War was almost certain. The longer a decisive trial of strength was put off, the worse would be our chances, at first of stopping Hitler without serious fighting, and as a second stage of being victorious after a terrible ordeal. . . . Nazi Germany had secretly and unlawfully created a military air force which, by the spring of 1935, openly claimed to be equal to the British. . . . Great Britain and all Europe, and what was then thought distant America, were faced with the organized might and will-to-war of seventy millions of the most efficient race in Europe, longing to regain their national glory, and driven—in case they faltered—by a merciless military, social, and party regime. Hitler was now free to strike. . . . The Berlin-Rome Axis was in being. There was now, as it turned out, little hope of averting war or of postponing it by a trial of strength equivalent to war. Almost all that remained open to France and Britain was to await the moment of the challenge and do the best they could.[19]

Churchill's misgivings turned out to be well founded, although none of his colleagues acted as decisively as he hoped they would. Between 1935 and 1939, Allied leaders engaged in what later became known as a "policy of appeasement," in which they granted Hitler various concessions, in effect allowing him to get away with the seizure of neighboring lands. These aggressions included Austria and Czechoslovakia, which came under Nazi domination in 1938. In each case, the Allies hoped that Hitler would keep his promises and make no more territorial demands. Apparently they still

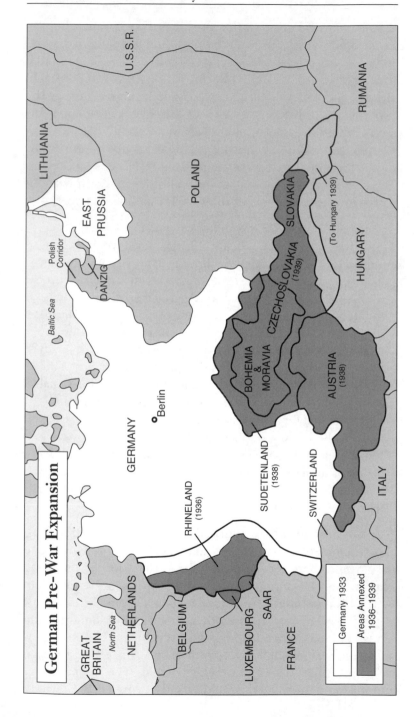

German Pre-War Expansion

GREAT BRITAIN

North Sea

NETHERLANDS

BELGIUM

LUXEMBOURG

SAAR

FRANCE

RHINELAND (1936)

GERMANY

Berlin

SUDETENLAND (1938)

SWITZERLAND

ITALY

Baltic Sea

LITHUANIA

EAST PRUSSIA

Polish Corridor

DANZIG

POLAND

U.S.S.R.

BOHEMIA & MORAVIA

CZECHOSLOVAKIA (1939)

SLOVAKIA

(To Hungary 1939)

HUNGARY

AUSTRIA (1938)

RUMANIA

Germany 1933	
Areas Annexed 1936–1939	

did not grasp that he actually meant to carry out the foreboding, violent plans he had outlined in *Mein Kampf*.

Poetic Justice?

Similarly, Soviet leader Joseph Stalin did not take Hitler's anti-Russian rhetoric seriously enough. Despite Hitler's earlier reference to the Soviets as the "scum of the earth," and Stalin's indictment of the Nazis as "bloody assassins of the workers," the two men stunned the world by signing a non-aggression pact in August 1939. According to historian Louis Snyder:

> The pact provided that the two parties would not resort to war against each other, would not support any third power in the event that it attacked either signatory, [and] would consult on all matters of common interest. . . . A secret protocol [clause] . . . divided eastern Europe into eventual German and Russian spheres, and each signatory was given territorial gains in the lands lying between them.[20]

Later, Hitler would turn on the Russians in order to implement his diabolical blueprint for *Lebensraum*. For the moment, however, his cynical, cold-blooded bargain with Stalin provided the Nazis with the means of launching full-scale war. One of the "lands lying between" Germany and Russia became the first battleground of that war when Hitler attacked Poland on September 1, 1939.

In a little less than twenty years, the Nazis had risen from obscurity to become a serious threat to global stability and human freedom. Within days following the German assault on Poland, most of the world's great powers were locked in a titanic death struggle that would end up killing tens of millions of people and disrupting and forever changing the lives of hundreds of millions more. Almost six long and bloody years later, the end would come with the capture of ruined Berlin by the Soviets and Americans.

Nothing could ever compensate for the mass death and misery Hitler and his Nazis had caused. But at least there was a small touch of poetic justice. In his final moments in that dismal underground bunker, as the Allied shells roared and pounded above him, the realization of a terrible truth must have filled him with rage and regret. The glorious reich he had vowed would last for a thousand years had rather pathetically missed the mark by 988 years.

Notes

1. John Toland, *Adolf Hitler.* Garden City, NY: Doubleday, 1976, p. xiii.

2. Adolf Hitler, *Mein Kampf*, trans. Ralph Manheim. Boston: Houghton Mifflin, 1971 (originally published in Germany in 1925–1926), p. 3.

3. Quoted in William L. Shirer, *The Rise and Fall of the Third Reich: A History of Nazi Germany.* Greenwich, CT: Fawcett, 1960, p. 29.

4. Quoted in Jeremy Noakes and Geoffrey Pridham, eds., *Documents on Nazism, 1919–1945.* New York: Viking Press, 1975, pp. 36–37. The idea that German Jews were not Germans, but were instead a separate and inferior race living inside Germany, was a product of Hitler's own ignorance and blind hatred. Jews had made up a small but important and productive minority of Germany's population for many centuries and considered themselves to be just as German as the nation's non-Jewish inhabitants.

5. Quoted in Shirer, *Rise and Fall of the Third Reich*, p. 54.

6. Crane Brinton et al., *A History of Civilization, 1815 to the Present.* Englewood Cliffs, NJ: Prentice-Hall, 1976, p. 759.

7. Erich Kahler, *The Germans.* Princeton, NJ: Princeton University Press, 1974, p. 280.

8. Hitler, *Mein Kampf*, pp. 223–24.

9. NSDAP stood for *National Sozialistische Deutsche Arbeiter Partei,* which translates into English as National Socialist German Workers' Party.

10. The swastika symbol has been found in the ruins of ancient Troy, in what is now Turkey, as well as among ancient Egyptian and Chinese artifacts. In modern times prior to Hitler's rise, the Baltic states of Estonia and Finland used it as a battle emblem. Various anti-Semitic German political groups then adopted it before Hitler made it nationally and internationally famous, or perhaps more properly, infamous.

11. Hitler, *Mein Kampf*, pp. 496–97.

12. Kahler, *The Germans*, pp. 277–78.

13. Quoted in Abraham Resnick, *The Holocaust.* San Diego: Lucent Books, 1991, p. 18.

14. Hitler originally titled the book *Four and a Half Years of Struggle Against Lies, Stupidity and Cowardice*, but his publisher informed him that such a long and ponderous title would not sell and insisted that he shorten it to the simpler and stronger *My Struggle.*

15. Hitler, *Mein Kampf*, pp. 138–40.

16. Under the Weimar Republic's constitution, the president served for seven years.

17. Hitler reckoned the medieval Germanic Holy Roman Empire as the First Reich and the German union forged in 1871 by Otto von Bismarck as the Second Reich. As leader of the so-called Third Reich, Hitler portrayed himself as the

successor to Germany's great past leaders and, for attacking the forces that had humiliated and destroyed the "glorious" Second Reich, the country's savior.

18. Quoted in Jeremy Noakes and Geoffrey Pridham, eds., *Nazism, 1919–1945, Vol. 1: The Rise to Power, 1919–1934, A Documentary Reader.* Exeter, Eng.: University of Exeter, 1983, p. 180.

19. Winston S. Churchill, *The Gathering Storm.* Boston: Houghton Mifflin, 1948, pp. 189–90.

20. Louis L. Snyder, *The War: A Concise History, 1939–1945.* New York: Dell, 1960, p. 91.

Chapter 1

The Causes of the Rise of Nazi Germany

Turning | Points

IN WORLD HISTORY

Lack of International Cooperation and Controls

Louis L. Snyder

One of the major factors that allowed Hitler and the Nazis to rise to power in Germany in the period between World Wars I and II was the atmosphere of animosity and distrust among the world's most powerful nations. Had they gotten along better, World War I might have been avoided, and Hitler would not have been able to exploit the trauma the Germans endured as a result of their war losses. In this concise essay, Louis L. Snyder, former professor of history at the City College of New York, describes the lack of effective international controls before World War I. He then shows how a major attempt to institute such controls, the League of Nations, ultimately failed, paving the way for the next great war.

[One] basic cause for both World Wars was the lack of effective machinery for regulating relations between nations. In their everyday life human beings found it expedient and necessary to use policemen to prevent asocial conduct. But what about the international scene? Here there was nothing to prevent a nation from going berserk as a result of its frustrating experiences.

The Need for International Law

In 1926, G. Lowes Dickinson, British essayist, published a significant book titled *International Anarchy, 1904–1913*, in which he recounted the selfish secret intrigues of all the

Reprinted with the permission of Simon & Schuster from *The War: A Concise History, 1939–1945*, by Louis L. Snyder. Copyright ©1960 by Louis L. Snyder.

Powers. This international anarchy culminated in World War I. "This much is true," Dickinson wrote, "that until men lay down their arms, and accept the method of peaceable decisions of their disputes, wars can never cease.". . .

In early modern times, the growth of commerce, the rise of national states, and frequent wars all combined to create the need for a legal code that would operate at a level above the laws of individual national states and restrict their irresponsible actions. Modern international law was systematized and popularized by a Dutchman, Hugo Grotius (1583–1645) in his *Law of War and Peace* (1625). Grotius held that international law embodies rules that each nation is morally required to obey, even if they could not be imposed by a superior force.

Considerable hope was aroused among reasonable men by the two international Peace Conferences organized by Czar Nicholas II of Russia . . . in 1899 and 1907. But little was done by the delegates to these meetings beyond passing resolutions calling for the promotion of international peace and for humane conduct of war, such as prohibiting poison gas, dum-dum bullets, or the launching of projectiles and explosives from balloons. Note the persistence of the idea of "the laws and customs of war." But the key problem was how to prevent sovereign states from going to war.

The League of Nations

World War I made it imperative that a global federation or world-state be formed to promote international accord. But how could international order be achieved on a scene marked by discontent of the defeated powers, disillusionment of the victors, and an America retreating into isolation? The League of Nations, brain-child of Jan Smuts, a South African leader, was offered as a solution.

From the beginning the League of Nations was the special project of [American] President [Woodrow] Wilson, who worked himself into the grave on its behalf. "The Covenant we offer," he said, "must be based primarily upon moral sanctions with resort to force only as a final means of action."

Wilson went to the Peace Conference at Versailles in 1919, the first American president to leave the United States during his term of office. The peoples of Europe welcomed him as if he were the Messiah, with cries that seemed to come from the heart of humanity. But the statesmen of Versailles denounced him as an impractical idealist who knew nothing of the realities of diplomacy. . . .

Wilson, his nerves shattered by the interminable bickering, was certain that the peoples of the world shared his hatred of war, militarism, and the old secret diplomacy. He did his best to purge the world of war through the instrument of the League of Nations. With great reluctance he even accepted some of the harsher terms of the Treaty of Versailles, the treaty of peace with Germany, in return for support of the League. He was successful in having the full Covenant of the League inserted into the Treaty of Versailles as the first of its 15 parts.

But once home, Wilson found himself embroiled in a battle with isolationist Republican senators who, among other reasons, resented having been left behind on the junket to Versailles. They viciously attacked the League. "The United States must not be trapped in foreign entanglements."

Wilson tirelessly traversed the country by railroad, literally begging the people for support. He warned that if we did not join the League there would certainly be another world war within another generation. After delivering his fortieth speech, at Pueblo, Colorado, he collapsed from nervous and physical exhaustion.

The abstention of the United States was a deadly blow to the League. In *Triumph and Tragedy* (Volume VI of his history of World War II), Winston Churchill states flatly that the League was ruined by the failure of the United States to take an active role. There were other contributing factors, such as the failure to include the defeated powers in the original membership list, the unwillingness of the major powers to disarm, and the survival of power diplomacy. But the League could not survive without American participation.

The League was able to dispose of several dozen minor disputes, most of them legacies of the war. Example—the dispute between Finland and Sweden over the Aaland Islands in the Gulf of Finland.

But observe that these were relatively minor quarrels. After 1931 came the major international disputes. The League failed to halt Japanese aggression in China, to check Italy in Ethiopia, or to handle the problems arising from the Spanish Civil War.

The Same Old Story

Still, despite its weaknesses, the League of Nations was the most promising institution as yet brought into existence to promote international understanding. A modest beachhead was established in the struggle to establish a world society with a formal constitution. With all its limitations, the first important step had been taken.

A Heritage of Suspicion and Bitterness

In this excerpt from his book Western Civilizations, *noted historian Edward M. Burns explains how, in the early years of the twentieth century, Europe was divided into hostile opposing camps. The nations making up these camps, including Germany, were those that would later wage both world wars.*

By 1907 the great powers of Europe had come to be arrayed in two opposing combinations, the Triple Alliance [Germany, Austria, and Italy] and the Triple Entente [Britain, France, and Russia]. Had these combinations remained stable and more or less evenly matched, they might well have promoted the cause of peace. But no such condition prevailed. Each grew weaker and less stable with the passage of time. The Triple Alliance declined in strength because of a growing coolness between Italy and Austria. Moreover, Italian nationalists coveted territory in North Africa, notably Tripoli, which they believed they could obtain only by supporting French ambitions in Morocco. Meanwhile, the Triple Entente was threatened by discord between Britain and Russia. Because their lifeline to the East might be imperiled, the British could not view with equanimity

The statesmen of the postwar era had learned little. Again they reverted to the futile behavior of the past in the search for security and disarmament. It was the same old story of combinations, treaties, *revanche* [revenge]. Germany and the Central Powers [name given to the alliance between Germany and Austria during World War I], defeated on the battlefields, were united in their desire to repudiate the peace settlements. The Western Powers feared the expansion of Bolshevism [Russian communism], while the Soviet Union was convinced the entire world wanted to destroy her. The French, even though counted among the triumphant Allies, were gripped by a feeling of insecurity. Britain persisted in an attempt to restore the old European balance of power, which would enable her to maintain a dominant position on the Continent. The United States,

---

the cardinal aim of Russia to "open the Straits" [the Bosporus, separating the Mediterranean and Black Seas] and gain control of Constantinople. Disharmony in the Triple Entente also increased when Britain and France refused to support Russia in her dispute with Austria over the latter's annexation of Bosnia and Herzegovina. In short, conflicts were so numerous that the members of neither alliance could be quite sure where their opposite numbers might stand in case of a real threat of a European war.

Between 1905 and 1913 five serious international crises endangered the peace of Europe. In a sense they were not so much causes as they were symptoms of international animosity. Yet each of them left a heritage of suspicion and bitterness that made war all the more probable. In some cases hostilities were averted only because one of the parties was too weak at the time to offer resistance. The result was a sense of humiliation, a smoldering resentment that was almost bound to burst into flame in the future.

Edward M. Burns, *Western Civilizations*. New York: W.W. Norton, 1973, pp. 759–60.

disgusted with the recurrent European crises, returned to isolation.

This was the soil of an uneasy Europe in which the dragon's teeth for the next war were being planted, soon to spring up as armed hordes. Many men saw it coming. Few could do anything about it.

The Myth of Germany's Betrayal Led to the Rise of Nazism

Hannah Vogt

Hitler effectively exploited the confusion and humiliation felt by the German people after their defeat in World War I. The German generals claimed that their forces had not been defeated. Rather, they said, the war effort had been betrayed by liberal politicians and other civilians at home, a theme that the Nazis emphasized again and again in their rise to power. German political scholar Hannah Vogt here shows that it was not civilian intrigues but the outright failure of the generals and their armies that brought about defeat. The famous "stab in the back" was therefore nothing but a myth that ended up playing right into the hands of right-wing politicians like Hitler.

In August 1919, the . . . first parliament of the German Republic appointed a Commission of Inquiry. Its task was to determine whether war could have been avoided, and, especially, whether it could not have been ended sooner. This commission, meeting in public session, was told by a former Secretary of State, [Karl] Helfferich, that Russian money had financed the German Revolution of November 1918 [the creation of the Weimar Republic by German democrats] and that its instigators had, as it were, attacked the German army from the rear. Soon afterwards, Field Marshal [Paul] von Hindenburg testified before the same body. He was asked some questions but disregarded them; instead, he read a prepared statement along the lines that the army and the military chiefs had always done their best. The German people and the political parties, however, had deserted the men fighting at the front, and, in the words of a British general, "stabbed the army in the back."

A Legend Is Born

Thus was born the notorious stab-in-the-back legend. It was accepted eagerly, for many Germans drew comfort from the idea that the German army had remained "unvanquished in battle." The stab-in-the-back legend afforded them a rationale for their hatred of democracy, of the Republic, of anything new. Later on, it was grist for the Nazi mill and thus it turned into one of the most pernicious political myths of the recent past. But how did Germany really lose the war?

Memoirs, newspapers, and pictures reflect the strange intoxication which overwhelmed the whole of Germany when war broke out. Men marched to defend their threatened fatherland, recalling the glorious campaigns of 1814 and 1870. Soldiers going to the front hoped to be "back with mother" within six weeks. Women and young girls pressed flowers and presents on the troops en route. Volunteers who lined up at recruiting stations were worried that the war would be over before they arrived at the front.

But very soon it became obvious that a quick military decision could not be reached. . . . Despite the courageous sacrifice of many young volunteers in the battle of Langemarck all exertions were in vain. The western front solidified into a war of position, corroding nerves and consuming material. Attempts made over many months to exhaust French manpower by attacking the fortifications of Verdun also failed. The Germans paid with 280,000 dead, wounded, and prisoners for the attack, while the defending French lost 300,000 men. . . .

A Deteriorating Situation

In the east, meanwhile, generals Hindenburg and [Erich] Ludendorff had won important battles. But these victories failed to force Russia to her knees, and were thus indecisive.

As the war spread to additional theaters, extending the battle lines to Italy and Turkey in 1915, Germany and her allies found themselves in a situation which was deteriorating. Well aware that it would be almost impossible to win the war by military means alone, the German Chief of Staff, General [Erich] von Falkenhayn, urged the Chancellor to seek a compromise peace. But nobody listened.

During the first few days of the war, the German industrialist, Walther Rathenau, 47 years of age and thus too old for the army, reported to the German Ministry of War and offered his services. He pointed out that manufacturers needed to be assured that they could continue to receive supplies of raw materials, and that central controls would have to be imposed. Thereupon he was entrusted with the control of German raw material procurement, and succeeded in organizing it with dedication, persistent effort, and intelligence. It was mainly due to his initiative that industry quickly made use of an invention of the German scientist Fritz Haber, by which ammonia was synthesized directly by combining hydrogen and nitrogen. Only by this means was the German production of ammunition assured.

The food situation was even less favorable than industrial production. As early as 1915, the sealing off of the North Sea by the British navy began to have a serious effect on Germany. It countered this breach of maritime law with submarine warfare, but this failed to improve its food supply or to force the English to their knees.

Since there was no way out of scarcity, the limited supplies had to be rationed. Food rationing, however, immediately produced a black market. The peasants resented enforced delivery quotas. The workers, especially in the big cities, were underfed, and were embittered because higher income groups escaped the general misery by buying under the counter. . . .

Constitutionally, the Kaiser [Emperor William II] was Commander in Chief of the Armed Forces as well as head of the government. During the war, however, he remained much in the background. [Theobald] Bethmann-Hollweg, the Chancellor, was a prudent and honest man, but he lacked creative imagination, and was unable to anticipate events or devise long-range plans. His foreign policy was half-hearted throughout, and he failed to carry out domestic reforms which would have given parliament greater responsibility. . . .

The Generals Interfere in Politics

In August 1916, the Kaiser appointed Field Marshal von Hindenburg as Chief of General Staff, and General Ludendorff Quartermaster General.

Both had earned high praise for their achievements on the eastern front. For purely military purposes the Kaiser could not have chosen better men. In fact, however, it was a fateful choice, for Ludendorff in particular chose to use his authority to overstep his military office and trespass upon politics. . . . Hindenburg's and Ludendorff's interference in political affairs turned warfare into an end in itself. Bethmann-Hollweg's carefully considered judgment was that "these men of genius aim purposefully at militarizing every aspect of the state." The abdication of the political way of thinking in the interest of the military is precisely what is called "militarism."

The military mind triumphed openly over political considerations in January 1917, when Hindenburg and Ludendorff pressed for unlimited submarine warfare to achieve the purely military objective of increasing the security and efficiency of the submarines. They were backed by navy experts, who claimed that if German submarines could operate without restrictions they could manage to sink on an average 600,000 tons of English shipping a month. This would so cripple England's food supply and industrial production that within six months the English government would be forced to capitulate.

In vain did Bethmann-Hollweg point out that unrestricted submarine warfare which would also affect neutral shipping in enemy waters would thus do irreparable damage to relations with the neutrals, especially the United States. The generals appealed to the Kaiser, who allowed himself to be persuaded by their arguments. Thus, unrestricted submarine warfare was unleashed on February 1, 1917, and had the immediate effect of bringing the USA into the war. But even the hoped-for military effects failed to materialize, in spite of heroic efforts by German submarine crews, and in spite of the experts' calculations, which incidentally had been based on inadequate statistics. The six months passed during which these tactics were supposed to defeat England, but England showed no sign of yielding. . . .

The German military chiefs gave conclusive proof of their political ineptitude by being unable to produce even one rational plan for terminating the war. Nothing characterizes this better than Ludendorff's question to a conservative representative (November 1916): "Is there any way at all to end this war?" He should have been racking his brains day and night over this very political question, but his military mind grasped only the concepts "victory or defeat." He was unable to realize that victories can have value only if they lead to an enduring peace, and that it is possible to kill oneself with victories, allowing the enemy to win the last and decisive battle. Ludendorff identified defeat with "destruction," which made it sound somber and hollow, and neglected the fact that 60 million people could survive even a defeat.

Public Opinion Determined by Hot-Heads

There actually were some clear-thinking, farsighted men in Germany, who, even during the first intoxication brought on by the victories of 1914, had pondered ways of bringing about a peace. . . . But these moderates had no influence on the public. Opinion was determined by the so-called "Pan-German League," which was a hodgepodge of hot-headed nationalists. The league wanted "global prestige" and colonies for Germany; they held that in politics no holds were barred, that might makes for right, and that Germany had to wage an aggressive "struggle for existence." Mixed with these goals were a hatred of socialists, antisemitism, and a rejection of the democratic way of life. The Pan-Germans further increased their influence because censorship, instituted at the outbreak of the war, impeded public discussions. As a result, matters were continually presented in a rosy light. The government wished to create a mood of optimism, and prop up state authority. They suppressed unfavorable facts, and failed to explain the truth about doubtful "conquests." Instead, loudmouthed show-offs took the lead, and spread the illusion that Germany would obtain "peace with victory" and dictate its demands.

Two memoranda of 1915 illustrate the war goals of the annexationists. In one of these, the six most powerful German business associations called for the complete annexation of Belgium, a strip of the French coast reaching to the Somme, the iron ore of Longwy and Briey, and coal mines in some French departments. To balance this gain in industrial power, "an equivalent agricultural area to be acquired in the east" was considered necessary.

The second memorandum, nearly topping the first in its demands, was signed by German university professors and civil servants. They advised making maximum demands. France was to be ruthlessly subjugated politically and economically, and forced without mercy to pay the highest war indemnities. Belgium's annexation was demanded "by the most immaculate concept of honor." No demand for reparations could be high enough for England, that "nation of shopkeepers." Russia was to cede land expropriated from previous owners. . . .

The Appeal for an Armistice

The German Supreme Command [made] one more attempt to take the initiative in the west. They planned to launch another attack with 200 divisions (3.5 million men), which gave them a slight numerical superiority over the French and English. The plan was to drive a wedge between the English and the French, to pin the English on the Channel, and to beat the French in a vast encirclement battle of the type that had been envisioned in 1914 but had failed then. There was hope that the Americans would get out of the war, once the planned operation had succeeded. Such a foolish hope, of course, cast doubt on the whole scheme. How could a great power be expected to fail its allies so miserably! England, moreover, was supported by a whole empire.

In all probability, then, final military victory had eluded Germany. At that moment, it would have been much better to offer peace. . . . The enemy powers would certainly have thought twice before they dismissed an offer backed up by the threat of 200 divisions.

German politics, however, were decided by military leaders, and thus the great offensive in the west began on March 21, 1918. It was a well-planned military operation, for as a soldier Ludendorff knew his job. One must admire him if merely for his ability to turn the war of position once more into a war of movement in a narrow segment of space where 7 million soldiers had been massed. Equally astonishing was the spirit of the soldiers, who after three years of exhausting trench warfare, made a last supreme effort.

Five times decisive attacks were launched during this last German offensive. Each time these attacks achieved some tactical success, but decisive victory still eluded the German forces. Each month the number of Americans in the European theater grew; there were 300,000 men in March, but already 1.2 million by July. After the fifth attack had spent itself in July 1918, the enemies, led by Marshal [Ferdinand] Foch, began counter-attacks. Superior in troops and material, they scored quick triumphs, especially since the German army had nothing to match a new British weapon—the tank. With the tank the British succeeded in slashing a deep gap into the German front lines on August 8. Ludendorff called the day the "black day of the German Army." From that day on at least, he must have known the war was lost militarily. . . .

In September 1918 . . . Hindenburg and Ludendorff, facing up to facts, demanded that armistice negotiations be undertaken immediately. They knew full well that only a new government would be able to undertake such negotiations. Ludendorff passed word to the party leaders in the German *Reichstag*. Political reforms, blocked so long by the Supreme Command, were now ordered in the very face of defeat.

The *Reichstag* accepted Prince Max von Baden, a liberal, as Chancellor. Prince Max energetically opposed issuing a precipitate appeal for an armistice, since, in his opinion, such a step was bound to decrease the influence his new government hoped to exert on the peace. He made it clear that he would go ahead only if he received a written request from the Supreme Command. Thereupon, Hindenburg, in a letter of October 3, unequivocally established that the Supreme Command was responsible for the termination of the war in form as well as in substance:

> The Supreme Command continues to insist on its demands of Sunday, September 29, of this year that an appeal for an Armistice should be issued forthwith. . . . We cannot make good the severe losses which we have suffered in battle during the last few days. We cannot force a peace any longer on our enemies, as far as it is humanly possible to judge. The enemy, on his side, keeps throwing new and fresh reserves into the battle. . . . Under such circumstances, the fighting must be broken off in order to spare the German people and its allies needless sacrifices. Each day that is lost costs the lives of thousands of brave soldiers.

This left Prince Max no choice. With a heavy heart he addressed a note to President [Woodrow] Wilson on October 4, asking him to act as mediator in the arrangement of an armistice. . . .

Hindenburg's letter needs to be read with great care. It includes not a word about a failure on the part of the people, or about a revolution, or even a revolutionary mood that made necessary a termination of hostilities. This makes it even harder to understand how, little more than a year later, the writer of this letter dared to deny his own responsibilities, and to blame the loss of the war on the German nation and the revolution.

In view of this legend, it must be stated with utmost clarity that, from the very beginning, a total German victory was hardly possible, and that each passing year made it even less likely. Total defeat perhaps could have been avoided if the political leaders had been determined to use military successes at the proper time, and had sought a moderate peace of understanding. The German nation also bears responsibility in so far as it surrendered to authoritarian leadership all too willingly, and failed to demand more energetically its right to a share in the making of decisions. The revolution of November 1918 was an effect not a cause of the defeat.

The Terms of the Versailles Treaty Led to the Rise of Nazism

E.J. Feuchtwanger

The German people were insulted, traumatized, and angered by the harsh terms of the 1919 Treaty of Versailles, imposed on Germany by the victorious Allies at the conclusion of World War I. Besides forcing the Germans to pay huge reparations (payments for damages) and to give up various borderlands, the Allies forbade any attempt at *Anschluss*, the reunification of Germany and Austria. The Allies also denied Germany membership in the League of Nations, the new international organization championed by U.S. president Woodrow Wilson. The Germans particularly resented the treaty provision calling for the detainment of "war criminals," including the former German kaiser William II, who had taken refuge in Holland at war's end. In the years following the war, Adolf Hitler gained popularity by successfully exploiting the sense of outrage that most Germans felt about the treaty. This summary of the treaty's terms and their effects on the German people is by E.J. Feuchtwanger, former reader of history at the University of Southampton.

The implications of military defeat had overshadowed developments in Germany from the moment when at the end of September 1918, [General Erich] Ludendorff had pressed for an immediate armistice. Those forces in Germany that had asked for more moderate war aims and an approach based more on international cooperation and less on power were vindicated. . . .

Even if the situation in October 1918 had been better managed on the Allied as well as on the German side, the psychological readjustment required of the great majority of the German population was too great and the time for making it too short. A simplistic expectation was created among the masses that if they divested themselves of their discredited rulers with all possible haste, they would be spared the consequences of defeat. . . . Thus a thoroughly unrealistic mood of illusion and aggrieved sense of national honour pervaded both the political establishment and public opinion at large as the process of peacemaking began.

The armistice agreement of 11 November 1918 anticipated many aspects of the ultimate peace settlement. In the West there was to be a return of all German-occupied territories. . . . The German areas on the left bank of the Rhine were to be occupied by the Allies. . . . There were to be far-reaching handovers of assets such as gold, foreign currency and railway rolling stock, anticipating later reparation demands. German forces were to be disarmed and demobilised to a low level. In the East . . . German troops were to evacuate their current positions in former Russian territory, such as the Baltic states, only when the Allies demanded it. . . . The armistice hardly fell short of a total submission of Germany to the victorious Allies. It came as a cold douche [splash of water] to the German government and a public high on illusions.

Nevertheless the German government made extensive preparations for the peace negotiations in which they now hoped to engage. Presiding over these efforts was Count [Ulrich von] Brockdorff-Rantzau, who took charge of German foreign policy in December 1918. He was a liberal aristocrat, a professional diplomat with an internationalist outlook. He also had somewhat old-fashioned ideas of national honour. Brockdorff-Rantzau engaged a wide circle of advisers, prominent among them businessmen and bankers of again liberal and internationalist outlook, such as the Hamburg banker Max Warburg. . . .

The course of the peace conference from its first meeting in January 1919 gave the Germans virtually no opportunity to engage in serious negotiations with their former enemies. The divisions on the Allied side, between [U.S. president Woodrow] Wilson's vision of a new world order on the one hand and the French requirement for security against a German revival, were so great that the hammering out of some kind of agreed settlement formed the main theme of the negotiations in Paris. If the Germans had been allowed to engage seriously in these negotiations the task of peacemaking would have become almost impossible. German hopes of separate and detailed talks with major and minor allies therefore never became a reality.

On 7 May 1919 the German delegation was asked to receive a completed draft of the treaty and invited to make written comments only. On this occasion Brockdorff-Rantzau delivered a speech from a seated position to express his utter contempt for the way the German delegation was being treated. He voiced perfectly the mood of impotent rage and the profound sense of injustice that was sweeping the German nation. . . . Even the most representative organ of the liberal press, the *Frankfurter Zeitung*, declared, on 8 May 1919, that 'in this document the delusions of an all-conquering materialism had reached . . . their peak. If this draft, or a similar one, should be put into operation, then it is time to despair of the future of mankind.'

The Reparations Question

The depth and unanimity of revulsion in Germany from the proposed treaty was above all due to article 231, the war guilt clause. It did not explicitly proclaim Germany's war guilt. Its wording was: 'The Allied and Associated Governments declare, and Germany acknowledges, that Germany and her allies are as perpetrators responsible for all the losses and damages suffered by the Allied and Associated Governments and their citizens, as a result of the war forced upon them by the attack of Germany and her allies.' The main purpose of the article was to pin on Germany the responsibility for reparations and to provide a moral justification for this responsibility.

The reparations question had loomed increasingly large during the peace negotiations. The final and unfortunate outcome, which was to poison international relations for over a decade, was the product of the difficult economic and fiscal situation which a war of unprecedented destructiveness had created in most of the combatant nations. The leading politicians were under great pressure to mislead their public into thinking that the defeated enemy could be forced to make good these losses.

The notion that the Germans should be made to pay 'until the pips squeak' figured prominently in the British general election of 1918. National interests clashed on the definitions of damage and compensation. The French might initially have been satisfied if they had received a large measure of help in repairing the physical damage to their economically crucial northern departments [provinces]. This could hardly have suited the British who had suffered great financial losses, but not much physical damage. The Americans were not prepared to forgo repayment of the loans which they had provided for the European belligerents, which in turn reinforced the need of the Europeans for heavy reparation payments. . . . The differences over reparations and the complexity of the question made for a wide definition of German liability, which, given the climate of public opinion, had to be based on a moral responsibility. Even so it proved impossible to arrive at concrete figures, which were to be left to a future reparations commission. Meanwhile Germany was obliged to make an interim payment of 20 billion gold marks by May 1921. . . .

Leaving aside the emotional issues of war guilt and reparations the provisions of the treaty fall into four main categories: territorial cessions, occupation of territory subject to time limits and without permanent loss of sovereignty, limitation of forces and armaments and demilitarised zones, and cession of economic assets over and above reparation liabilities.

In the west the principal territorial cession was Alsace-Lorraine [a section of eastern France seized earlier by Germany], a forgone conclusion, which aroused relatively little immediate resistance. There were minor adjustments of the German-Belgian frontier around Eupen and Malmedy. . . . Much more deeply resented were the losses to Poland, West Prussia and Posen, which gave Poland direct access to the sea and left East Prussia separated from the main body of Germany by the so-called Polish corridor. . . .

Any border line between Poland and Germany would have left sizeable ethnic groups on the wrong side and this settlement certainly left more than a million Germans under Polish sovereignty. The frontiers chosen did, however, have some historical validity, in that they were similar to the dividing line of 1772 between the rising state of Prussia and the then Polish state. The depth of German resentment can only be understood in the light of the tradition, going back at least into the nineteenth century, of growing hostility between German and Polish nationalism, tinged on the German side with racial contempt.

The German grievance about the eastern borders was aggravated by the fact the principle of national self-determination . . . was here applied to Germany's disadvantage. . . . The Austrian provisional assembly had voted in November 1918 to join the German Reich. . . . The veto on the *Anschluss* implicit in article 80 of the Treaty of Versailles and formalised in the Treaty of St Germain with Austria reinforced the sense of injustice felt among virtually all sections of German opinion. It was claimed that German territorial losses had deprived the country of 14.6 per cent of its arable land, 74.5 per cent of its iron ore, 68.1 per cent of its zinc ore, and 26 per cent of its coal production. . . .

Other "Unreasonable" Demands

Germany was effectively barred for the foreseeable future from becoming a great power again in a military sense. The major force limitations were a ceiling of 100 000 men on the army, of 15 000 on the navy, the prohibition of conscription and the abolition of the General Staff. Offensive weapons, such as tanks, aeroplanes and submarines, were not permitted. . . .

Finally, the surrender was required of many economic assets: merchant marine, patents, overseas investments and property. The Allies were to be granted most-favoured-nation treatment and there was a five-year ban on protective tariffs. The loss of all German colonies was seen as a special attack on German honour, for it seemed to impugn Germany's ability to act as trustee for less developed peoples. Although many Germans regarded the League of Nations with suspicion as one more example of Wilsonian trickery and illusionism, Germany's exclusion from it was seen as another instance of the Allied determination to degrade their former enemy to a power of the second rank.

The extradition of German political figures seen in Allied countries as war criminals, led by the Kaiser, was regarded in Germany as a totally vindictive, dishonourable and insupportable demand. It caused the first major tussle between the Allies and the German government. The Dutch government in any case refused to hand over the Kaiser and official Germany remained totally adamant in its refusal to comply with this aspect of the treaty. All that was conceded was that proven war crimes, such as firing on civilians in lifeboats after a submarine sinking, would be tried in German courts. . . .

The cliff-hanging drama around the rejection or acceptance of the peace terms in June 1919 . . . highlighted the atmosphere of hysteria and unreason which engulfed most of the German public. The grand reorientation of Germany's vision of herself in the international community received a setback from which it never fully recovered, even if in due course underlying realities were bound to reassert themselves. An acute observer, the liberal theologian and sociologist Ernst Troeltsch, caught something of the prevailing total loss of composure: 'grim community of people, but the old legends about defeat due to Jews and SPD [democratic party] surface again . . . Prof. X calls the peace a catastrophe which could only happen to a people whipped up by Jews and SPD.'. . . Even pacifists joined in the universal chorus of condemnation and self-pity. A German historian speaking on 16 June 1919 in commemoration of students fallen in the war said portentously: 'Our misfortune is boundless and we cannot reach its limits in our lifetime.'

Germany's Post–World War I Economic Troubles

Simon Taylor

In the early 1920s, Germany suffered from serious inflation, defined in the simplest sense as a rise in prices accompanied by a decrease in the value of money. Often referred to as the "great" or "hyper-" inflation, it caused
severe deprivation among the middle and lower classes.
Along with the economic ravages of the Great Depression
that struck a few years later, the poverty and misery caused
by the great inflation strengthened the Nazis, who
claimed to have the solutions to the nation's problems. As
explained here by scholar Simon Taylor, an authority on
Germany in the period between the world wars, many factors contributed to the inflation. These included too
much concentration of wealth in the hands of a few
wealthy industrialists and a lack of an effective system of
taxation. Also, most average investors put their money in
government bonds, which meant that when the government suffered financial losses, so did they.

The hyper-inflation that raged during 1922 and 1923 and the
world economic depression which broke towards the end of
1929 are normally seen as the decisive events which destroyed
the fabric of Weimar society and prepared the way for the rise
of German fascism. The hyper-inflation was decisive in that
it had psychological and political effects far beyond the impact of the actual economic chaos caused by the collapse of
the German currency. The Depression was crucial, because it

Reprinted from *The Rise of Hitler: Revolution and Counterrevolution*, by Simon Taylor (London: Duckworth; New York: Universe Books), ©1983 by Simon Taylor, by
permission of the publishers.

provoked a widespread and bitter class polarisation in German society during a period of political instability.

In order to understand the long-term political effects of the hyper-inflation it is necessary to examine not only how inflation affected different social classes, but equally how the inflation affected the different sections of the middle class. For the inflation finally and spectacularly demonstrated to those members of the *Mittelstand* [middle classes] who considered themselves 'above politics' that political organisation was necessary in order to guarantee their very survival. Even more alarmingly, it demonstrated that the *Mittelstand*, far from being the vital middle estate of society, was in fact an amorphous mass of individuals with few common interests; nor could they rely upon the political parties of the working class or the upper classes to represent their particular economic demands.

The hyper-inflation had its origins in the general system of finance practised by German industry. Unlike Britain and the USA, where commercial banks acted as sources of credit for the wider financial market, Germany had banks which were originally planned as institutions for the *direct* financing of heavy industry. Funds were mainly used for loans to industrial and commercial customers, and either one bank or a consortium of banks would lend money for projects such as the construction of a steel works, a new mining venture or the building of a chemical refinery. In return, the banks gained the majority of shares issued by the company to finance its expansion. Conversely the general public, instead of investing widely in shares issued on the Stock Exchange, subscribed to government savings bonds.

The relationship between banks and heavy industry naturally became very close, and every major bank had its boardroom connections with at least one branch of heavy industry. This interrelationship fostered a process of capital concentration [massing of a great deal of money in the hands of a few], for it became necessary to raise huge sums of capital as industry became increasingly mechanised. Another factor which promoted capital concentration was the status of trusts and cartels [monopolies of industries, each by one

Six Weeks' Pay for a Pair of Boots

From his book Modern Germany, *Koppel S. Pinson, a noted scholar of German history, provides some of the startling facts and figures of German inflation in the early 1920s.*

The German mark which had stood at 4.2 per dollar before the war and at 8.9 in 1919, after the conclusion of hostilities, continued to decline steadily for the next three years. In the middle of 1922 the decline began to assume fantastic and astronomical proportions. By November, 1923, the German mark reached the dizzy figure of 4,200,000,000 to the dollar. Those were mad days in Germany. The daily dollar quotation took the place of the weather as the standard subject of conversation. The American dollar became the measure of value in Germany, and prices were adjusted to the dollar rather than to the mark. The situation developed with such speed that paper mills and printing presses could not keep pace with the need for supplies of paper money. Over 300 paper mills and 2,000 printing establishments worked on 24-hour shifts to supply the Reichsbank with the needed bank notes.

The mark lost all value and a wild scramble ensued for real goods of all kinds. Barter replaced the use of money for large sections of the population. . . .

The inflation left havoc and distress among the workers and especially among the middle classes. Soaring prices far outdistanced increases in wages, and there were resulting strikes and unemployment. Workers had to pay the equivalent of nine to ten hours of work for a pound of margarine, several days' work for a pound of butter, six weeks' pay for a pair of boots, and twenty weeks' pay for a suit of clothes. The most disastrous effects of inflation, however, were felt by the urban middle classes, especially fixed income groups and those living on savings and pensions. These classes suffered economic and psychic damage that left permanent injuries to the social body of Weimar Germany.

Koppel S. Pinson, *Modern Germany: Its History and Civilization.* New York: Macmillan, 1966, pp. 446–47.

or a few large companies] in German law. While in the United States anti-trust laws made the infringement of free competition a criminal offence, in Germany cartel agreements had legal status and could be enforced in the courts. Even in the mid 1890s there were official cartels in iron, steel, coal, cement, plate glass and chemical manufacturing. By 1914 the framework of the German cartel structure was well established, with either rigid or loose systems of production quotas, market sharing and price-fixing agreements. Among small producers the formation of producers' and buyers' co-operatives had much the same effect in severely limiting free competition and legitimising cartel policies.

More and More Paper Money Printed

The war had two major effects on the structure of the German economy. First, . . . the production of armaments at the expense of consumer goods favoured heavy industry and accelerated capital concentration. Secondly, the cost of the war had severely inflationary effects because the government, fearing to harm the interests of its political backers, lacked the will to impose a progressive taxation system. Instead of imposing tax increases upon industry and the wealthy (which was done only belatedly and ineffectually), the authorities attempted to cover the mountain of debt by issuing war bonds. And although the purchase of such bonds by the German public became increasingly less 'voluntary' as the war progressed, the sums so raised never remotely paid for the billions of marks' worth of munitions shot off by the armed forces. The government's response was to print more money, and by the end of the war the amount of paper money in circulation had risen six-fold in comparison with 1913.

Hence the German inflation really began in 1914, although its effects were disguised by the closing of the foreign exchanges for the duration of the war and the introduction of rationing. By November 1918 the German mark had declined to half its former gold value on neutral money markets, although only after the total collapse of the controlled war economy did the full extent of Germany's economic dislocation become apparent.

Chapter 2

The Birth and Early Growth of the Nazi Party

Turning | Points

IN WORLD HISTORY

The Origins of Hitler and the Nazi Party

Marshall Dill Jr.

In this essay, historian Marshall Dill Jr. chronicles Adolf Hitler's early years and traces the social and ideological forces that shaped the young man's thinking. Dill then tells how, after serving in the German army during World War I, Hitler became involved with the German Workers' Party in Munich, the chief city of the southern German region of Bavaria. After examining Hitler's reorganization of the party, Dill concludes with useful thumbnail sketches of some of the führer's most important Nazi assistants, including Hermann Göring, Rudolf Hess, and Alfred Rosenberg.

Adolf Hitler was born on April 20, 1889, in the village of Braunau-on-the-Inn on the Bavarian frontier of Austria, where his father, Alois Hitler, was a customs official. All members of the Hitler family, as far back as it can be traced, were peasants working the land of Upper Austria near the border of Bohemia [a region of Czechoslovakia]. Alois was the first to improve his social status. As a civil servant of the Austrian Empire, he was entitled to wear a uniform and exert his minor authority. Thus his son was born into that lower middle class of which he was to become the prophet.

Adolf and his father were a bad combination. The father wanted to make a civil servant of his son, but as early as his eleventh year Adolf was determined to become an artist. . . . The problem was solved by the death of Alois in 1903, after

Reprinted from *Germany: A Modern History*, by Marshall Dill Jr. (Ann Arbor: University of Michigan Press), ©1961 by The University of Michigan, by permission of the publishers.

which the indulgent Clara Hitler supported her son by her own drudgery and permitted him to continue at school in Linz and even to take art lessons. His aim was to enter the Vienna Academy of Fine Arts, to which he applied . . . [but] he was refused admission on the grounds that the samples he had supplied were unsatisfactory. Hitler would not believe this; he preferred to think that he was the victim of a conspiracy, that some undefined "they" were against him. Soon afterwards he was also refused at the Technical Building School where he hoped to be trained as an architect.

On the Streets of Vienna

In 1908 Hitler's mother died, and Adolf found himself without family or financial security. He made his way back to Vienna where he stayed until 1913 earning a precarious living by painting postcard views of the monuments of the city and also shaping his political opinions. These were the decisive formative years.

Vienna was a cosmopolitan city, inhabited by the numberless ethnic groups that composed the old Austro-Hungarian Empire. It was also a cauldron of raging political controversy. Socialists, racialists, and nationalists of all hues held constant meetings and published endless pamphlets. It was a tailor-made atmosphere for the young wastrel who liked to wander from meeting to meeting.

People who knew Hitler during his Vienna period tell of his way of life. He was usually desperately poor. When he managed to sell a few pictures, he lived in a furnished room; more often he slept in flophouses maintained by the city or charitable institutions for the down-and-out. His clothes were shabby; he did not always have enough to eat. At times when his income was especially poor he took whatever job offered itself in the construction industry. . . .

In his autobiography *Mein Kampf*, Hitler maintains that his basic political attitudes were formed in Vienna. He writes lyrically of his pride in being a German; his rabid nationalism was fully developed thus early and correspondingly his loathing for "inferior" races, especially if they were in any position of authority over real Germans. . . . For him all men were not brothers; and of all the peoples to whom Hitler refused to be a brother, he felt most virulently about the Jews. To him Jews were an alien malignant growth sapping the roots of Germanism. One looks in vain for any rational ingredient when Hitler writes of the Jews. It is pure emotion and hatred. The Jews were responsible for everything Hitler disliked in art, politics, social life, etc. A psychologist might say that Hitler made the Jews a scapegoat for his own inadequacies.

Hitler grew to hate the city of Vienna and the Austrian state in general. He was infuriated by what he felt was the undue power given to non-German elements in the society. More and more he longed for a purely German state. Accordingly in 1913 he moved across the border to Munich, with which he fell immediately in love. He led more or less the same sort of life in Munich that he had in Vienna; yet this time he was happier, for he was in a completely German atmosphere. . . .

The German Workers' Party

[The following year, World War I began and Hitler enlisted in the German army. After serving for four years, he] made his way, still in uniform, across Germany to his beloved Munich. However, it was a different Munich now, having been racked by revolution and insecurity. . . . He saw and heard Communists, socialists, nationalists, Bavarian separatists, all making full use of the newly granted freedoms of speech and press. It would have been impossible for him to find any laboratory richer in political viruses.

In mid-1919 Hitler got a job with the army as a sort of political training official to keep the men away from left-wing infection and to investigate new political groups that were spawning. Here he came in contact with the general in command in Bavaria, Major General Ritter von Epp, later to become Hitler's regent (*Statthalter*) in Bavaria; and with Captain Ernst Röhm, one of the most important figures in the early days of the Nazis. Röhm was a swashbuckling freebooter, happy only when fighting or in the company of fighting men, but nevertheless a person of real administrative and organizational ability. As one of his routine duties, Hitler was told in September 1919 to attend and report on a meeting of a new, small party called the German Workers' party. This little group descended from a circle organized about a year earlier by Anton Drexler, a toolmaker, who had conceived the idea of founding a rigidly nationalist party but on a principle different from existing nationalist groups, which tended to appeal to the upper and middle classes. He had the insight to realize that nationalism needed mass support, and thus he proposed that his party would appeal to the working classes. This was undoubtedly one of the aspects that appealed to Hitler. . . . Drexler had very little success at first, even when he merged with another circle led by a journalist named Karl Harrer. In 1919 a few interesting persons joined the group. One was Major Röhm; another was Dietrich Eckart, a journalist and poet of extreme nationalist views; still another was Gottfried Feder, an odd economist, who was in thrall to his hatred of big business and the "slavery of interest" and who wanted a world safe for the proprietor of the corner grocery store.

Hitler, angered at a speech favoring Bavarian separatism, arose at the first meeting he attended and delivered himself on the theme of German unity. The party leaders were impressed and invited Hitler to a meeting of their committee soon afterward. In a short time he became member number seven of the committee of the German Workers' party. This was the germ of the future Nazi party.

Hitler as Orator and Organizer

Within a few months Hitler discovered two gratifying things about himself. One was that he had competent, if unorthodox, organizational ability; the other, that he was an extraordinarily persuasive public speaker. At first he was nervous about facing an audience, but as his audiences grew, he developed the techniques which made him one of the greatest demagogues in history. Endless repetition, short powerful slogans, no concepts inaccessible to the meanest mentality: these were the keys to his oratorical success. His voice was harsh; his German had a strong Austrian accent; but he managed to exercise an almost hypnotic power over his hearers.

Soon Hitler quit his job with the army and devoted himself full time to the party.

In early 1920 the party, soon to be renamed the National Socialist German Workers' party (the German initials N.S.D.A.P. or the slang term Nazi were used in abbreviations), issued its twenty-five point program, which remained official until the end. It was drawn up by the early leaders of the party, and though Hitler occasionally paid lip service to it, he certainly never felt bound to it. The first point reads: "We demand the union of all Germans to form a Great Germany on the basis of the right of self-determination enjoyed by nations." The treaties of 1919 were to be abolished; Germany was to regain her colonies; no Jew was to be a member of the nation. . . . The program ends by calling for general progressive reforms in such fields as health and education.

Although the Twenty-Five Points were never officially abandoned, a characteristic of Nazism is its lack of positive program. It is easy to say what Hitler opposed; it is almost impossible to give a neat list of the issues he supported. During the twenties in particular, the movement was destructive rather than constructive. The Nazis were against communism, socialism, democracy, liberalism, the Jews . . . the Western powers, the treaties of 1919, etc. Those things were clear, but as far as a positive program was concerned, there was nothing but vague mouthings about racial purity, national regeneration, the leadership principle, etc. Both Nazism and its Italian cousin, Fascism, were essentially opportunistic. The genius of Hitler and [Italian dictator Benito] Mussolini was their ability to take advantage of a given situation using shopworn slogans of easy application. Their failure lay in their increasing belief that they were invincible and their consequent wild overreaching.

Between 1920 and 1923 Hitler hammered out the main bases that were to characterize the party for its entire existence. Less and less is heard of Drexler, Eckart, and Feder. Hitler quickly assumed complete command. . . . He was an expert psychologist of the classes he was dealing with, and knew the importance of such details as the party uniform, its flags, and its songs. He was giving to an uprooted people a sense of "belongingness" that had been lost with the old traditional society. The arresting character of the swastika emblem; the memories of the old imperial red, black, and white colors; the simplicity of the brown shirt and arm band: these were appreciated by Hitler who labored over them personally. As early as 1920 Hitler decided that the party must have a uniformed group of strong, devoted young men to protect the meetings from violence. They had another use, which was not kept secret: preventing and breaking up meetings of any opposition groups. This was the kernel from which grew the *Sturm Abteilung* (otherwise known as S.A., the fighting wing or "storm troop"), which was composed of . . . [military] veterans and hoodlums. It took part in all sorts of demonstrations and made the nights hideous with street fighting and bloodshed.

Hitler's Nazi Companions

Another important step forward was taken in late 1920 when Röhm persuaded General Ritter von Epp to raise a collection to enable the new party to buy a . . . Munich newspaper, the *Völkischer Beobachter* (*"Racial Observer"*). Now the party had an organ, at first weekly but soon afterwards daily, which could spread the word beyond the beer halls in which meetings were held. Eckart became the first editor, but not for long. He was succeeded by Alfred Rosenberg.

Some of the men who later became paladins [champions] of Nazi Germany joined Hitler in these early years. The most interesting of them was Hermann Goering, born on January 12, 1893, the son of a German consular official. He became a professional soldier, . . . entered the new flying corps, and by the end of the war was the leading German war ace. . . . The armistice took him from the heights to the depths. He left Germany for Sweden, became a commercial pilot, contracted the morphine habit, and married a wealthy Swedish noblewoman. The Goerings returned to Germany and settled near Munich, where Hermann heard of the National Socialist party. He joined it and soon found himself at the head of the S.A. A fat, bluff, flamboyant character with an almost pathological love for uniforms and ostentation,

Goering possessed considerable personal charm which disguised a brutal and amoral ruthlessness.

The relationship between Hitler and Rudolf Hess was more personal. Like a number of the important Nazis, Hess was not a native German. He was born in Alexandria, Egypt, son of a German merchant there. He was only twenty when the war broke out; he fought throughout it, first as an infantry man and then as a flyer. . . . Hess became Hitler's secretary and in the mid-twenties recorded *Mein Kampf* as the leader dictated it. A colorless personality, Hess was content to remain in Hitler's shadow. As deputy leader of the party, he did much of the dirty work. He was like a puppy dog following his master. . . .

Alfred Rosenberg was an even more pitiable case. Born of German stock in the Baltic provinces of Russia, Rosenberg was trained for architecture at Russian schools. He fled from the Russian Revolution with a passionate hatred for Bolshevism [Russian communism] and also for the Jewish people, whom he equated with the Bolsheviks. He was a natural candidate for the new party and soon rose to a high position, succeeding Eckart as editor of the *Völkischer Beobachter*. He took his ideology seriously, even to the point of recommending a return to the worship of the old Nordic Germanic gods. As party ideologist he penned a long, turgid, racialist book called *The Myth of the Twentieth Century*, which became after *Mein Kampf* the second Nazi bible, although toward the end of his life Hitler himself admitted that he had never read it through.

With these companions and with this preparation, Hitler marched into the turbulent year 1923, a year which was to have great importance for his thinking and for the future of National Socialism.

The Nazis' Failed "Beer Hall *Putsch*"

Otis C. Mitchell

Adolf Hitler's first serious bid for power occurred late in 1923. This was a period of extreme tension between German leaders in Munich, the capital of the state of Bavaria, and the central government in Berlin, then headed by President Friedrich Ebert. The three most powerful men in Bavaria at the time were Gustav von Kahr, the state commissioner; Colonel Hans von Seisser, leader of the state police; and General Otto von Lossow, commander of the army units in the Munich area. Borrowing the ancient Roman term for a three-way ruling coalition, many referred to them as the "Bavarian triumvirate." Because they wanted to see the Weimar democracy replaced by a more autocratic government, preferably one led by Bavaria, these men sympathized with right-wing patriotic groups. As University of Cincinnati scholar Otis C. Mitchell explains in this essay, Hitler thought the three men could be coerced into helping him stage a *putsch*, or coup, that would topple the Berlin government. And to that end, on the night of November 8 he disrupted a meeting they were holding in a Munich beer hall.

It should be noted . . . that the aims of Hitler and the three men who governed Bavaria—Kahr, Lossow, and State Police Chief Hans Seisser—were not the same, particularly with respect to the type of action they wanted to take against the

Reprinted from *Hitler over Germany: The Establishment of the Nazi Dictatorship (1918–1934)*, by Otis C. Mitchell (Philadelphia: Institute for the Study of Human Issues, 1983), by permission of the author.

Berlin government. The triumvirate that ran Bavaria were separatists at heart; they were thus primarily interested in Bavarian autonomy. Hitler wanted to overthrow the republican government and eventually build a new state for all Germany, a dictatorship. It was this divergence in aims that caused Hitler to launch his Beer Hall Putsch. If he had not done so, the dispute between Berlin and Munich might have dragged on interminably. During the latter part of October and the first week of November, Germany stood close to civil war. . . .

Thus, Hitler's putsch broke up the Berlin-Munich impasse, unintentionally of course. It seemed to Hitler that events had produced a fortuitous time to strike. The Berlin government he so hated was swimming in a sea of troubles. The troops stationed in Bavaria, constituting a substantial part of the entire German army, were in a virtual state of mutiny. Hitler believed that there was a good chance that prominent rightists, including the men who ran Bavaria, might well join him in a . . . march on Berlin. He had been hinting at such a tactic for some time in many of his public pronouncements. . . .

Now Hitler began to consider dates. Finally, the Nazis . . . decided on 8 November 1923 . . . because Kahr had called a mass meeting in Munich's Bürgerbräukeller [a large beer hall] for that date, during which he planned to reveal whatever plans or programs for the future he had in mind. The official announcement said that, in his speech, Kahr would protest the growth of Bolshevism in Germany.

Hitler States His Demands

Hitler had worked up the enthusiasm of his followers to a fever pitch. He could not afford a long delay. Surely this crisis would not last forever, and it might well ameliorate before turning into the civil war he wanted.

Once the meeting at the Bürgerbräukeller, one of Munich's giant beer halls, began, Hitler had some 600 of his storm troopers surround the meeting place. Hitler then made his entrance, attired in a frock coat, prominently displaying his Iron Cross. . . . The Nazi leader . . . shouted loudly that the national revolution had commenced and that he had the hall surrounded. Squat, swarthy, his massive head set between hunched shoulders, Dr. Gustav Ritter von Kahr stared at Hitler. . . . After a brief conversation with Kahr, Lossow, and Seisser at the front of the auditorium, Hitler went into a side room with the three men who formed the Bavarian triumvirate.

Once alone with the three dignitaries, Hitler called out to his subordinates in a typically theatrical gesture: "No one leaves the room without my permission." Hitler then announced the formation of new Bavarian and Reich governments. He said that in Bavaria Ernst Pöhner would act as Prime Minister. In the Reich he would himself temporarily direct affairs. [General Erich] Ludendorff was to lead the army. He then threatened the three men: he told them they had two choices—they could either fight and achieve victory at his side or they could die on the spot. He had four bullets in his pistol, he said, one for each member of the triumvirate and one for himself. At this point, Hitler was asked by Lossow: "What is Ludendorff's attitude toward this affair?" The answer was: "Ludendorff is ready and will soon be fetched."

Before Ludendorff arrived, however, the crowd in the hall had become quite impatient. . . . Some of them began insulting the surrounding Nazis, deprecating the theatricality of the proceedings. Hitler returned to the hall and fired a shot into the air with a weapon he had pulled from his back pocket. He told the crowd: "If you are not quiet, I will have a machine gun put up in the gallery." The crowd quieted.

The Coup Collapses

When Ludendorff finally appeared, he was disgruntled to learn that Hitler had appointed himself President of the Reich without consulting him. Hitler had often portrayed himself as "The Drummer," the man who was to beat the drums in public to announce the coming of one greater than he, the one who would lead Germany out of her sorry state. Ludendorff had always assumed that he himself was the one who was greater. Despite this imagined reversal, however, Ludendorff promised to cooperate in the national revolution.

Finally, Kahr agreed to join Hitler in his great adventure. . . . How serious Kahr, Lossow, and Seisser really were is not all that certain. They had barely reached an agreement with Hitler, when the Nazi chief was called away to settle a quarrel [among some of his supporters]. . . . As soon as he had gone, the crowd poured out of the hall. Lossow, Kahr, and Seisser also left unobtrusively.

By about 1 A.M., however much inclined the Bavarian leaders may have been to go along with Hitler's revolutionary intent, Kahr, Lossow, and Seisser had decided that their best course of action was to withdraw from the whole affair. Of course, in an attempt to assess the seriousness of their intentions, it is certainly worthwhile to remember that there was no reason for Kahr, Lossow, or Seisser to have been particularly enthusiastic about entering a government where they would have been forced to serve under the upstart Hitler. At any rate, around 3 A.M. a statement was signed by Lossow and sent to all local radio stations. The broadcast to the Munich area indicated that Kahr and his associates were revoking an agreement made at gunpoint. The following morning placards that bore a similar statement and had been signed by Kahr were put up around Munich.

The previous night, in spite of all the marching and the tumult . . . only one stronghold had been occupied by the putschists. Ernst Röhm had taken army headquarters in Munich at the head of a troop known as the Reich War Flag. Bearing the unit's banner, as the War Flag marched up to the military district headquarters and seized it without a struggle, was a shortsighted twenty-three-year-old man named Heinrich Himmler [who would later become leader of the Nazi SS]. . . .

Also on the previous night, President [Friedrich] Ebert had resorted to an emergency powers article in the Weimar Constitution (Article 48). The Reich President, acting under the auspices of Article 48, gave General [Hans] von Seeckt temporary dictatorial powers. Seeckt at once called upon the army to resist all attempts to draw it into Hitler's adventure. There was some sympathy for the putsch among junior officers, but the loyalty of the army as a whole was never in question. Reinforcements soon entered the Bavarian capital. As it turned out, perhaps the most effective measure in suppressing the attempted coup was a telegram from Seeckt to Lossow. It warned Lossow that, if he did not subdue Hitler, Seeckt would displace him, move into Bavaria, and quash the Nazi-led uprising himself.

Hitler Is Arrested

These were great setbacks for Hitler. At this point, a more prudent man might have terminated his attempt at revolt. By the morning of 9 November, it had become clear to Hitler and the rest of the putsch leaders that the plot had miscarried. Ludendorff, however, still believed that his personal prestige could carry the coup through to a successful completion. He persuaded Hitler, against the Nazi's better judgment, that the putschists should take the offensive and march on Lossow's headquarters near Odeonsplatz. Ludendorff misguidedly believed that, if he were present, the officers and men of the army would follow the great hero of World War I and not Lossow.

Even as these discussions were being held, . . . across the River Isar regular army troops had surrounded Röhm and his men. No shots were fired, but the War Flag men were unable to leave the occupied building.

Around noon on 9 November . . . a long column in ranks of about 2000 men left the beer hall where they had spent the night, located only a short distance from Ludwig's Bridge across the Isar. At the bridge they met and overpowered a police contingent.

Once the river had been breached, the column marched on to . . . the city hall, there to be greeted by an enthusiastic crowd. There were various routes to Odeonsplatz from the town hall, and the police attempted to cordon these off. One of these was the narrow Residenzstrasse. The police gathered at Residenzstrasse were hastily called-in state troopers; the Munich police was too infected with nationalist and racist sentiments to be relied upon.

The leaders of the marching column finally decided upon Residenzstrasse as their route. Quickly, the marchers came within shouting distance of the state police. The state troopers' calls of "Stop! Don't go on!" were not obeyed. According to one participant eyewitness, a policeman who later made an official report, one of the Nazis fired a shot as soon as they were within range. . . . Three policemen and sixteen Nazis were killed in [the brief exchange of gunfire that ensued]. . . . One man alone among the putschists kept his head. Erect and unperturbed, Ludendorff marched on, pushed through the police line, and reached Odeonsplatz beyond. There a police officer went up to him and said, "Excellency, I must take you into custody." The general replied, "You have your orders. I will come with you.". . .

Hitler was apparently dragged to the ground, when the man next to him, with whom he was walking arm-in-arm, was knocked over backward by the bullet that ended his life. Hitler scrambled to his feet, stumbled backward, and allowed himself to be pushed into a friend's automobile. He was then taken by car to a hiding place in the countryside, where he was arrested two days later.

The putsch was a miserable failure. Hitler had lacked support from two crucial elements—the army and the police. In truth, Hitler had never wanted to use force against either of these elements. He later said: "We never thought to carry through a revolt against the army; it was with it we believed we could succeed." The Beer Hall Putsch was, on the whole, an ill-prepared and amateurish affair. . . .

The Lesson Learned

Among the most important effects of the putsch were the political lessons Hitler learned from his failure. He learned just how dangerous it was to underestimate the power of the state and to overestimate his own strength. He pledged, thereafter, to work within the system, if only *just* within it on occasion. He would use the flaws and weaknesses in the Weimar system to overthrow it. In ensuing years, even while his storm troopers were breaking the law, Hitler constantly harped on the necessity for at least technical legality within Nazism. He soon became dubbed by the press—Adolfe Légalité ("Adolf the Legal").

The Beer Hall Putsch, failure though it had been, became enshrined in Nazi mythology. Hitler and his comrades returned every year to Munich on 8 November. There, once again, the "old fighters" of National Socialism would walk the route from the Bürgerbräu to Odeonsplatz. They would carry with them the so-called blood flag, the swastika banner supposedly stained with the blood shed by National Socialists on that day. This became the Nazi passion play. When Hitler spoke of it, his words were full of pseudo-Christian references. The putsch, he liked to say, had caused "the blood of its martyrs to become the baptismal waters of the Third Reich."

Hitler Writes *Mein Kampf,* the Nazi Bible

William L. Shirer

During the mid- to late 1930s, American journalist William L. Shirer worked in a Western news bureau in Berlin and witnessed firsthand Hitler's repressive new dictatorship. Years later Shirer published his massive *Rise and Fall of the Third Reich*, which has been called "the definitive work on Nazi Germany." In this excerpt from the book, Shirer discusses the ideas and impact of *Mein Kampf*, which Hitler began writing in 1924 while serving a jail sentence for attempting an antigovernment coup the year before. As Shirer points out, though the so-called Nazi Bible is a rambling, boring, and demented work, it had far-reaching repercussions for Germany, Europe, and the world, for it plainly outlined the plans for conquest, dictatorship, and persecution of minorities that Hitler later actually put into effect.

Not every German who bought a copy of *Mein Kampf* necessarily read it. I have heard many a Nazi stalwart complain that it was hard going and not a few admit—in private—that they were never able to get through to the end of its 782 turgid pages. But it might be argued that had more non-Nazi Germans read it before 1933 and had the foreign statesmen of the world perused it carefully while there still was time, both Germany and the world might have been saved from catastrophe. For whatever other accusations can be made against Adolf Hitler, no one can accuse him of not putting down in writing exactly the kind of Germany he intended to make if he ever came to power and the kind of world he meant to create by armed German conquest. The blueprint of the Third Reich and, what is more, of the barbaric New Order which Hitler inflicted on conquered Europe in the triumphant years between 1939 and 1945 is set down in all its appalling crudity at great length and in detail between the covers of this revealing book. . . .

The Law of Self-Preservation

Hitler's basic ideas were formed in his early twenties in Vienna, and we have his own word for it that he learned little afterward and altered nothing in his thinking. When he left Austria for Germany in 1913 at the age of twenty-four, he was full of a burning passion for German nationalism, a hatred for democracy, Marxism [i.e., communism] and the Jews and a certainty that Providence had chosen the Aryans, especially the Germans, to be the master race.

In *Mein Kampf* he expanded his views and applied them specifically to the problem of not only restoring a defeated and chaotic Germany to a place in the sun greater than it had ever had before but making a new kind of state, one which would be based on race and would include all Germans then living outside the Reich's frontiers, and in which would be established the absolute dictatorship of the Leader—himself—with an array of smaller leaders taking orders from above and giving them to those below. Thus the book contains, first, an outline of the future German state and of the means by which it can one day become "lord of the earth," as the author puts it on the very last page; and, second, a point of view, a conception of life, or, to use Hitler's favorite German word, a *Weltanschauung*. That this view of life would strike a normal mind of the twentieth century as a grotesque hodgepodge concocted by a half-baked, uneducated neurotic goes without saying. What makes it important is that it was embraced so fanatically by so many millions of Germans and that if it led, as it did, to their ultimate ruin it also led to the ruin of so many millions of innocent, decent human beings inside and especially outside Germany.

Now, how was the new Reich to regain her position as a world power and then go on to world mastery? Hitler pondered the question in the first volume, written mostly when he was in prison in 1924, returning to it at greater length in Volume Two, which was finished in 1926.

In the first place, there must be a reckoning with France, "the inexorable mortal enemy of the German people." The French aim, he said, would always be to achieve a "dismembered and shattered Germany . . . a hodgepodge of little states.". . . Therefore, there must be "a final active reckoning with France . . . a last decisive struggle . . . only then will we be able to end the eternal and essentially so fruitless struggle between ourselves and France.". . .

In this manner Hitler leads to the core of his ideas on German foreign policy which he was to attempt so faithfully to

---

How the Jews Twist the Truth

In this excerpt from Mein Kampf, *Hitler claims that Jews purposely lie and states that this is one of the reasons he has come to hate them.*

The more I argued with them, the better I came to know their dialectic [method of argument]. First they counted on the stupidity of their adversary, and then, when there was no other way out, they themselves simply played stupid. If all this didn't help, they pretended not to understand, or, if challenged, they changed the subject in a hurry, quoted platitudes which, if you accepted them, they immediately related to entirely different matters, and then, if again attacked, gave ground and pretended not to know exactly what you were talking about. Whenever you tried to attack one of these apostles, your hand closed on a jelly-like slime which divided up and poured through your fingers, but in the next moment collected again. But if you really struck one of these fellows so telling a blow that, observed by the audience, he couldn't help but agree, and if you believed that this had taken you at least one step forward, your amazement was great the next day. The Jew had not the slightest rec-

carry out when he became ruler of the Reich. *Germany, he said bluntly, must expand in the East—largely at the expense of Russia.* In the first volume of *Mein Kampf* Hitler discoursed at length on this problem of *Lebensraum*—living space—a subject which obsessed him to his dying breath. . . . But the soil of Europe was already occupied. True, Hitler recognized, "but nature has not reserved this soil for the future possession of any particular nation or race; on the contrary, this soil exists for the people which possesses the force to take it." What if the present possessors object? "Then the law of self-preservation goes into effect; and what is refused to amicable methods, it is up to the fist to take.". . .

Can anyone contend that the blueprint here is not clear and precise? France will be destroyed, but that is secondary to the German drive eastward. First the immediate lands to

---

ollection of the day before, he rattled off his same old nonsense as though nothing at all had happened, and, if indignantly challenged, affected amazement; he couldn't remember a thing, except that he had proved the correctness of his assertions the previous day.

Sometimes I stood there thunderstruck.

I didn't know what to be more amazed at: the agility of their tongues or their virtuosity at lying.

Gradually I began to hate them.

All this had but one good side: that in proportion as the real leaders or at least the disseminators of Social Democracy came within my vision, my love for my people inevitably grew. For who, in view of the diabolical craftiness of these seducers, could damn the luckless victims? How hard it was, even for me, to get the better of this race of dialectical liars! And how futile was such success in dealing with people who twist the truth in your mouth, who without so much as a blush disavow the word they have just spoken, and in the very next minute take credit for it after all.

Adolf Hitler, *Mein Kampf.* Trans. Ralph Manheim. Boston: Houghton Mifflin, 1971, pp. 62–63.

the East inhabited predominantly by Germans will be taken. And what are these? Obviously Austria, the Sudetenland in Czechoslovakia and the western part of Poland, including Danzig. After that, Russia herself. Why was the world so surprised, then, when Chancellor Hitler, a bare few years later, set out to achieve these very ends?

On the nature of the future Nazi State, Hitler's ideas in *Mein Kampf* are less concise. He made it clear enough that there would be no "democratic nonsense" and that the Third Reich would be ruled by the *Fuehrerprinzip*, the leadership principle—that is, that it would be a dictatorship. There is almost nothing about economics in the book. The subject bored Hitler and he never bothered to try to learn something about it. . . .

What interested Hitler was political power; economics could somehow take care of itself. . . .

Therefore, as Hitler said in a speech in Munich in 1923, "no economic policy is possible without a sword, no industrialization without power." Beyond that vague, crude philosophy and a passing reference in *Mein Kampf* to "economic chambers," "chambers of estates" and a "central economic parliament" which "would keep the national economy functioning," Hitler refrains from any expression of opinion on the economic foundation of the Third Reich. . . .

Considerable editorial advice and even pruning on the part of at least three helpers could not prevent Hitler from meandering from one subject to another in *Mein Kampf*. Rudolf Hess, who took most of the dictation first at Landsberg prison and later at Haus Wachenfeld near Berchtesgaden, did his best to tidy up the manuscript, but he was no man to stand up to the Leader. More successful in this respect was Father Bernhard Stempfle, . . . an anti-Semitic journalist of some notoriety in Bavaria. This strange priest . . . corrected some of Hitler's bad grammar, straightened out what prose he could and crossed out a few passages which he convinced the author were politically objectionable. The third adviser was Josef Czerny, of Czech origin, who worked on the Nazi newspaper, *Voelkischer Beobachter*, and whose anti-Jewish poetry endeared him to Hitler. Czerny was instrumental in revising the first volume of *Mein Kampf* for its second printing, in which certain embarrassing words and sentences were eliminated or changed; and he went over carefully the proofs of Volume Two.

Nevertheless, most of the meanderings remained. Hitler insisted on airing his thoughts at random on almost every conceivable subject, including culture, education, the theater, the movies, the comics, art, literature, history, sex, marriage, prostitution and syphilis. Indeed, on the subject of syphilis, Hitler devotes ten turgid pages, declaring it is *"the* task of the nation—not just *one more* task," to eradicate it. To combat this dread disease Hitler demands that all the propaganda resources of the nation be mobilized. "Everything," he says, "depends on the solution of this question." The problem of syphilis and prostitution must also be attacked, he states, by facilitating earlier marriages, and he gives a foretaste of the eugenics [attempted improvement of a species or race through genetic manipulation] of the Third Reich by insisting that "marriage cannot be an end in itself, but must serve the one higher goal: the increase and preservation of the species and the race. This alone is its meaning and its task."

Life as an Eternal Struggle

And so with this mention of the preservation of the species and of the race in *Mein Kampf* we come to the second principal consideration: Hitler's *Weltanschauung*, his view of life, which some historians, especially in England, have seen as a crude form of Darwinism but which in reality . . . has its roots deep in German history and thought. Like Darwin but also like a whole array of German philosophers, historians, kings, generals and statesmen, Hitler saw all life as an eternal struggle and the world as a jungle where the fittest survived and the strongest ruled—a "world where one creature feeds on the other and where the death of the weaker implies the life of the stronger."

Mein Kampf is studded with such pronouncements: "In the end only the urge for self-preservation can conquer . . . Mankind has grown great in eternal struggle, and only in eternal peace does it perish. . . . Nature . . . puts living creatures on this globe and watches the free play of forces. She then confers the master's right on her favorite child, the strongest in courage and industry. . . . The stronger must dominate and not blend with the weaker, thus sacrificing his own greatness. Only the born weakling can view this as cruel . . ." For Hitler the preservation of culture "is bound up with the rigid law of necessity and the right to victory of the best and strongest in the world. Those who want to live, let them fight, and those who do not want to fight, in this world of eternal struggle, do not deserve to live. Even if this were hard—that is how it is!"

And who is "nature's favorite child, the strongest in courage and industry" on whom Providence has conferred "the master's right"? The Aryan. Here in *Mein Kampf* we come to the kernel of the Nazi idea of race superiority, of the conception of the master race, on which the Third Reich and Hitler's New Order in Europe were based. . . .

> Blood mixture and the resultant drop in the racial level is the sole cause of the dying out of old cultures; for men do not perish as a result of lost wars, but by the loss of that force of resistance which is continued only in pure blood. All who are not of good race in this world are chaff.

Chaff were the Jews and the Slavs, and in time, when he became dictator and conqueror, Hitler would forbid the marriage of a German with any member of these races, though a fourth-grade schoolmarm could have told him that there was a great deal of Slavic blood in the Germans, especially in those who dwelt in the eastern provinces. In carrying out his racial ideas, it must again be admitted, Hitler was as good as his word. In the New Order which he began to impose on the Slavs in the East during the war, the Czechs, the Poles, the Russians were—and were to remain, if the grotesque New Order had endured—the hewers of wood and the drawers of water for their German masters. . . .

Hitler's Feverish Brain

Such were the ideas of Adolf Hitler, set down in all their appalling crudeness as he sat in Landsberg prison gazing out at a flowering orchard above the River Lech, or later, in 1925–26, as he reclined on the balcony of a comfortable inn at Berchtesgaden and looked out across the towering Alps toward his native Austria, dictating a torrent of words to his faithful Rudolf Hess and dreaming of the Third Reich which he would build . . . and which he would rule with an iron hand. That one day he would build it and rule it he had no doubts whatsoever, for he was possessed of that burning sense of mission peculiar to so many geniuses who have sprouted, seemingly, from nowhere and from nothing throughout the ages. He would unify a chosen people who had never before been politically one. He would purify their race. He would make them strong. He would make them lords of the earth.

A crude Darwinism? A sadistic fancy? An irresponsible egoism? A megalomania? It was all of these in part. But it was something more. For the mind and the passion of Hitler—all the aberrations that possessed his feverish brain—had roots that lay deep in German experience and thought. Nazism and the Third Reich, in fact, were but a logical continuation of German history.

Who Joined the Nazi Party?

Robert Edwin Herzstein

The Nazi Party was ultimately successful because over the course of the 1920s and early 1930s it drew in millions of new members and received the support of numerous well-to-do and/or well-known individuals. In this essay, University of South Carolina professor Robert Edwin Herzstein discusses the various kinds of people attracted to Nazism. He begins with free booting military adventurers, such as Ernst Röhm (who became the head of the SA), men itching for a fight and eager to shake up the established order. Then Herzstein identifies some of the group's financial supporters, including the daughter of the great nineteenth-century German operatic composer Richard Wagner, whose music Hitler found inspiring. Many lower-middle-class men, Herzstein explains, turned to Nazism as a way of maintaining traditional patriotic values at a time when German society was undergoing radical political changes. And finally, there was the Nazi appeal to anti-Semitic sentiments that were particularly strong in Germany at this time.

Hitler drew into his party men such as Captain Ernst Röhm, still officially with the Reichswehr [German army] command in Bavaria, and the former head of the Richthofen air squadron in 1918, Hermann Göring. Göring was a high-living, intelligent, cynical, self-proclaimed Renaissance man, married to a beautiful Swedish wife. Men such as Röhm and Göring wanted adventure—they wanted a nationalist uprising against the Republic. They, in turn, through their mili-

From *Adolf Hitler and the German Trauma*, by Robert E. Herzstein. Copyright © by Robert Edwin Herzstein. Originally published by G.P. Putnam's Sons, New York. Reprinted here by permission of the author and his literary agent, Susan Ann Protter.

tary prestige, brought hundreds of other men into the paramilitary arm of the Nazi Party, the Sturmabteilung or SA. Hitler was always troubled by this Freikorps [i.e., freebooter, or soldier of fortune] adventurer type. Contrary to what one might assume, he was suspicious of such men. His direction was entirely political and he saw paramilitary groups such as the SA as an arm of his political leadership of the National Socialist German Workers' Party. Men like Röhm and Göring, at least in this period, saw things quite differently. They wished to use the SA and other paramilitary groups as a sort of surrogate army. . . . In this SA they would perpetuate military values, hide weapons, and prepare for the day of reckoning with the Weimar Republic. They hoped to play a major role in obliterating the Treaty of Versailles and its main sponsor, France. . . .

The Party's Supporters

Several elements made up the early Nazi Party: petit bourgeois [lower-middle-class shopkeepers and artisans]; servicemen and adventurers such as Göring, Rudolf Hess, and Ernst Röhm; the fanatically ambitious, embittered revolutionary orator, Adolf Hitler; anti-Semitic pornographers and dregs such as Julius Streicher. There is a further problem concerning the early Party which is more difficult to pinpoint, but it is undoubtedly there. The Party spent far more than it took in from selling subscriptions to the *Völkischer Beobachter* [the party's right-wing newspaper] and charging admission to Nazi rallies. What was the nature of the financial support for the Party? Certain elements in Munich society, afraid of Bolshevik revolution and hating the Weimar Republic in Berlin, were willing to give money to Adolf Hitler. At first, Hitler bowed and scraped in the presence of such individuals of superior social status. Hitler clearly was ill at ease. He would scream too much and then turn on his heels and take his leave. But individuals such as . . . Helene Bechstein, wife of the famous piano manufacturer, Putzi Hanfstaengl, of the famous art-collecting family, and Winifried Wagner, daughter-in-law of the great composer [Richard Wagner], took Hitler under their protection in this period, taught him better manners and better dress, and gave

Do You Want to Be Jewish Slaves?

These are excerpts from a 1920 pamphlet written by Anton Drexler, one of Hitler's colleagues in the group that would soon become the Nazi Party. This is a clear example of how the group tried to appeal to anti-Jewish feelings that were widespread in Munich and other German cities at the time.

National Socialist German Workers Party

A Political Awakening

Dear Colleagues,

It is a workmate who is speaking to you—one who still stands at the lathe.

What he has to say to you might seem rather strange and surprising; since it sounds very different to what you are accustomed to hear. . . . I am a socialist like yourselves, and want manual workers to gain equality with all other creative groups, as well as the annihilation of layabouts and drones and the confiscation of profits earned without work or effort. . . .

But I am convinced that we are not on the right path to reach this goal. . . .

Many of our leaders are indeed honest men, and want the best for the workers. But there are also a number who are in the service of a foreign power.

They have used the workers' movement as an instrument for certain special interests. . . . As a result of my investigations, I am convinced:

There is a secret world conspiracy, which while speaking much about humanity and tolerance, in reality wants only to harness the people to a new yoke.

A number of workers' leaders belong to this group. The leaders are big capitalists. . . .

300 big bankers, financiers and press barons, who are interconnected across the world, are the real dictators. They belong almost exclusively to the 'chosen people'. They are all members of this same secret conspiracy, which organises world politics. . . . Their aim is:

the Party some money. At this and later times Hitler seems

THE DICTATORSHIP OF MONEY OVER WORK. . . .
When will we finally see through the false friends of our
movement? The Jewish big capitalist always plays our friend
and dogooder; but he only does it to make us into his slaves.
The trusting worker is going to help him to set up the world
dictatorship of Jewry. Because that is their goal, as it states in
the Bible. 'All the peoples will serve you, all the wealth of the
world will belong to you'. . . . In the Talmud it says, 'a time is
coming when every Jew will have 2800 slaves'.
Comrades, do you want to be Jewish slaves?
. . . An end to false pride! We workers always give it out that
we have created all human culture with our bare hands. But is
that right? . . . What about teachers, inventors, artists, re-
searchers and technicians?
Are the middle classes, the bourgeoisie and the farmers not
productive? . . . and don't they also suffer under the dictatorship
of big capital, just like us? Wouldn't it make more sense to offer
them our hand and together turn on our common enemy? . . .
It is the particular trick of the capitalist exploiters that they are
able to play the workers and the bourgeoisie off one against the
other, and thereby keep them powerless.
Shake off your Jewish leaders, and those in the pay of Judas!
. . . And one final point. Don't expect anything from Bolshevism [Russian communism]. It doesn't bring the worker freedom. . . . In Russia the eight-hour day has been abolished.
There are no more workers' councils. All cower under the dictatorship of a hundred government commissars, who are nine-
tenths Jewish.
Bolshevism is a Jewish swindle.

Anton Drexler, toolmaker.
Munich
1920

Simon Taylor, *The Rise of Hitler: Revolution and Counter-revolution in Germany,
1918–1933*. New York: Universe Books, 1983, pp. 63–64.

to have had a particularly winning way with middle-aged women, and he used this charm to the utmost. Some very few industrialists, such as Fritz Thyssen, may have given Hitler some funds early in the 1920's, but it would be absurd to state that Hitler was a tool of the German industrialists during this period. He was not nearly that important until 1931–1932.

Winifried Wagner, who was particularly enamored of Hitler, was an important conquest for him. . . . It was on paper supplied by Winifried Wagner that Hitler dictated the first draft of Volume I of *Mein Kampf*. Through her he came into contact with the infirm Houston Stewart Chamberlain, archpoet of German racialism, the author in 1899 of the famous *Foundations of the Nineteenth Century*. How closely Hitler had read Chamberlain is difficult to determine. . . . In his table talk during World War II, Hitler criticized Chamberlain for trying to fuse Germanic and Christian concepts. For Hitler, Christianity was a part of the Jewish poison which had infected the Aryan peoples. . . . Nevertheless, Hitler knew the prestige of this fanatical racial theorist in right-wing circles, and he paid a symbolic visit to Chamberlain in Bayreuth in October, 1923. Chamberlain, in a now famous letter to Hitler, soon thereafter avowed his belief in the Nazi cause and his personal faith in the Führer's messianic mission. When Chamberlain died in 1927, the Nazi daily gave him a five-column obituary.

The Influence of Anti-Semitism

Thus, before 1923 Hitler and the Nazis drew almost exclusively upon fringe fanatical elements in German society, elements which were at the time without a national base. We must question what type of a society it was in which such elements could eventually mold the destiny of Europe. But such financial and social contacts were not the only important new acquaintances made by Hitler in these early years of the *Bewegung* or the Nazi movement. Through the agency of Alfred Rosenberg, a German . . . who had been in Russia during the Bolshevik Revolution, Hitler met many of the White Russian refugees who flocked to Munich after the failure of the Russian counterrevolution in 1919–1920. These individuals, already strongly anti-Semitic, helped convince Hitler that the Russian Revolution was a revolt of the racial underworld provoked by the Jews in order to destroy the Aryan peoples. . . .

It is difficult to portray the moral and intellectual atmosphere in Bavaria and indeed in much of Germany during this period. Students went about quoting the "Protocols of the Elders of Zion," a notorious forgery which claimed that a Jewish world conspiracy existed. Anti-Semitism was more rife than ever before and was openly advocated by leading academics. The so-called Revolution of 1918 [in which democratic factions established the Weimar Republic] had not been a revolution in terms of replacing judges and teachers, most of whom stayed on and continued to hold their old imperial, reactionary German attitudes. They often treated the left harshly and the right, however murderous, kindly.

Reaffirming Traditional Values

In the midst of all of this decadence and despair, great innovative work flourished in the Weimar Republic. Such creative work, whether in architecture, painting, or literature, tended to have an aesthetically or politically radical impulse behind it. This further annoyed large segments of the frightened German middle class, while the very real decadence of the SA, Freikorps men, and Nazis was successfully concealed behind the torrent of abuse which they visited upon the . . . experimental German intellectual scene. . . . The artistic outsider of the prewar days was now the artistic insider. The bourgeoisie, however, was troubled by the revolutionary implications of the new art and the new values. Under these unsettled conditions, thousands of men flocked into groups such as the Nazis and the SA in order to reaffirm traditional patriotic virtues. Solidarity as expressed in military music and marching, the use of the Aryan sign or swastika (which had first been used by the Austrian Nazis), parading about in uniforms, and above all, the continuation of the officer-enlisted man relationship—this was the manner in which men like Röhm and Hitler answered the chaos and innovation of the early Weimar period.

The Nazi Party in Germany was not the only National Socialist organization in Europe. The Sudeten Germans and the Austro-Germans had similar if weaker organizations, and at least until the early 1920's there was a sort of Nazi international [brotherhood] among the three of them. The German Party, however, had by 1923 eclipsed the others in both fame and strength, and Hitler was the undisputed leader of this Nazi Party by 1922. It was clear that the other members of the steering committee could not do without him, that he was the main reason why the halls were filled when the NSDAP [Nazi Party] held a rally.

Chapter 3

Hitler Comes to Power

The Nazis Gain Strength by Exploiting the Electoral System

Crane Brinton, John B. Christopher, and Robert Lee Wolff

In the late 1920s, while Germany experienced increasing prosperity, most Germans supported moderate parties such as the Social Democrats. But as unemployment, poverty, and other severe effects of the Great Depression increased after 1929, the German people began to lean more toward right-wing groups. Among these were the *Stahlhelm*, or "Steel Helmets," a conservative organization of army veterans, and the Nazis. The aging president, former general and war hero Paul von Hindenburg, himself leaned increasingly toward the right, believing that more autocratic rule was needed to alleviate the growing economic emergency, which, of course, played into the Nazis' hands. In this essay, Crane Brinton and John B. Christopher of the University of Rochester and Robert Lee Wolff, the Archibald Cary Coolidge Professor of History at Harvard University, explain how Hitler took advantage of the changing political situation and made impressive gains in a series of elections. By making backroom deals and thereby manipulating Hindenburg and other leading politicians at the same time, Hitler managed to become chancellor largely by legal means.

During . . . [the] middle years of the Weimar Republic, economic recovery proceeded steadily, until, in 1929, German industrial output exceeded that of 1913. First-rate German

From *A History of Civilization: 1815 to the Present*, by Crane Brinton, John B. Christopher, and Robert Lee Wolff, 5th ed., ©1976. Reprinted by permission of Prentice-Hall, Inc., Upper Saddle River, N.J.

equipment, coupled with superb technical skill and a systematic adoption of American methods of mass production, created a highly efficient industrial machine. . . . The emphasis was always on heavy industry, which meant that continued prosperity would depend upon a big armaments program.

All through this period, [war] reparations were paid faithfully, with no damage to the German economy. Indeed, more money flowed into Germany from foreign, especially American, investment than flowed out from reparations. Dependence on foreign capital, however, which would cease to flow in time of depression, made German prosperity artificial.

In 1925, after President [Friedrich] Ebert died, a presidential election was held in which three candidates competed. The Catholic Center, the Democrats, and the Social Democrats supported the Center leader, Wilhelm Marx. The Nationalists, People's party, and other right-wingers joined in support of Field Marshal Hindenburg, then seventy-seven years old. The communists ran their own candidate and thus contributed to the election of Hindenburg, who won by a small plurality. Abroad, the choice of a man so intimately connected with imperial militarist Germany created dismay; but until 1930 Hindenburg acted entirely in accordance with the constitution, to the distress of most of the nationalist groups. The domestic issues of this period all aroused great heat, but were settled by democratic process. In the elections of 1928, the Social Democrats were returned to power and the Nationalists and Nazis were hard hit. All in all, prosperity encouraged moderation and a return to support of the republic. . . .

The Impact of the Depression

But even before the last achievements of this "period of fulfillment," the depression had begun to knock the foundations out from under prosperity and moderation. Unemployment rose during 1929. After the American stock-market crash in October, foreign credits, on which prosperity had so largely depended, were no longer available to Germany. Short-term loans were not renewed, or else were recalled. Tariff barriers were hurting foreign trade. Hunger reappeared.

Although unemployment insurance cushioned the first shock for the workers, the lower middle classes, painfully recovering from the inflation, had no such barrier between them and destitution. Their desperation helped Hitler, whose fortunes during the years of fulfillment had fallen very low, although he had attracted a number of new followers who were later to be important in his movement. . . .

The Republic in Danger

The government fell in 1930 over a disagreement on a question of unemployment insurance benefits. Hindenburg appointed to the chancellorship Heinrich Bruening, a member of the Catholic Center party. Bruening would have liked to support parliamentary institutions . . . but he was to find it impossible. . . . President Hindenburg, now eighty-two, had fallen more and more under the influence of General Kurt von Schleicher, an ambitious political soldier who had intrigued himself into the president's favor.

Hindenburg was now itching to rule by decree, as the constitution authorized him to do in an emergency. By failing to pass Bruening's economic program, the Reichstag gave Hindenburg the opportunity he wanted. Bruening agreed, partly because he felt that a genuine emergency existed, but partly because he was determined to keep his bitter political rivals, the Social Democrats, from replacing him in office.

A presidential decree proclaimed the new budget. When the Reichstag protested, Hindenburg dissolved it and called new elections (September 1930). Nazis and communists fought in the streets, but both gained greatly at the expense of the moderates. The Nazis' Reichstag representation rose from 12 to 107 and the communists' from 54 to 77. Bruening had to carry on against the wishes of the electorate; supported only by Hindenburg, he too now turned authoritarian.

In order to avoid a new government in which Nazis would participate, the Social Democrats decided to support Bruening. When the Reichstag met, Nazis and communists created disorder on the floor, but voted together in opposition to government measures. These measures passed only because the Social Democrats voted for them. . . .

Now Nazis, Nationalists, the veterans organization of the Steel Helmets [and other right-wing groups] . . . formed a coalition against Bruening. This coalition had great financial resources and a mass backing, chiefly Nazi. It had its private armies in the SA, in the Stahlhelm [army veterans], and in other semimilitary organizations. Because the left was split and the communists in effect acted as political allies of the right, nothing stood between this new right-wing coalition and a political victory except the person of Hindenburg, who controlled the army, and by virtue of the Weimar Constitution was able to keep Bruening in office. Early in 1932, the great industrialist Fritz Thyssen invited Hitler to address a meeting of coal and steel magnates. Hitler won their financial support by convincing them that if he came to power he would be their man. Though some of Hitler's followers were now impatient for a new putsch, he curbed them, believing that the Nazis could come to power legally.

In the presidential elections of March 1932, Hitler ran as the candidate of the Nazis, and Hindenburg as the candidate of the Center, Social Democrats, and other moderate parties. The Nationalists nominated a Stahlhelm man, and the communists of course ran their own candidate. Hitler polled 11,338,571 votes, and Hindenburg polled 18,661,736, only four-tenths of a percent short of the required majority. In the run-off election, the Nationalists backed Hitler, whose total rose to 13,400,000 as against Hindenburg's 19,360,000. The eighty-four-year-old marshal reelected as the candidate of the moderates was, however, no longer a moderate himself, but the tool of the . . . military.

Although the government now ordered the Nazi SA and SS disbanded, the decree was not enforced. In April 1932 the Nazis scored impressive victories in local elections, especially in all-important Prussia. Bruening was unable to procure in time either an Allied promise to extend the moratorium on reparations payments or permission for Germany to have equality in armaments with France. Schleicher, who was now deeply involved in intrigue against Bruening, worked on Hindenburg to demand Bruening's resignation. This Hindenburg did on May 29, 1932, the first time a president had dismissed a chancellor simply because he had lost personal confidence in him. Bruening's successor was Franz von Papen, a rich Catholic nobleman and a member of the extreme right wing of the center, who installed a cabinet composed of nobles. Papen was Schleicher's man—or so Schleicher thought. The Center disavowed Papen, who had the real support of no political party or group, but whom the Nazis temporarily tolerated because he agreed to remove the ban on the SA and SS. . . .

On July 31, 1932, new elections for the Reichstag took place, called by Papen on the theory that the Nazis had passed their peak, that their vote would decrease, and that they would then be chastened and would cooperate in the government. But the Nazis won 230 seats and became the biggest single party in the Reichstag; the communists gained also, chiefly at the expense of the Social Democrats. The Democrats and the People's party almost disappeared, while the Nationalists suffered, and the Center scored a slight gain. Papen had failed. He now wanted to take some Nazis into the government, but the Nazis demanded the chancellorship, which Hindenburg was determined not to hand over to Hitler. Papen now planned to dissolve the Reichstag and to call new elections. By repeating this process, he hoped to wear down Hitler's strength each time, until he brought Hitler to support him and accept a subordinate place. As Papen put pressure on the industrialists who had been supporting Hitler, the Nazi funds began to dry up, leaving Hitler seriously embarrassed. The elections of November 6, 1932, bore out Papen's expectations. The Nazis fell off from 230 seats to 196; and, although the communists gained substantially and ominously, Papen too won some support. . . .

The Republic Was Doomed

Had Papen been permitted to continue his tactics, it is possible that Hitler might have been kept from power. But Papen resigned as a matter of form because he could not count on majority support in the Reichstag. Angry with Schleicher and sorry to lose Papen, Hindenburg forced Schleicher himself to take the office on December 3, 1932.

Now the backstairs general was chancellor, but he had no political support whatever, and had alienated even Hindenburg. He lasted in office only about eight weeks. . . .

Schleicher did [make] . . . every effort to appeal to all shades of opinion except the extreme left. But this attempt in itself alienated the . . . industrialists. The tortuous Papen, eager for revenge, intrigued with these enemies of Schleicher. Early in January 1933 Papen met Hitler at the house of the Cologne banker Baron Kurt von Schroeder. The industrialists, who had temporarily abandoned Hitler, now agreed to pay the Nazis' debts. Hitler, in turn, no longer insisted on the chancellorship. He thus led Papen to hope that he would come back into office with Hitler's backing. Hindenburg, too, was enlisted. When the president refused to give Schleicher the authority to dissolve the Reichstag at its first new session, which would surely have voted him down, Schleicher had no choice; he was forced to resign (January 28, 1933).

But Hitler had now raised the ante, and demanded the chancellorship for himself. Papen consented, provided Hitler undertook to govern in strict accordance with parliamentary procedure. Papen was to be vice-chancellor, and still thought he could dominate the government, since only three of its eleven ministers would be Nazis. He therefore persuaded Hindenburg to accept Hitler as chancellor. But Papen underestimated Hitler. Though Hitler swore to Hindenburg that he would maintain the constitution, he had no intention of keeping his oath. The Weimar Republic was doomed from the moment Hitler came to the chancellor's office on January 30, 1933.

Hitler Consolidates Power by Eliminating the SA and Other Potential Opponents

A.J. Ryder

Even after he had made himself dictator in 1933, Hitler realized that his power was not yet completely secure. Many of the numerous SA storm troopers under Ernst Röhm did not belong to the Nazi Party. This fact, coupled with the desire of Röhm and other SA leaders to achieve important positions in the government and to absorb and control the *Reichswehr*, the regular German army, made the SA a serious threat to Hitler's continued power. Hitler decided it was essential to purge the SA, along with many other potential political opponents and rivals. The bloody process began on June 30, 1934, which later became known as the infamous "Night of the Long Knives." In the span of only a few days, Hitler both eliminated the main threats to his position and demonstrated to the nation how he planned to deal with anyone who might dare to oppose him.

There comes a time in all revolutions when disagreement breaks out among the revolutionaries. The leaders, having achieved their immediate aims, wish to consolidate and enjoy their gains, while their more radical rivals, still struggling for power, insist on a further turn of the revolutionary wheel. In the eyes of the radicals the moderates are opportunists if not traitors; in the eyes of the moderates the radi-

From *Twentieth-Century Germany: From Bismarck to Brandt*, by A.J. Ryder (New York: Columbia University Press), ©1973, A.J. Ryder. Reprinted by permission of Macmillan Ltd., London.

cals are fanatics or utopians. Behind the ideological catch-words lie personal rivalries. Such a situation existed in Germany at the end of 1933. The Nazi leaders were tasting the fruits of power; they sat in the government, directed civil servants, humiliated their opponents, developed their economic policy, but they also adapted themselves to the realities in which they found themselves. There remained the vast army of rank and file party members and the storm-troopers, most of whom were still insufficiently rewarded for their contribution to the Nazi victory. Their dissatisfaction made them a danger to Hitler. He was now more concerned with government and foreign policy than with the fulfilment of the vaguely radical aspirations of his left-wing followers. He knew that the civil servants wanted the country to settle down, and he wished to show the world that the new Germany was a land of peace and order. He had no intention of allowing the S.A. to let loose a second wave of revolution. In a speech on 7 July he warned the state governors that the time had come to call a halt to party excesses: 'The revolution is not a permanent state of affairs. . . . The stream of revolution that has been released must be guided to secure the bedrock of evolution.' And he spoke equally bluntly to the leaders of the S.A. and S.S.: 'I will suppress every attempt to disturb the existing order as ruthlessly as I will deal with the so-called second revolution.' Röhm, Chief of Staff of the S.A., rejected this view. The revolution, he complained to his senior colleagues, had fallen into stagnation, and the S.A. and S.S. might sink into mere propaganda bodies. To imagine that order was the citizen's first duty was to betray the cause, and the struggle must be continued.

A Showdown with the S.A. Inevitable

Differences between Hitler and the S.A. widened after Hitler's assumption of power. While up to then all storm-troopers belonged to the N.S.D.A.P. [the Nazi party], by the summer of 1934, when the S.A. numbered four and a half million, only about a quarter were party members. Their loyalty was doubtful, and their lack of a definite role made them restless. Though in December 1933 Röhm became a minister in the cabinet, he had no executive power and felt frustrated. His ambition had been to become Minister of War.

Hitler Arrests Röhm

One of Hitler's chauffeurs, known as Kempka, later testified to the events of the night of June 30, 1934. This excerpt from Kempka's account reveals Hitler's personal participation in the arrest of Röhm and other SA brownshirts.

Hitler sits down beside me and gives the order: 'To Wiessee, as fast as possible!'

It must have been about 4.30 a.m., the sky has cleared up, it is nearly bright daylight. We meet watering carts and people on their way to work. . . . Hitler sits beside me in silence. . . .

Just before Wiessee, Hitler suddenly breaks his silence: 'Kempka,' he says, 'drive carefully when we come to the Hotel Hanselbauer. You must drive up without making any noise. If you see an SA guard in the front of the hotel, don't wait for them to report to me; drive on and stop at the hotel entrance.' Then, after a moment of deathly silence: 'Röhm wants to carry out a *coup*.'

An icy shiver runs down my back. I could have believed anything, but not a *coup* by Röhm!

I drive up carefully to the hotel entrance as Hitler had ordered. . . . Right behind us another car stops with a squad of detectives which had been raised in Munich.

As soon as I have turned the car so that it is ready to leave in a moment, I rush into the hotel with my gun at the ready. . . .

I run quickly up the stairs to the first floor where Hitler is just coming out of Röhm's bedroom. Two detectives come out of the room opposite. One of them reports to Hitler: 'My Führer . . . the Police-President of Breslau is refusing to get dressed!'

Taking no notice of me, Hitler enters the room where Obergruppenführer Heines is remaining. I hear him shout: 'Heines, if you are not dressed in five minutes I'll have you shot on the spot!'. . .

Meanwhile, Röhm comes out of his room in a blue suit and

The S.A. chiefs would have liked to run the army, with the much smaller *Reichswehr* absorbed in what Röhm called the

with a cigar in the corner of his mouth. Hitler glares at him but says nothing. Two detectives take Röhm to the vestibule of the hotel where he throws himself into an armchair and orders coffee from the waiter.

I stay in the corridor a little to one side and a detective tells me about Röhm's arrest.

Hitler entered Röhm's bedroom alone with a whip in his hand. Behind him were two detectives with pistols at the ready. He spat out the words: 'Röhm, you are under arrest.' Röhm looked up sleepily from his pillow: 'Heil, my Führer.' 'You are under arrest' bawled Hitler for the second time, turned on his heel and left the room.

Meanwhile, upstairs in the corridor things are getting quite lively. SA leaders are coming out of their rooms and being arrested. Hitler shouts at each one: 'Have you had anything to do with Röhm's schemes?' naturally, they all deny it, but that doesn't help them in the least. . . .

No shot, no sign of resistance. All this time, Röhm is sitting unsuspectingly drinking his third cup of coffee. Only a single word from him, and the whole thing would have worked out differently. . . .

Now the bus arrives which has been fetched [to take the prisoners away]. . . . Quickly, the SA leaders are collected from the laundry room and walk past Röhm under police guard. Röhm looks up from his coffee sadly and waves to them in a melancholy way. . . .

At last Röhm too is led from the hotel. He walks past Hitler with his head bowed, completely apathetic. Now Hitler gives the order to leave. I sit at the wheel of the first car with Hitler beside me and our column, which in the meantime has grown to about twenty cars, starts moving.

Jeremy Noakes and Geoffrey Pridham, eds., *Nazism, 1919–1945, Vol. 1: The Rise to Power, 1919–1934, A Documentary Reader.* Exeter, Eng.: University of Exeter, 1983, pp. 178–79.

'brown flood' of the S.A. 'I regard the *Reichswehr*', he wrote to one of his senior officers, 'only as a training school for the German people . . . the conduct of war and therefore of mobilisation too in future is the task of the S.A.' To subordinate the highly professional army to the semi-trained mass of brownshirts was quite contrary to Hitler's plans. [President Paul von] Hindenburg, whose attachment to the *Reichswehr* was exceeded only by his veneration for the monarchy, would have vetoed it. Nor did Hitler himself believe that the stormtroops were capable of playing the part assigned to the army. The *Reichswehr*, with its expertise and proud traditions, was indispensable. Hitler knew that the generals had no love for the S.A., and that once conscription was introduced the latter would be superfluous [unneeded]. There was another consideration: Hitler was soon to offer the western powers a reduction of the S.A. as a contribution to disarmament and proof of his sincerity. For all these reasons, a showdown between Hitler and Röhm was becoming inevitable.

Hitler Prepares to Strike

On New Year's Day 1934 Hitler publicly thanked Röhm for his 'imperishable services' to the Nazi movement and the German people, but relations between them became increasingly strained. In an address . . . on 2 February Hitler again emphasised that the revolution was over and that stability was now the party's duty. All internal quarrels must be set aside in the interest of unity: 'Especially for reasons of foreign policy it is necessary to have the whole nation hypnotically behind us.' On 28 February Hitler persuaded Röhm to sign an agreement . . . which stated that the *Reichswehr* Ministry bore sole responsibility for national defence and left only training functions to the S.A. Röhm did not hide his annoyance, and told his followers privately that he did not intend to keep the agreement. This was reported to Hitler, whose reaction was: 'We must allow this affair to ripen fully.' He made his preparations for the expected Putsch. Heinrich Himmler, the head of the S.S., was put in charge of Herman Göring's political police, the Gestapo. The S.S. were to be the executioners in the forthcoming purge. But the army, the main immediate beneficiary, was to provide arms, barracks and transport. . . . Hitler knew that time was short, for he wanted to settle accounts with Röhm before the approaching death of Hindenburg. He may also have been stung into action by a speech made by Vice-Chancellor Franz von Papen at Marburg on 17 June attacking Nazi lawlessness and warning against a second wave of revolution. This was a reminder that the regime had critics on the right as well as on the left.

Opponents of All Shades Purged

Early in June Hitler, after summoning Röhm for a long conference, ordered the S.A. to go on leave for the whole of July. Röhm himself was given sick leave to attend a sanatorium for treatment of a painful nervous malady. The future of the S.A. was to be discussed at a meeting of senior S.A. officers at Bad Wiessee in Southern Bavaria. Suddenly, at the end of June, Hitler struck. He himself arrested Röhm and others in their Bad Wiessee hotel. Similar arrests of S.A. leaders took place in other parts of Germany, especially in Berlin and Silesia. The victims were usually taken to a barracks or prison and executed summarily. Röhm himself, understandably bewildered by the whole action, was shot in a Munich prison after refusing to commit suicide. Hitler took advantage of the opportunity to settle a number of grudges with past and present political opponents of all shades. Those murdered included [Gustav von] Kahr, the former Special Commissioner for Bavaria who had 'betrayed' Hitler in November 1923; [General Kurt von] Schleicher and his wife, accused posthumously of plotting with Röhm and with the French ambassador François-Poncet; [leading Nazi] Gregor Strasser, with whom Hitler had broken in December 1932; [Erich] Klausener, a well-known Catholic leader and civil servant; and Papen's legal adviser, Edgar Jung, also a Catholic. . . . Hitler admitted to 77 deaths; the exact number is not known, but was certainly much bigger. According to the Ministry of Justice, the total was 207. The S.A. was also disarmed. Papen himself had a narrow escape, which he owed to the friendship of Hindenburg . . . or possibly to the fact that he was Vice-Chancellor. The army made no effort to save Schleicher. . . . Though the Officers' Corps was furious, it was powerless. . . . Nor did the Roman Catholic Church protest at the murder of Klausener and Jung. The jurists abjectly accepted Hitler's claim that on 30 June he had acted as the supreme judge of the German nation against a National-Bolshevik rising, and an article in the *Deutsche Juristenzeitung* of 1 August 1934 carried the cynical title: 'The *Führer* protects the law.' The allegation that Röhm was about to lead a revolt against Hitler was virtually disproved by his behaviour just before the purge, and no serious evidence incriminating him was ever produced. Yet in a more general sense Röhm and his S.A. did represent a genuine threat to Hitler's regime. Henceforth German law was the will of the Führer. The claims of the S.A. were disposed of for ever, but the forces of order, which had defeated them, were in the hands of a gangster. Many Germans were now disillusioned about the Third Reich, but too frightened to act or speak against it. The real victors were the S.S., who were now placed directly under Hitler. Two years later the S.S. leader, Himmler, was put in charge of all the police in Germany. Hitler had promised the army that it would be the sole bearer of arms, but in time the S.S. was to become a more dangerous rival to the army than the S.A. and to achieve the kind of dominance Röhm had only dreamt of.

The SS and Gestapo Enforce the Nazi Police State

Roger Manvell

Adolf Hitler could not have maintained his dictatorial powers over Germany without an effective, fanatically loyal police force. Once Hitler eliminated the SA in 1934, the highly regimented and supposedly "racially pure" members of the *Schutzstaffel*, known more simply as the SS, became his enforcers. SS leader Heinrich Himmler oversaw the organization's secret branch, the Gestapo, whose agents were essentially political police who used arbitrary arrests, torture, and murder to maintain a reign of terror for the führer. From his informative and disturbing book *SS and Gestapo: Rule by Terror*, historian Roger Manvell describes the leaders, aims, and brutal tactics of the special security forces that kept Hitler in power.

What does it mean to live in a police state? More particularly, what did it mean to live in a police state administered by the agents and collaborators of the nazi regime in Germany? . . .

Learning to Live Without Civil Rights

For the ordinary citizen, living in a police state means the disappearance of most, if not all of one's civil rights. There is no protection from the peremptory knocking on the door, or the terror of sudden arrest and the disappearance of any individual, often without trace, utterly lost to his relatives and friends. The ordinary citizen who suffers from the common anxieties about the safety and security of himself and his family, soon learns to pay lip-service to the regime, and keep his nose clean. He does his daily job, performs his military service, wears the prescribed badges, pays the right dues, gives the right salutes, and keeps quiet about anything dubious he may know or suspect is going on. As the economy of his country grows straitened through war, or the preparation for it, he learns to do without the consumer goods that other people in the state, more politically privileged than himself, may still be able to enjoy. He turns on his radio receiver, tuned to receive the national service only; like the press and publishing he knows it is strictly censored and ideologically indoctrinated. He may even for a moment wonder why it is so strictly forbidden to listen to broadcasts from abroad. If in his frustration he may grumble just a little, he refers to his leaders by initials only and speaks the words beneath his breath. He has learned always to be wary of strangers, wary of his friends, wary even of the members of his family, more especially the younger generation who have been warned to watch their parents. Above all, he is careful to let slip nothing which might be held politically suspect, let alone subversive, and he shies away from acquiring any knowledge which could conceivably be judged as dangerous. He is always the very last person to know who has just been arrested, or what they may be thought to be suffering in the concentration camps. This kind of unpleasant business is the sole concern of the authorities. Nevertheless, he becomes the constant, if unwilling recipient of rumour; when all forms of news or information are known to be controlled or doctored, the winds of curiosity are inevitably stirred by the rustle of gossip, innuendo, and whispered warnings.

The Nazi Regime

The Nazi regime created an exceptional, virulent [unusually harsh] form of police state. It stemmed directly from an exceptional, virulent ruler, who, as everyone knows, came to power in Germany in January 1933, after he was created Chancellor. Little more than a dozen years before Hitler had been living the life of a back-street agitator. Nine years before he had served a term of imprisonment for conducting an abortive, armed uprising in Munich. Once installed as Chancellor, he so rapidly entrenched himself that within months he was ruling Germany virtually by personal decree. During his reign of terror, which lasted a bare twelve years, Hitler reformed and greatly expanded the frontiers of the German Reich, 'uniting' those whom he regarded as belonging to the common German stock, rearming his newborn nation, and, within six years, leading it into war. . . .

Hitler's record remains without true parallel in human history. He did what he did through the rapid establishment of a highly organized and ruthless police state. Behind the evident strength of the German army and that of the civic police stood the far less evident, and largely 'secret' forces of the SS and their colleagues of the Gestapo, the political police. Though elements in the German army serving Hitler's regime were guilty of criminal acts going far beyond the 'accepted' horrors of 'legal' total war, the crimes against humanity for which Hitler's name must stand forever execrated [hated] were undertaken in his name by these extraordinary secret forces. . . .

Racial 'Purity' and Aryan Ceremony

From the smallest beginnings—a mere handful of men intended to exercise strong-arm methods to protect the speakers at Nazi rallies—the SS came to assume immeasurable power under the tutelary leadership of Heinrich Himmler, an obsessive nationalist whose gradual ascent in the Nazi hierarchy was won by backstairs intrigue. While others . . . expended their undoubted talents in the limelight, Himmler grew in authority with the SS forces which sustained him until he became by far the most formidable of the subleaders working in close association with the Führer. Unlike most of the others, Himmler had no trace of cynicism in him. He knew precisely what he believed in—the racial superiority of the Nordic, 'Aryan' peoples and the establishment of an imperial world system under German domination, the rule of the master-race.

So it was to Himmler and to certain reliable members of

the SS that Hitler finally entrusted the highly secret operation of the 'final solution', the mass-extermination of the European Jews, the ultimate crime of genocide which came to a head during the middle and final years of the war [World War II]. It was the SS, and in particular Himmler's deputy, Reinhard Heydrich, who master-minded the plan for genocide which led to the mass-destruction within three years of over five million Jews and as many again of the other 'unwanted' peoples of Europe—Slavs, Gypsies, and those who for one reason or another had the fires of resistance burning in their bellies.

The SS therefore came to occupy a very special place in the Nazi conspiracy for power. In the public eye, before the war, they shone with a certain, elite splendour in their immaculate black uniforms edged with silver facings. They demonstrated, or were said to demonstrate, the glory of racial 'purity', with two full centuries of unsullied German stock standing to their credit. Lawyers and intellectuals, even certain aristocrats, let alone bishops, pulled what strings they could to be admitted to the SS ranks, proud of their honorary officer status and the uniform which confirmed it. They accepted with good grace, or with a cynical humour, the bogus 'Aryan' ritual and folkloric ceremonial which Himmler had devised—as if it were the Knights of the Round Table he was convening, and not an organisation whose prime function was, in the end, to murder their fellow-men.

The Trivial and the Terrible

Certain details in this grim, extraordinary history possess a kind of dark comedy—for example, Himmler zealously competing for an SS athletics badge with his aides surreptitiously upgrading his lamentable performance, the endless fuss of racial 'purity' when any SS man felt the urge to marry, or the pagan ceremonials invented to celebrate Nazi anniversaries or replace Christian ceremonies for marriage, birth, and death. The more cynical merely laughed at Himmler behind his back, until the day came when they had to hear one of his grim speeches delivered before private gatherings of his SS officers. Here, as nowhere else, Himmler frankly outlined the need to exterminate the Jews and work his prisoners to death for further German victory. Most of them would listen to such things with a cold detachment, because it was not likely they would themselves in person have to spill a victim's blood. This, after all, was normally left to the SS rank and file, the trained killers, men recruited for front-line duties in the so-called Action Groups, or to the labour squads assembled to carry out the extermination routines developed by the technicians of mass-genocide.

The absurd, the trivial, the macabre, the terrible, all make up the SS story, which imposed the ultimate in human suffering on many millions of innocent people. The smiling VIP at a Party reception, dusting his new black uniform as he sips his black-market liquor, stands at one end of the sinister SS spectrum, while at the other, hidden away from public sight, some terrorized woman screams as a man in the same elegant garb hits her across the face. There is polite applause for Himmler . . . while in the confines of some backroom Adolf Eichmann [one of Himmler's henchmen] plans the logistics of transportation for the next fifty thousand Jews to be exterminated. . . .

The Gestapo

All this, and more than this, became the punitive function of the SS, once the Nazis had achieved full power. And behind them, working in close alliance with the SS, were the men and women of the Gestapo, police either in uniform or plain clothes with the special function of maintaining political security in Germany and later in the German-occupied countries. These were the men who came for you in the small hours of the night, their cars, tires screaming, braking suddenly to a halt in the street below, snatching you, half-awake and terrified, from the arms of your wife and children. They were the specialists in brutal interrogation, with or without their medieval machines of torture, who knew by hard experience the finer limits of human endurance and the stages by which any information they required, true or false, could be most effectively extracted.

Better even than the SS, the Gestapo learnt the melodramatic techniques of terrorization which form an inevitable part in the conduct of a police state. A melodramatic style in terrorization is a psychological factor in conditioning those who must be pursued, harried, and punished. Sheer uncertainty is a further factor; when a person does not know through months or even years what may happen to him from day to day or night to night, powers of resistance in the most resilient can be gradually worn away.

The network of administrative machinery which lay behind this arbitrary form of power grew up largely behind the backs of the German public. They saw it only in its outward manifestations—the undergrowth of published decrees, laws, and regulations which finally hedged them in. Behind the scenes, at the desks of ministries and Party offices, the conspiracy of the bureaucrats had also taken place, created by men with a genius for stopping up the loopholes of civil liberty and the citizen's right of protest. On the whole, the German public took it meekly, with a fatalistic shrug of the shoulders; they saw it as a gradually encroaching *fait accompli* [a done deal], far too dangerous to resist.

These then were the conditions in Germany, and eventually in the occupied territories of Europe, which began in 1933 and lasted until the final defeat of Hitler brought liberation for the living. Some two-thirds of Europe became subject to this organized form of tyranny.

Nazi Persecution of Jews and Christians

Robert-Hermann Tenbrock

One of the most visible signs of Hitler's assumption of power in Germany in 1933 was the widespread persecution of religious groups, mainly Jews and Christians. In this essay from his history of his native country, noted German scholar Robert-Hermann Tenbrock first summarizes the Nazis' systematic denial of the Jews' civil rights as Germans. Then he describes the culmination of pre–World War II anti-Jewish savagery, the frightening *Kristallnacht*, translated variously as "Crystal Night" or "Night of the Broken Glass." This was the name coined to describe the widespread destruction of property and physical violence directed against German Jews by the SS and other thugs on the night of November 9/10, 1938. Tenbrock concludes with a brief account of Nazi attempts to suppress and silence Christian leaders.

German Jewry had won a position of respect for itself in Germany. . . . The tendency to merge entirely with the German people had become more pronounced in proportion to the ever-increasing social, economic and professional equality. Conversions to either of the two great Christian confessions [Catholicism and Protestantism] were not infrequent and marriages with non-Jews were no longer looked upon as something out of the ordinary. During the Great War, the percentage of Jews who laid down their lives for their country was completely in accord with their numbers in the pop-

Reprinted from *A History of Germany*, by Robert-Hermann Tenbrock (London: Longmans, Green). Copyright ©1968 by Max Hueber Verlag, Muenchen, and Ferdinand Schoeningh, Paderborn.

ulation. Many of them left the army with high decorations. Since the war the Jews had provided a remarkable number of internationally recognised scientists like Einstein, artists like Max Reinhardt, musicians like Bruno Walter and [Arnold] Schönberg, writers like [Franz] Kafka, and philosophers like Martin Buber. In spite of anti-Semitic speeches and writing before and after the First World War . . . the tendency towards assimilation had continued among the majority of German Jews.

The Brutal Anti-Jewish Campaign

This fruitful development was brought to an abrupt end, when Hitler assumed power. Completely misunderstanding Hitler's real intentions, only very few German Jews, mainly those active in politics, got out of harm's way. But as early as 1 April 1933 a public boycott hit Jewish shops, lawyers and doctors hard. The SA provided sentries to supervise its observance. By the law for the "Restoration of the Civil Service" all Jews and officials descended "from at least three grandparents of pure Jewish race", as well as political opponents, lost their posts. The Jews in the liberal professions were also deprived of their livelihood, for since the *Gleichschaltung* (the coordination of the *Reich*), all self-employed persons were obliged to enroll in a Nazi organisation.

The "Nuremberg Laws" of 15 September 1935 distinguished between "Aryan citizens of the *Reich*" enjoying full rights and mere "subjects", prohibited marriages between Aryans and Jews, and brutally punished the so-called "racial stain". Thus, in one fell stroke, the Jews were cast back to their state of pre-emancipation days.

The assassination of a counsellor at the German embassy in Paris by the 17-year-old son of a Jewish family deported to Poland in the most shameful fashion was the opportunity for an organised outbreak of "spontaneous" terror by plainclothes [storm troopers] . . . against all Jews in the night of 9/10 November 1938 (called the *Kristallnacht* or "Night of the Broken Glass" on account of the shattered windows of Jewish shops). In this one night practically all the synagogues in Germany were set on fire, Jewish cemeteries desecrated, and brutalities practiced on Jewish men, women and children. In addition a fine of 1,250 million Marks was imposed on the Jews. From now on, Jews were forbidden to take part in cultural events or attend German schools. Naturally they were regarded as "unfit for military service", too. In order to make any relations with a German impossible, in accordance with Hitler's will, they were bound as from 15 September 1941 to wear a "Star of David", several inches across, attached to their clothing on the left hand side of the breast, and to add "Israel" or "Sarah" to "Aryan" sounding names. Many Jews proudly conformed to this decree to bear the names of great biblical personages. A kind of "Jewish Renaissance" flowered out of the isolation into which the Jews were now forced. Hitler's final aim was the physical extermination of the whole of European Jewry, a goal for which he felt the time was not yet ripe merely for reasons of foreign policy. A war would, in his opinion, provide him with the opportunity he was looking for.

Christian Leaders Arrested and Imprisoned

The two great Christian confessions, but especially the Catholic Church, had met Hitler's seizure of power with reserve or open disapproval. The assertion in the Nazi programme that the party "rests on the foundation of positive Christianity" was generally regarded as pure rhetoric. The Catholic Church had even attached penalties to membership of the National Socialist Party. After he came to power, Hitler's political conduct towards the Churches at first seemed to give the lie to this attitude. In July 1933 he concluded a concordat with the Catholic Church, in which he recognised the Church's right to its own Catholic youth organisation and to denominational schools. But immediately after signing it, he had Catholic youth leaders arrested in Berlin. A little later he tried to shake the Catholic population's confidence in its pastors by bringing "scandal cases" against Catholic priests.

Hitler thought the Protestant Church would be easy meat. Ludwig Müller, a former army chaplain, was placed at the head of a Hitler-inspired splinter group which called it-

Night of the Broken Glass

This is part of the report filed on November 21, 1938, by David Buffum, the American consul in the German city of Leipzig who witnessed firsthand the terrifying night of anti-Jewish persecution earlier that month.

The shattering of shop windows, looting of stores and dwellings of Jews which began in the early hours of 10 November 1938, was hailed subsequently in the Nazi press as a 'spontaneous wave of righteous indignation throughout Germany, as a result of the cowardly Jewish murder of Third Secretary von Rath in the German Embassy at Paris'. So far as a very high percentage of the German populace is concerned, a state of popular indignation that would spontaneously lead to such excesses, can be considered as nonexistent. On the contrary, in viewing the ruins and attendant measures employed, all of the local crowds observed were obviously benumbed over what had happened and aghast over the unprecedented fury of Nazi acts that had been or were taking place with bewildering rapidity throughout their city. . . .

At 3 a.m. on 10 November 1938 was unleashed a barrage of Nazi ferocity as had had no equal hitherto in Germany, or very likely anywhere else in the world since savagery began. Jewish buildings were smashed into and contents demolished or looted. In one of the Jewish sections an eighteen-year-old boy was hurled from a three-storey window to land with both legs broken on a street littered with burning beds and other household furniture and effects from his family's and other apartments. This information was supplied by an attending physician. It is reported from another quarter that among domestic effects thrown out of a Jewish building, a small dog descended four flights on to a cluttered street with a broken spine. Although apparently centred in poorer districts, the raid was not confined to the humble classes. One apartment of exceptionally refined occupants known to this office was violently ransacked, presumably in a search for valuables which was not in vain, and one of the marauders thrust a cane through a priceless medieval painting portraying a biblical scene. Another apartment of the same category is known to have been turned upside down in the frenzied pursuit of whatever the invaders were after. Reported loss by looting of cash, silver, jewellery, and otherwise easily convertible articles, has been apparent.

Jewish shop windows by the hundreds were systematically and wantonly smashed throughout the entire city at a loss estimated at several millions of marks. There are reports that substantial losses have been sustained . . . as many of the shop windows at the time of the demolition were filled with costly furs that were seized before the windows could be boarded up. In proportion to the general destruction of real estate, however, losses of goods are felt to have been relatively small. The spectators who viewed the wreckage when daylight had arrived were mostly in such a bewildered mood that there was no danger of impulsive acts, and the perpetrators probably were too busy in carrying out their schedule to take off a whole lot of time for personal profit. At all events, the main streets of the city were a positive litter of shattered plate glass. According to reliable testimony, the debacle was executed by SS men and Stormtroopers not in uniform, each group having been provided with hammers, axes, crowbars and incendiary bombs.

Three synagogues in Leipzig were fired simultaneously by incendiary bombs and all sacred objects and records desecrated or destroyed, in most cases hurled through the windows and burned in the streets. No attempts whatsoever were made to quench the fires, the activity of the fire brigade being confined to playing water on adjoining buildings. All of the synagogues were irreparably gutted by flames, and the walls of the two that are close to the consulate are now being razed. The blackened frames have been centres of attraction during the past week of terror for eloquently silent and bewildered crowds.

Jeremy Noakes and Geoffrey Pridham, eds., *Nazism, 1919–1945, Vol. 2: State, Economy and Society, 1933–1939, A Documentary Reader.* Exeter, Eng.: University of Exeter, 1984, pp. 554–55.

self the "German Christians' Faith Movement". He had Müller appointed *Reichsbischof* ["Bishop of the Reich"]. After Müller had been confirmed in this position by synodal elections which resulted in a German Christian majority in all the regional churches, with the exception of Westphalia, Hitler regarded him as the official representative of the Protestant Church. But now representatives of the Protestant Church in all the German *Länder* [provinces] took up the struggle against the distortion of the Christian message by the German Christians. They formed the "Confessing Church", which took its stand on the bible and the creeds. The best brain among them was Karl Barth, their best known member Martin Niemöller, former submarine commander during the First World War and now pastor in Berlin-Dahlem. Niemöller was placed in a concentration camp in 1937 because of his resistance to the National Socialists, and remained there until the end of the Second World War.

Chapter 4

The Nazis Transform German Society

Turning | Points

IN WORLD HISTORY

Strict Nazi Controls of the Press and Other Forms of Communication

David Welch

One of the grim realities of life in Nazi Germany was government censorship. David Welch, a professor of history at the University of Kent at Canterbury in England, describes how the Nazis controlled and censored Germany's radio, press, and film industries. Under Hitler's propaganda minister, Joseph Goebbels, the Ministry for Popular Enlightenment and Propaganda (RMVP) and Ministry of Culture tightly regulated these means of communication. The media became a tool to help spread conformity to the ideals of the Third Reich.

When Goebbels became Minister for Propaganda, the [German] newspaper and film industries were still privately owned; the broadcasting system, however, had been State-regulated since 1925 by means of the Reich Radio Company [RRG]. . . . However, the RRG had little say over programme content, which was the responsibility of nine regional broadcasting companies. . . .

Although the Nazis had failed to gain access to this medium while in opposition, once in power the 'coordination' of German radio proved comparatively easy, despite a few initial setbacks. From the moment he assumed power, Goebbels recognised its propaganda potential and he was determined to make the most of this relatively new medium. In his address to representatives of the press on 15 March

Reprinted from *The Third Reich: Politics and Propaganda*, by David Welch (London: Routledge), ©1993 by David A. Welch, by permission of the publishers.

1933, Goebbels had revealed that the radio would have the responsibility of bringing the people closer to the National Socialist State. He hinted that the Nazis had already gone some way to achieving this, because

> our radio propaganda is not produced in a vacuum, in radio stations, but in the atmosphere-laden halls of mass gatherings. In this way every listener has become a direct participant in these events. I have a vision of a new and topical radio, a radio that really takes account of the spirit of our time . . . a radio that is aware of its great national responsibility.

Goebbels clearly saw in radio an instrument not only to create uniformity but also to guide public opinion towards the Nazi concept of 'national community' as the ideological obverse to the class conflict that had been such a feature of Weimar politics. . . . In his efforts to consolidate his control over radio, Goebbels' immediate problem was to break down the federal structure, over which the Reich possessed limited economic and political control. . . . Thus before Goebbels could assert his new ministry's control over radio, indeed over all rival agencies, he was obliged to persuade Hitler to issue a supplementary decree on 30 June 1933 which laid out in detail those responsibilities which were to be transferred to RMVP from other ministries and rival agencies. The regulations stated:

> The Reich Minister for Popular Enlightenment and Propaganda is responsible for all influences on the intellectual life of the nation; public relations for the State, culture, and the economy, for instructing the domestic and foreign public about them and for the administration of all the institutions serving these purposes.

The "People's Receivers"

The first important step towards integrating the technical, commercial and listening side of radio came with the formation on 8 July 1933 of the RRG under the new Director of Broadcasting, Eugen Hadamovsky, a former motor mechanic, who had originally formed a 'voluntary' organisation called the 'National Socialist Radio Chamber' on 3 July. Six months later this would become the official Reich Chamber of Radio. Hadamovsky was also given the additional title of Reich Transmitter Leader and in his capacity as overlord for broadcasting he quickly established a direct link to Goebbels and was largely responsible for approving all important broadcasts. Membership of the RRG now became compulsory for everyone connected with broadcasting, whether radio engineers or salesmen of wireless sets. . . .

The technical mobilisation of German radio as the 'voice of the nation' is a history of remarkable accomplishment. To increase the number of listeners, the Nazis persuaded manufacturers to produce one of the cheapest wireless sets in Europe, the VE 3031 or *Volksempfänger* ('people's receiver'). The 'people's radio' was heavily subsidised so that it would be affordable to all workers. In fact two versions of radio receivers were quickly produced: one for 75RM, and the *Volksempfänger* for 35RM payable in instalments. A poster issued by the RMVP advertising the *Volksempfänger* showed one of these uniform radio sets surrounded by thousands of people, with the caption: 'All Germany listens to the Führer with the People's Radio.' One-and-a-half million sets were produced during 1933, and in 1934 the figure for radio sets passed the 6 million mark, indicating an increase of more than 1 million in a single year. The long-term aim was to install a set in every home in Germany. Indeed, by the beginning of the war over 70 per cent of all households owned a wireless set— the highest percentage anywhere in the world. The 'people's receivers' were designed with a limited range, which meant that Germans who purchased them were unable to receive foreign broadcasts. . . .

The Nazis' "Spiritual Weapon"

The radio soon came to be regarded as the Nazi regime's principal propaganda medium for the dissemination of National Socialist ideas and in the creation of a single public opinion. In order to achieve these objectives, special emphasis was placed on political broadcasts. Listeners soon learned to associate signature tunes with various Party leaders who would make regular speeches over the radio. Hitler's speeches were preceded by his favourite march, the *Badenweiler*; Goebbels' annual eulogy on Hitler's birthday was accompanied by [German composer Richard] Wagner's 'Meistersinger' overture, and the Führer's speech on Heroes' Day by Beethoven's 'Eroica' symphony. It has been estimated that in 1933 alone, fifty speeches by Hitler were transmitted. By 1935, Hitler's speeches reached an audience of over 56,000,000. The radio was, not surprisingly, described as 'the towering herald of National Socialism', the means of expression of a united State. In his desire to create 'one single public opinion' Goebbels maintained that it was imperative that this 'spiritual weapon of the totalitarian State' should enjoy the confidence of the people. With the radio, he declared, 'we have destroyed the spirit of rebellion'. . . .

The Press Must "Instruct" as Well as Inform

The press proved infinitely more complicated for the Nazis than the radio, which had, for some time, experienced a degree of State involvement. The press, on the other hand, was associated with a whole plethora of political parties, pressure groups, religious bodies and private companies. In 1933 Germany could boast more daily newspapers than the combined total of Britain, France and Italy. . . .

The Third Reich adopted a three-pronged approach to the control of the press: first, all those involved in the press industry were rigorously controlled; second, the Party's publishing-house, the Eher Verlag, gradually acquired the ownership—directly or indirectly—of the vast majority of the German press; and, finally, the RMVP controlled the content of the press by means of the State-controlled press agency and daily press briefings and directives. The response of the publishers and journalists to the Nazi take-over is most revealing. The publishers' association effectively 'coordinated' themselves. They immediately sought a *modus vivendi* [compromise] with the new regime by first of all replacing politically 'unacceptable' members and then appointing Max Amann, the head of Eher Verlag, as chairman of their organisation, under the revised title of the 'Association of German Newspaper Publishers'. . . . On 30 April 1933, the Association announced that membership would be compulsory and that all members of the Association would be screened for their 'racial and political reliability'.

In his speech to the press of 15 March 1933, Goebbels referred to the press as a piano on which the Government could plan to influence the public in whatever direction it desired. However, although the Nazis looked upon the press as an instrument of mass influence, they were aware that their success had been due more to the spoken than to the printed word. In order to reassure his audience, Goebbels presented himself to the press as a fellow-journalist who had experienced the frustrations of working in opposition to the Government of the day: 'If opposition papers claim today that their issues have been forbidden, they can talk to me as a fellow-sufferer. There is, I think, no representative of any newspaper banned fifteen times, as mine was!' According to Goebbels, the press must not 'merely inform; it must also instruct'. He argued that there was 'no absolute objectivity', and the press should expect to receive not simply information from the Government but also instructions: 'We want to have a press which cooperates with the Government just as the Government wants to cooperate with the press. . . . We do not want a state of daily warfare.' He also urged the press to change its style of reporting in order to reflect the 'crusading' spirit of the time: 'The reader should get the impression that the writer is in reality a speaker standing behind him.' Newspapers in the Third Reich were to capture the atmosphere of the emotion-laden mass meetings. In this respect, the Party newspaper, the *Völkischer Beobachter*, would give the lead. . . .

The Government's Strait-Jacket on the Press

Having regulated both entry into the profession and the flow of news from its source, Goebbels then tackled the problem of editorial policy and content. From 1933 the press department of the RMVP took over the daily press conferences which had been a regular feature of journalistic life during the Weimar Republic. The content of the newspapers was rigidly controlled through the very detailed directives issued by the RMVP, which even covered the length of articles on particular topics and where they should be placed in the paper. Admission to these conferences was now severely controlled along Party and racial lines. As one senior journalist for the *Frankfurter Zeitung* observed:

> The press conference *with* the Reich Government established in 1917 was changed by the National Socialists on their seizure of power in Germany in 1933 into a 'press conference of the Reich Government'. So it was now an institution of the Government. There it gave directives, laid down language variations, and brought the 'press into line'. . . . Before 1933, these press conferences were run by journalists and the Government was their guest; after they were run by the Government.

. . . The overriding feature of the press until the outbreak of war at least was the deliberate sacrifice of speedy reportage of news in favour of staggeringly comprehensive, but unwieldy, press directives. In many respects Nazi propagandists favoured broadcasting at the expense of the press. Hitler, who was a voracious newspaper reader, is said to have been hostile to the press and to journalists. Not only did he believe that pictures and spoken words had greater impact than printed words, but he also resented the press for its vehement criticism of him during the years when the Nazis were in opposition. Although he rarely received journalists, he would occasionally praise the press for their performance. . . . Goebbels, on the other hand, who recognised good journalism, was never entirely happy about the drab uniformity of the German press which was the outcome of his policy. He nevertheless defended the [restrictive Nazi] press laws by arguing that the free expression of opinion could seriously threaten the National Socialist State, and continued to reject suggestions that problems should be frankly discussed in the press. His directives became so minutely detailed that the papers were virtually written for the editors by the Ministry for Propaganda. The Government strait-jacket so destroyed journalistic initiative that Goebbels was prompted to remark in his diary: 'No decent journalist with any feeling of honour in his bones can stand the way he is handled by the press department of the Reich Government. . . . Any man who still has a residue of honour will be very careful not to become a journalist.'

Nazi Control of the Film Industry

Hitler and Goebbels shared an interest in film. Shortly after his appointment as Minister for Popular Enlightenment and Propaganda, Goebbels declared that the German cinema had been given the mission of conquering the world as the vanguard of the Nazi troops. Film propaganda was Goebbels' special interest, for he believed in the power of the cinema to influence people's thoughts and beliefs, if not their actions.

As early as the 1920s the National Socialists had infiltrated their members into many spheres of public life. The entire organisation of the Party, the division into administrative sectors and the structure of leadership were built up as a state within a state. The Nazis were therefore well placed to take control of a film industry which had to a large extent prepared itself to be controlled. . . . The German cinema was affected behind the scenes by a process of which the ordinary citizen was largely unaware. To achieve this end, a plethora of complex laws and decrees and an intricate state machinery were instigated to prevent non-conformity. Pursuing a policy that was to become traditional in the Third Reich, the Party organisation was kept separate from State administration at both national and regional levels, while at the same time remaining closely linked with it. . . .

The film industry presented a number of structural, economic and artistic problems for the builders of the new German society. Significant of the high estimation of the cinema in the Third Reich is the fact that the Reich Film Chamber [RFK] was founded by Goebbels some months before the Reich Chamber of Culture, of which it became a part. The creation of the RFK on 14 July 1933 is an excellent example of the process of coordination in that it allowed the RMVP to exert its control over both film-makers and the film industry as a whole. . . .

Apart from regulating the financing of films, one of the main purposes of establishing the RFK was the removal of Jews and other *entartete Künstler* (degenerate artists) from German cultural life, since only racially 'pure' Germans could become members. Whoever wished to participate in any aspect of film production was forced to become a member of the RFK. By 1936, the Party had begun publishing a new illustrated film magazine, *Der deutsche Film*, with the intention of disseminating party policy relating to the film industry through consciously anti-Semitic propaganda. Statistics were published in film magazines and books, which purported to expose an overwhelmingly Jewish influence in film production. Although the industry had been heavily dependent on Jewish artists and executives, these figures were a gross exaggeration. However, because Nazi propaganda identified Jewish influence with the downfall of German culture, it was only to be expected that the Party would use the struggle in the film industry to stir up racial hatred. Not surprisingly, these policies resulted in the emigration of all those who either could not or would not submit to such conditions. The loss of talent was severe, but the Nazis were able to retain a reservoir of talented actors, technicians and artistic staff. . . .

Film Censorship

According to Goebbels, the German cinema was in a state of spiritual crisis which 'will continue until we are courageous enough radically to reform German films'. National Socialist film-makers, he argued, 'should capture the spirit of the time'. What was not required in these films was 'parade-around marching and the blowing of trumpets'. In calling for the industry's cooperation in this new venture Goebbels concluded by declaring that with this new conviction 'a new moral ethos will arise', allowing it 'to be said of German films, as in other fields, "Germany leads the world!"'.

To consolidate his position, Goebbels still desired more power than he had hitherto secured through the Reichskulturkammer legislation. He also needed some form of legal confirmation to be able to supervise films in the early stages of production. Goebbels settled both these issues by creating a revised version of the Reich Cinema Law, which became law on 16 February 1934. This legislation attempted to create a new 'positive' censorship by which the State encouraged 'good' National Socialist films instead of merely discouraging 'bad' ones. . . .

The new film legislation greatly extended the powers of censorship, which it prescribed in some detail. It replaced the original law of 12 May 1920, which had regulated films during the Weimar Republic. Although the Weimar censorship was initially a democratic one—'films may not be withheld on account of political, social, religious, ethical, or ideological tendencies'—the intervention of the censor was permitted when 'a film endangers public order or safety . . . or endangers the German image or the country's relationship with foreign states'. The examination of films was delegated to two censorship offices, in Berlin and in Munich. Each office had two chairmen, who examined films with the aid of four assessors drawn from the teaching and legal professions and the film industry itself. . . .

According to Paragraph 4 of the 1934 Cinema Law, all kinds of films were to be submitted to the censor. Public and private screenings were made equal in law. Even film advertising in the cinemas was censored. For each print of a film a censorship card had to be issued which contained the official report on the film together with an embossed stamp of the German Eagle. In all matters concerning censorship, the Minister for Propaganda had the right of intervention. . . .

Reinforcing the Existing Order

Secure in the knowledge that film censorship had been reorganised according to the principles of the NSDAP [Nazi Party], Goebbels now embarked on his next project, the nationalisation of the film industry. In fact this would be carried out in two stages, largely through a process of which the ordinary citizen was totally unaware. When the Nazis came to power there were four major film companies operating in Germany. To have nationalised them immediately would have damaged their contacts with foreign distributors, which in turn would have reduced the not inconsiderable revenue and foreign currency earned from Germany's film exports. It seemed advisable, therefore, to proceed warily with the nationalisation of the cinema industry and not alarm the outside world unnecessarily. However, as German film exports continued to decline under the Nazis and production costs continued to increase, the RMVP decided secretly to buy out the major shares in the film companies. . . .

Of the entire production of feature films, virtually half were either love stories or comedies, and a quarter dramatic films like crime thrillers or musicals. Yet all went through the pre-censorship process and all were associated with the National Socialist ideology in that they were produced and performed in accordance with the propagandist aims of the period. In a highly politicised society like the Third Reich, even the apolitical becomes significant in that so-called 'entertainment films' tend to promote the official world-view of things and to reinforce the existing social and economic order. Propaganda is as important in reinforcing existing beliefs as it is in changing them, and even the most escapist entertainment can, as Goebbels noted, be of value to the national struggle, 'providing it with the edification, diversion and relaxation needed to see it through the drama of everyday life'. The comparatively small number of overt political films was supplemented by documentary films and newsreels, which became increasingly important during the war.

Thus the themes that recur in the Nazi cinema are central to their *Weltanschauung* [view of life], and these ideas were repeated at carefully chosen intervals. . . . Perhaps the two best-known documentaries of the Nazi period are Leni Riefenstahl's *Triumph des Willens* (*Triumph of the Will*, 1935) about the 1934 Party rally in Nuremberg, and *Olympiade* (*Olympia*, 1938), a four-hour record of the 1936 Olympic Games held in Berlin, which proved an ideal vehicle for Nazi propaganda to foreign countries. . . .

Unlike Hitler, Goebbels believed that propaganda was most effective when it was insidious, when its message was concealed within the framework of popular entertainment. Goebbels therefore encouraged the production of feature films which reflected the ambience of National Socialism rather than those that loudly proclaimed its ideology. The result . . . was a monopolistic system of control and organisation which maintained profits and managed to quadruple the annual number of cinema-goers between 1933 and 1942. Film was only one factor in reaching an uncritical audience; but it had an important function, in the sense that when people read newspapers or listened to the radio they were more conscious of the propaganda content. The cinema, on the other hand, was associated with relaxation and entertainment and was therefore all the more dangerous. . . . It is clear that when the Nazis assumed power they thought highly of film as a propaganda weapon. The need for conformity in a police state meant that the film industry had to be reorganised according to the ideals of the NSDAP. Like all forms of mass communication, film had to correspond to the political *Weltanschauung* and the propaganda principles of the Party. The communications media—the press, radio and film—had a circular interrelationship in that they supplied each other with themes in the manner prescribed by the State, and supported each other in their effect by a simultaneous and graduated release of information, which was circulated, controlled, and modulated by the State. This control remained of paramount importance to Goebbels and Hitler, both of whom continued to recognise its importance as a source of their 'popularist' appeal. In his diary entry for 20 June 1941, Goebbels recorded: 'The Führer praises the superiority of our system compared with liberal-democratic ones. We educate our people according to a common world-view (*Weltanschauung*), with the aid of films, radio and the press, which the Führer sees as the most important tools of popular leadership. The State must never let them out of her hands.'

Capturing the Minds and Hearts of Germany's Youth

Stephen H. Roberts

The late Stephen H. Roberts, a professor of modern history at the University of Sydney, spent two years in Germany in the late 1930s. There, he witnessed firsthand the everyday lives of Germans in Hitler's new Third Reich. In this essay, taken from *The House That Hitler Built*, his powerful book describing what he saw, Roberts reveals what he terms the "distressing" manner in which the Nazis politically indoctrinated young people. First, he explains how the Hitler Youth movement got started; then describes its fanatical leaders, Kurt Grüber and Baldur von Schirach; and finally details the methods these men used to twist children's minds until they became, in Roberts's words, "unquestioning automata [robots]."

For the young, National Socialism is primarily a spiritual movement, a development through constantly renewed ecstasy to endless achievement. Why talk of past crusades and wars of liberation when they have before them the *Führer*? ... In a great boys' camp in Franconia, I saw sentries on duty in front of a column, round which heaps of banners were piled. I moved to approach the monument to read the names of the boy-martyrs inscribed on it, but my road was barred. 'This is holy ground, untouchable,' said one of the sentries who stood there night and day. A week before it had been a run for cattle!

The Youth Movement is nothing intrinsically new in Germany. Many such movements existed before the war [World War I], and many of the political and religious organizations after the war had youth subsidiaries. The difference between the Hitler Youth Movement and the many that it superseded is that it is now nation-wide, and includes 6,000,000 young people in what is practically a State department. . . .

After the war . . . it was a long time before the Nazis realized the importance of appealing to the very young. They used instead the cynical prematurely-aged youths who had borne a part of the actual fighting in the last years of the war. The children were overlooked until 1926, when, at . . . Weimar, Hitler made Kurt Grüber National Leader of the 'Hitler Youth'. Grüber had formed a cell of children in Plauen (Saxony), and now Hitler gave him an opportunity to spread his ideas throughout the nation. The name 'Hitler Youth' was suggested by Julius Streicher, the leader of the anti-Semites, and it was meant to include boys from the ages of fourteen to eighteen. Two years later, plans were made to have similar organizations for girls (the *Schwesternschaften*, after 1930 the 'German Maidens') and for boys from ten to fourteen (the *Jungmannschaften*, later the *Jungvolk*, as we know them to-day).

From its administrative centre in Plauen, the movement grew rapidly. It was soon banned in Bavaria, Hanover, Hesse, and elsewhere, but as usual it throve on persecution. By the beginning of 1929, steps were taken to link it on to the Storm Troopers. Henceforth the boy of eighteen passed from the *Hitler Jugend* into the Party and the Storm Troopers. That year Grüber proudly led 2,000 Hitler Youth past the *Führer*, and received banners for each of his provinces. The children marching behind their red flags with the hammer-and-sword insignia were now definitely part of the movement.

Expansion Under New Leadership

A somewhat stormy period then ensued, in which there were quarrels about leadership and methods of organization. The seat of the movement was transferred from Plauen to Munich; the whole of Germany was mapped out into ten Youth Groups; and Grüber came to be overshadowed by Hitler's

twenty-three-year-old protégé, Baldur von Schirach. Towards the end of 1931, Hitler made von Schirach chief-of-
staff of each of the three Nazi organizations for young persons (not only the Hitler Youth but the Union of Students
and the Union of Scholars as well). Grüber resigned, and his
successor survived for less than eight months, making way
for von Schirach as National Leader of the Hitler Youth
(June 1932). At that moment . . . there were only 35,000
members; but von Schirach began to plan a great army of
Germany's childhood, with himself as commander-in-chief.

Their organization henceforth duplicated that of the
Brown Army [i.e., the SA "Brownshirts"], from the smallest
band of ten comrades up to the *Gau* (or province) and the
nation as a whole. Indeed, the Hitler Youth frequently
thought it their main duty to follow the Brownshirts into the
street mêlées. In one of these fights, the fifteen-year-old
Herbert Norkus was murdered by Communists, and before
Hitler came to power no less than twenty boys lost their lives
in the street fighting.

A great expansion took place under von Schirach. Hitler
himself claims that the 35,000 members of June 1932 had
swollen into 1,000,000 six months later, when he became
Chancellor; but, however this may be, membership jumped up
phenomenally once the Nazis were in office. One by one the
other children's organizations fell into the Nazi maw. . . .
Their formal parades were now heralded by 600 banners,
while their camps had representatives of the fifty-three foreign
countries in which Germans residing abroad had dressed their
children in the brown shirts and shorts of the Hitler Youth. . . .

Stamping All in the Same Mould

A word must be said about the leader. Baldur von Schirach is
a plump self-satisfied young man of just thirty years of age.
When he was an art student ten years ago, Hitler, his intimate
friend, was able to discern exceptional qualities in him. He has
one of the longest entries in the Nazi *Who's Who*, telling at
length how frequently he communed with the *Führer* or how
often he consulted the Ministers. Described as 'Journalist
(Editor)', it is related how millions of his verses sold and how

two of his books, *The Unknown Hitler* and *The Triumph of the Will*, were the best sellers of 1932. His base-known poem is the song of the Hitler Youth, *Forward*, which commences:

Forward! Forward! Let the bright trumpets sound,
Forward! Forward! Youth knows no peril,

and goes on with this repetitious cacophony to the climax: 'We will march for Hitler through night and through danger, With the flag of youth for freedom and bread', and ends with the line: 'The standard is better than death.'. . .

Von Schirach has been pampered with posts of great responsibility since his seventeenth year. He has never had time to think, has never had his actions questioned, and has been saved from criticism by his friendship with Hitler. Apparently nobody can check him. He creates political difficulties by his open attacks on the Christian religion. His onslaughts three years ago on the youth organizations of the various churches are still in memory as cases of brutal suppression of opinions other than his own. . . .

His power continued to grow, and more and more impressionable children listened to his commands: 'Join no organizations but Hitler's and be ready to die for Hitler.' 'Forward! Forward! The banner leads us to eternity.' So he goes on; and the tragedy is that he is shaping the mentality of the next generation of Germans. But he takes no heed of the future, and the psychological problems of childhood and adolescence mean nothing to him. The song of the banner is enough, provided that 6,000,000 young Germans are all stamped into the same mould and emerge as unquestioning automata, physically fit and mentally sponges for the official Hitler hero-worship. The goal and the methods are simple, and all complexities are ignored. 'Command and we follow . . . the standard is more than death'—that is all. Whatever may be said of him, Baldur von Schirach is a great educational simplist.

Hitler Has Captured Their Hearts and Souls

The fight for the mind of youth starts in the cradle. The baby's earliest fairy tales must be in accordance with Nazi ideas. The *Führer* is 'the man sent from Heaven', who triumphed over some evil people called the Allies and who started a long fight to kill the bad ogre—the Bolshevik [Russian communist]—who is for ever trying to eat up honest little German children.

At the age of ten, each little boy gets a brown shirt . . . or, if he is too poor, his comrades often subscribe for him. Henceforth he belongs to the 'Young Folk'. The little girl will join the 'Union of German Maidens', and is supposed to be dressed in a uniform of white blouse and blue skirt, but, for some reason or other, the girls have to go without the uniforms more often than the boys. Little boy and girl alike are pledged to sacrifice everything for the *Führer* and are taught that he is everything and themselves nothing. After four years of this, the boy of fourteen joins the Hitler Youth, the outward symbol of his promotion being the change to brown trousers and the presentation of a red swastika armband as worn by adult members of the Brownshirt organization. Henceforth he is a Storm Trooper in miniature, and Hitler has arranged that the boy will have the same unit-numbers as his father.

When grown up, the boy goes to a camp for six months, compulsory labour service, for the most part working, stripped to the waist, in the fields. This is followed by two years' service in the army as a conscript, but, by the time the army gets hold of him, he is saturated with Nazi ideology, a fact which caused much friction in the early days of Hitler's power. . . .

It would be foolish to underestimate the enthusiasm of young Germany for their *Führer*. All other interests are disappearing, and it would be misleading to think that the religious bodies which are so vocal abroad are holding their own with the children. Again and again in Germany, even in Catholic Bavaria and the Black Forest, I found cases of children whose Roman Catholic parents tried to keep them in the few struggling Church societies that still exist for children. In every case the children wanted to join the *Hitler Jugend*. The brown shirt or drab blouse of Hitler won every time; the children wanted to follow the drums and the fifes of their playfellows' bands and, as they saw it, be normal. To be outside Hitler's organization was the worst form of punishment. Hitler has captured the children heart and soul, and it is one of the oldest adages of dictatorship that he who has control of the elementary schools for five years is established in power for ever. . . .

Their attitude of mind is absolutely uncritical. They do not see in Hitler a statesman with good and bad points; to them he is more than a demigod. Times out of number they answered my queries why they believed or did so-and-so by the reply: 'Because the *Führer* wills it!' There was no use going behind such a mandate; questioning was worse than heresy. The children of Germany believe that right and wrong are as distinct as black and white. Germany is always right, the rest of the world always wrong, and as for the Russians, they are literally devils from hell. It was this utter lack of any objective or critical attitude on the part of youth, even with university students, that made me fear most for the future of Germany. They are nothing but vessels for State propaganda. . . .

Every previous movement marked a revolt against authority; the youths of ten years ago who became front-line fighters in the service of Hitler were also rebels; but the youth of to-day are taught unquestioning obedience to authority. To rebel is unthinkable, to argue for themselves equally so. They must submit to a mental uniformity which by its nature is degrading. . . . The Hitler Youth Movement may be bigger than any of its predecessors; it may have the blessing of the State; but the sacred breath of liberty and of intellectual striving has gone from it. It resembles a giant with glandular trouble. The outward husk is imposing, but beneath is only mental aridness. If only one of the boys I saw in the most impressive Hitler camps would have questioned the propagandist lectures to which they were listening, if only one of them had asked a penetrating question, I would have felt more hope for the future of Germany.

Education in the Third Reich

Michael Freeman

While the Nazis indoctrinated young Germans in the "proper" political beliefs via the Hitler Youth movement, the authorities also exerted strict control of schools, teachers, and textbooks and other educational materials. Teachers who were of the "wrong" race or who did not conform in other ways to the new Nazi ideals were rooted out. And the curriculum was rewritten and specifically shaped to reflect Adolf Hitler's distorted views on history, biology, and other academic subjects. As University of Oxford scholar Michael Freeman explains in this essay, the "nazification" of education was an important part of *Gleichschaltung*, the process of reorganizing all social institutions to better serve the Nazi state.

The ultimate goal of Nazi education policy was the creation of 'the political, National Socialist, human being'. Education was not to be a training towards free, independent activity, but to develop the abilities of young Germans so that they fulfilled the aims and desires of the Nazi state. The reorganisation of the education system on Nazi lines had a number of distinctive dimensions. It involved an extensive revision of the curriculum. It involved the progressive removal of political and racial undesirables from the profession of teachers. It embraced the establishment of a stream of specialist schools where the future Nazi elite was to be trained. Finally, it applied the Fuehrerprinzip [leadership principle] to the whole structure of educational administration and brought the professional teaching organisations firmly within the

Nazi orbit. Certain of these aims were more quickly achieved than others: the purge of teachers, as well as the coordination of administration in accordance with the Fuehrerprinzip. . . . The enormous stress that the Nazis laid on physical education also slowed the learning process, regardless of the burdens that may have been imposed by a novel ideology. Pupils could spend up to five hours a day engaged in sports. There was also a latent conflict with the Hitler Youth, which set a rival focus for children's energies and loyalties.

The Universities Decline

Under National Socialism, the German universities saw a substantial decline in the numbers of both students and

---

A Nazi Biology Text

This is an excerpt from a German school text written in 1935— Heredity and Racial Biology for Students, *by Joseph Graf. Subtitled "The Aryan: The Creative Force in Human History," the tract tells students that the superior "racial soul" of white, blond Aryans has dominated history and calls for critical examination of the "obviously inferior" traits of Jews. Excerpted here is the assignment section that students were asked to complete after reading the text.*

How We Can Learn to Recognize a Person's Race
ASSIGNMENTS

1. Summarize the spiritual characteristics of the individual races. . . .

3. What are the expressions, gestures, and movements which allow us to make conclusions as to the attitude of the racial souls?

4. Determine also the physical features which go hand in hand with the specific racial soul characteristics of the individual figures.

5. Try to discover the intrinsic nature of the racial soul through the characters in stories and poetical works in terms of their inner attitude. Apply this mode of observation to persons

teachers, as well as a steady diminution in the range and quality of scholarship. Between the winter of 1930–1 and the summer of the outbreak of war [in 1939], the number of matriculated students fell from just under 96,000 to a little over 39,000. The nazification of curricula and the . . . restrictions upon academic freedom made university life increasingly unattractive. Non-Aryans were excluded from university; and those who could not show a satisfactory record in the Hitler Youth were also ineligible. Other explanations were found in the increasing career opportunities in business and in the armed forces as the Third Reich moved towards a war footing. Earlier, in 1933, the number of students had actually been cut by law, on account of very high

in your own environment. . . .

7. Collect from illustrated magazines, newspapers, etc., pictures of great scholars, statesmen, artists, and others who distinguished themselves by their special accomplishments (for example, in economic life, politics, sports). Determine the preponderant race and admixture, according to physical characteristics. Repeat this exercise with the pictures of great men of all nations and times. . . .

9. Observe people whose special racial features have drawn your attention, also with respect to their bearing when moving or when speaking. Observe their expressions and gestures.

10. Observe the Jew: his way of walking, his bearing, gestures, and movements when talking.

11. What strikes you about the way a Jew talks and sings?

12. What are the occupations engaged in by the Jews of your acquaintance?

13. What are the occupations in which Jews are not to be found? Explain this phenomenon on the basis of the character of the Jew's soul.

George L. Mosse, *Nazi Culture: Intellectual, Cultural, and Social Life in the Third Reich*. New York: Grosset and Dunlap, 1966, pp. 79-81.

graduate unemployment.

During the great phase of Nazi *Gleichschaltung* (1933–4), the universities lost some 16 per cent of their staff in a wave of ejections. The technical institutes lost around 10 per cent, the law schools some 21 per cent. Many of the more distinguished scholars took to emigration.

The Text-Books Rewritten

Curriculum development in the service of National Socialism presented a formidable task for party and state officials. That progress was haphazard and the actual results often dubious is a reflection of this, especially given the regime's relatively short life-span. The censorship of school text-books was one of the first and perhaps most readily implemented strategies, and yet this was not directed centrally until the spring of 1938; up to that time teachers performed the task of censoring. The institution of guidelines for elementary and secondary school curricula was similarly slow, even given that the task was no simple one. The brakes to more rapid progress were the desires of the various power groups within the Third Reich to influence education for their own ends. Subjects such as history and geography were variously recast to reflect Nazi racial doctrines. *German* history was studied largely to the exclusion of all other, and focused on Hitler and the rise of National Socialism. Vain attempts were made to interpret the Third Reich as the apotheosis [splendid culmination] of specified developments and trends in German history. German literature was sifted and categorised so that blood ties and sense of community were thrown into greater relief, and explicitly *völkisch* literature [that promoting a racially pure German community] was emphasised as part of this. Religious instruction was increasingly replaced by a motley collection of anti-Christian nationalist ideas, the change enhanced by the steady abolition of confessional schools. In the natural sciences, biology (predictably) was revised in accordance with Nazi racial theories, and *racial science* was granted an academic status which justified the establishment of new professorships in the universities. Many of the more mature among the German people held undeniable misgivings about the distortion of historical perspectives and the ascientific [non-scientific] nature of some of the regime's teachings. In German youth, however, Nazism found an understandably more receptive constituency, one which was cultivated as much outside the schoolroom as in it. The ideological campaign in the schoolroom was complemented in the machinery of the Hitler Youth.

Women's Roles in Nazi Germany

Richard Grunberger

One of the Third Reich's greatest challenges and largest overall efforts consisted in making German women conform to the ideal female image envisioned by Hitler and other leading Nazis. As English historian Richard Grunberger points out here, that image was not completely one-sided. While Hitler believed that ideally women belonged in the home, he allowed, and indeed expected, many of them to work as laborers in factories and in other jobs essential to the German economy. Still, he kept them out of politics and off of juries, maintaining that men were superior for such tasks. And even working women were expected to fulfill their main role for the "fatherland," namely to maintain the "Aryan race" by giving birth to at least four strapping children. Grunberger concludes with a brief description of Hitler's so-called cult of female admirers, many of whom preferred death to a Germany without him.

Women's role in [Nazi] society tended to become oversimplified in direct proportion to the increased diversification of their lives—to reach absolute intellectual bedrock in the slogan *'Kinder, Kirche, Küche'* (kids, kirk and kitchen). The cry 'Woman's place is in the home' found an ever-wider echo the more the logic of circumstances—economic necessity, wartime industrial mobilization, post-war demographic imbalance (the surplus of 1.8 million marriageable women) and inflation—forced female labour into factories and offices.

From *The Twelve-Year Reich: A Social History of Nazi Germany, 1933–1945*, by Richard Grunberger (New York: Holt, Rinehart and Winston). Copyright 1971 by Richard Grunberger. Reprinted by permission of Sterling Lord Literistic, Inc.

Between 1907 and 1925 the female labour force increased by over one-third (8.5 million to 11.5 million), whereas the net population growth amounted to a mere seventh (54.5 million to 62.4 million). But change was more than a matter of numbers; the Weimar constitution gave women the vote, and a feminist élite . . . had helped shape the political post-war scene. Interposed between these national figures and the army of working women was the professional vanguard of the second sex: nearly 100,000 women teachers, 13,000 women musicians and 3,000 women doctors. The last figure indicated a male/female ratio in medicine of fourteen to one, the same, incidentally, as among Reichstag deputies [members of Parliament]. . . .

The Depression naturally intensified the sex war in the labour market as employers held on to cheaper female labour while laying off expendable men. The drastic economic deterioration made the three K's *Kinder, Kirche, Küche* sound equally attractive to dole-receivers and to middle-class conservatives. As mass unemployment reinforced the after-effects of war and inflation as an impediment to marriage, the average woman began to look upon the three K's in a much more favourable light.

Nazi Anti-Feminism

It was in this situation that Hitler—with a unique blend of cynicism and psychological insight—assured a delegation who had come to discuss women's rights with him that in the Third Reich every woman would have a husband. . . .

The kernel of Nazi thinking on the women's question was a dogma of inequality between the sexes as immutable as that between the races. While this did not exactly degrade women to the status of Jews in the sex war, it did signify their irremediable confinement within the domestic round. The visible badge of feminine unworthiness was debarment from the political kingdom: one of the earliest Nazi Party ordinances (of January 1921) excluded women for ever from all leading positions in the Party.

Anti-feminism served as a non-lethal variant of anti-Semitism. . . .

Hitler called the emancipation of women a symptom of depravity. . . . Walter Darré, the pig-husbandry theorist turned Nazi Minister for Agriculture, attributed the desire for feminine emancipation to frustrations set up by malfunctioning sex glands. [Propaganda minister Joseph] Goebbels actually turned to animal life for corroborating the role assigned to women in the Nazi scheme of things. 'Woman has the task of being beautiful and bringing children into the world, and this is by no means as coarse and old-fashioned as one might think. The female bird preens herself for her mate and hatches her eggs for him.'. . . Goebbels cynically seized on . . . age-old German distaste for politics to turn the Nazi derogation of women into its fake opposite. 'Our displacement of women from public life occurs solely to restore their essential dignity to them.' 'It is not because we did not respect women enough but because we respected them too much that we kept them out of the miasma of parliamentary democracy.'

Goebbels's cabinet colleague, [Wilhelm] Frick (Minister of the Interior), talked of grading women according to their child output, a point which Hitler put less succinctly: 'Equal rights for women means that they receive the esteem they deserve in the sphere nature has assigned to them. . . . Woman has her battlefield too; with each child that she brings into the world for the nation she is fighting her fight on behalf of the nation.'. . .

Women Labourers

Though there was much talk of forcing married women back into their home to provide jobs for men, this mainly affected the professions, and fluctuations in the female labour force were only marginal. The truth was that female labour was cheaper: skilled women earned 66 per cent of men's wages, unskilled ones 70 per cent, which explains why during the Depression nearly one man in three (29 per cent) was dismissed but only one woman in every ten (11 per cent). Furthermore women workers were indispensable. In 1933 women formed 37 per cent of the total employed labour force in Germany. Every second agricultural worker was female; in addition, 75 per cent of female labour on the land was not hired but consisted of members of the family.

Since the absorption of men into the resurgent economy proceeded at a much faster rate than that of women—between 1933 and 1937 800,000 newly married women received loans on condition of not seeking re-employment—the female proportion of the total labour force declined to 31 per cent in 1937, although the total numbers actually increased. By 1939, women again constituted exactly a third of the employed labour force, comprising nearly 7 million white-collar and blue-collar workers. In industry as a whole they represented almost a quarter (23 per cent) of the personnel, but in certain branches, such as clothing and textiles, they constituted two-thirds and just over half of the total respectively. Even in the metalworking industries every eighth employee was a woman. In the distributive trades and in food production two out of every five workers were female, and the same applied to office work, where, incidentally, women were generally confined to subordinate positions. . . .

Since there was now a strong tendency for female labour to seek better-paid jobs in the commercial sector and in the towns, the government instituted a compulsory 'duty year' for all unmarried girls or women under twenty-five entering the labour market as office workers or employees of the clothing, textile or tobacco industries; during this duty year they had to do either agricultural or domestic work (or alternatively two years as auxiliary nurses or social-welfare workers). This decree was passed early in 1938. By the end of that year it was extended to cover entry into all private or public undertakings. Within two years, as the result of this measure, the female section of the labour service totalled 200,000. Before the outbreak of war women were also being taken on as tram conductresses and postal workers in various parts of the country, and later on some worked on the railways. This demand for female labour improved their bargaining position, although women in agriculture, catering, and so on, whose work was a function of their family membership, derived no benefit from their relative scarcity. . . .

None of this could obscure the basic contradiction that

those whom Nazi rhetoric had destined for the kitchen and the nursery eventually formed three-fifths of Germany's wartime labour force.

Professional Women Discouraged

The Third Reich could be compared to a double-ended gun trained both on the twentieth century and the Treaty of Versailles, with nostalgia for a pre-industrial past speaking out of one barrel, and streamlined industrial preparation for war out of the other.

To gloss over the divergence between Nazi promise and fulfilment, propaganda scaled new heights. . . . 'It has always been our chief article of faith,' wrote an official in the Nazi Women's League, 'that woman's place is in the home—but since the whole of Germany is our home we must serve her wherever we can best do so.'. . .

[But the range of places where professional women could serve was steadily shrinking.] Married women doctors and civil servants were dismissed immediately after the seizure of power. The number of women teachers at girls' secondary schools had decreased by 15 per cent by 1935. In the following academic year the entry of girls to training departments for university teachers was completely suspended. By this time the number of women academics had declined from fifty-nine to thirty-seven (out of a total academic teaching body of over 7,000). . . .

From June 1936 onwards women could no longer act as judges or public prosecutors, and female *Assessoren* (assistant judges, assistant teachers, and so on) were gradually dismissed. Women were declared ineligible for jury service on the grounds that 'they cannot think logically or reason objectively, since they are ruled only by emotion'. (Even so, certain branches of the legal profession were still kept open to them.)

The Evangelical Church, too, joined in the process of eliminating women from leading positions. In 1935 the Bishop of Hamburg rescinded an ecclesiastical reform of the Weimar period, under which women were admitted to certain functions inside the Church.

The situation of female students underwent two drastic (and contrary) reversals during the Third Reich, one soon after the seizure of power and the other during the war [World War II]. In 1933 women had constituted about a fifth of the entire student body and the regime early on devised measures to reduce feminine representation at institutes of higher learning to a one-in-ten ratio of the undergraduate total. . . .

The Sexual-Biological Role of Women

The average marriage age had been creeping upwards ever since the Great War [World War I], but the seizure of power immediately reversed that trend. The Third Reich furthermore made a woman's child-bearing period the apogee of her life-cycle. Women basked in Nazi public esteem between marriage and the menopause, after which they imperceptibly declined into a twilight condition of eugenic superfluity [i.e., they were no longer needed to reproduce]. . . . Even before 1939 the practice of herding young men together in barracks or camps for long periods at a time had led to a stultifying [stifling] of contacts between the sexes before marriage. As a result young women tended to have affairs with older men; this was a sufficiently widespread phenomenon to provide the theme of two contemporary novels. . . .

Closely related to women's sexual role in society was the question of their dress and demeanour. The seizure of power betokened a drastic reversal of the role women's appearance had played before 1933, when it had helped to inject an air of elegance and lightness into German life. Party militants, predominantly lower middle class and provincial, poured forth an unstaunched flood of . . . threats to make German womanhood return to its alleged primordial virtues. The *Völkische Beobachter* [a popular Nazi newspaper] castigated make-up as blatantly un-German, defining it as suitable for the sensual faces and thick lips of Levantines [i.e., Semites or Asians]. . . .

The provincial factory-cell organization of the NSBO (forerunner of the German Labour Front) in Lower Franconia excluded all women wearing powder and lipstick from its meetings; those seen smoking in public automatically forfeited their membership. . . . Since slimness was held to be incompatible with bearing many children, women were to be persuaded not to trouble about their figures. An additional aspect of the anti-modernist and anti-glamour movement was the pseudo-socialist tinsel of the Nazi revolution. Because the Hitler Youth decked itself out with the anti-bourgeois ideology of the Youth Movement, some young women considered it an affirmation of principle not to be interested in smart clothes and cosmetics. Compounding these various considerations, the regime produced an ideal type of feminity, for which the leaders of the women's section of the Reich Labour Service were groomed as prototypes. They were trained in Spartan severity, taught to do without cosmetics, to dress in the simplest manner, to display no individual vanity, to sleep on hard beds, and to forgo all culinary delicacies; the ideal image of those broad-hipped figures, unencumbered by corsets, was one of radiant blondeness, crowned by hair arranged in a bun or braided into a coronet of plaits. As a negative counter-image Nazi propaganda projected the combative, man-hating suffragettes of other countries. . . .

Hitler's Cult of Female Admirers

The purge of women in public life was partly compensated for by the outlet that work in the Women's League and the People's Welfare provided for their displaced energies. In addition the regime catered for the psychological needs of women who craved vicarious identification by constantly keeping a number of exemplary female personalities in the public eye, such as the screen-idol-turned-film-producer, Leni Riefenstahl, who earned a place in the national pantheon with her documentaries of the 1934 Nuremberg Rally and the 1936 Olympic Games in Berlin. She was subsequently joined by Hannah Reitsch, the first German woman to be awarded the glider pilot's badge, the certificate of an aircraft captain and the Iron Cross (Second Class). Another feminine exemplar was Gertrude Scholz-Klink, the . . . housewife who managed to combine leadership of the Nazi Women's League with running a home and bringing up a real family (in the Nazi sense of the word, i.e., consisting of four children). In addition there were the wives of the two men ranking immediately below Hitler in the Nazi hierarchy: Emmy Goering, an ex-actress of Wagnerian proportions and demeanour, and the fashion-conscious Magda Goebbels. . . . But though this sort of projection was a factor in the fantasy life of women, it paled into insignificance beside the Führer-cult. . . .

On public occasions in the Third Reich the female section of the crowd often exhibited a form of mass hysteria known as *Kontaktsucht* or 'contact-seeking', an uncontrollable urge to touch him physically; at mass meetings . . . the eyes of women listeners . . . glazed with a religious sort of exultation.

At the end of the war, too, more women than men preferred self-immolation [suicide] to living in a world devoid of the Führer's presence; their suicides ironically corroborated the received Nazi truth about the congenital difference between reason-motivated man and emotion-guided woman.

Sports Used as Propaganda: The 1936 Olympic Games

John Toland

At first, Hitler did not give much, if any, thought to the role athletics might play in his new reich. But not long after he took power, he found himself forced to deal with the fact that the International Olympic Committee, or IOC, had chosen Germany's capital of Berlin as the site for the upcoming 1936 Olympic Games. Hitler's propaganda minister, Joseph Goebbels, soon convinced the führer that the Nazis could reap great public relations benefits by hosting the games. And it would be particularly good for the reich's international image if German athletes won many medals. In this excerpt from his masterful biography of Hitler, award-winning historian John Toland describes the Nazis' attempt to put on a good face for the world during the Olympics by allowing Jewish athletes to compete on the German team. Toland then summarizes the opening and closing ceremonies and the overall German success, both on and off the field. He also touches briefly on the controversy surrounding the black American runner and jumper Jesse Owens; contrary to the popular story that later circulated widely, Toland points out, Hitler did not refuse to shake Owens's hand.

That summer [of 1936] the Olympics were staged in Berlin despite efforts by liberals in Great Britain, the United States and France to boycott them, largely because of Germany's anti-Semitic policies. In his eagerness to turn the Olympics into a showcase for Nazi achievements, Hitler made a number of concessions. Token Jews—notably Helene Mayer, the fencer, and Rudi Ball, the hockey star—were allowed to represent the Reich, and Captain Wolfgang Fürstner, another Jew, was charged with erecting and organizing the Olympic Village. More important, anti-Semitic posters along the highways as well as notices barring Jews from resorts were removed. In Berlin, [Julius] Streicher's *Der Stürmer* [a blatant anti-Jewish newspaper] disappeared from the newsstands. The entire anti-Semitic campaign, in fact, was muted. These marks of conciliation were given such international publicity that foreigners thronged to Berlin, where they were greeted enthusiastically.

The Opening Ceremonies

The opening ceremonies on August 1 were blessed by a clear blue sky. That afternoon Hitler led the parade to the stadium down the Via Triumphalis. His car, followed by a long caravan, proceeded slowly down the ten-mile boulevard, protected from the crowds by 40,000 Brownshirts and other guards. When the procession reached the stadium Hitler, in the simplest uniform, and the two Olympic officials strode forward, followed by the King of Bulgaria, crown princes from Sweden, Greece and Italy, and [Italian dictator Benito] Mussolini's sons. They marched through the tunnel into the world's largest stadium to be greeted by a brassy voluntary [fanfare] from thirty trumpets. The orchestra, led by [the great German composer] Richard Strauss and assisted by a chorus of 3000, broke into "Deutschland über Alles" followed by the "Horst Wessel Lied" and the "Olympic Hymn," composed by Strauss for the occasion. The crowd of 110,000 cheered as Hitler took his place in the official stand. Some of the delegations used the Olympic salutation, a stiff right arm extended to the side but, to the delight of the audience, Austrians modified this to the Nazi salute. The Bulgarians outdid them by adding a smart goose step. The greatest applause came for the 250-member French team, whose salute was more Roman than Olympian. They were followed by the British in straw hats who, by merely executing an "eyes right," offended numerous onlookers. The Americans got the least applause, and some derogatory stamping of feet, as they passed the Tribune of Honor, eyes right, without even dipping their flag.

The next day Hitler was present to congratulate Hans Wölke, a German, for breaking the Olympic record for the shot-put. He also congratulated the three Finns who swept

---

Hitler Gives the Games His Stamp of Approval

In this excerpt from his history of the modern Olympic Games, Alan Guttmann tells how Hitler, who cared little about sports, came to see Germany's hosting of the 1936 Olympics as a good idea. To the delight of the leaders of the Organisationskomitee, *the German Olympic committee, Hitler even offered to pay for a majority of the Olympic expenses.*

Hitler's rule began only six days after the creation, on January 24, 1933, of the Organisationskomitee. This state of affairs was certainly not what the IOC had expected when Berlin was chosen as the site of the games.

Quite apart from any general concern they might have had about Nazism, there was reason for committee members to be worried. Although Hitler thought that German boys should learn to box, in order to steel themselves for the rigors of their role as natural rulers, neither he nor his cohorts were advocates of modern sports. Sports were almost unmentioned in *Mein Kampf* and in the pages of the party's newspaper, *Der Völkische Beobachter.* The problem in Nazi eyes was that modern sports had developed in England rather than in Germany. . . . Among the most important characteristics of modern sports—in theory if not in practice—is equality: neither race nor religion nor ideology should be a factor in the determination of athletic excellence. Such a notion was, of course, anathema [loathsome] to Nazis dedicated to a primitive belief in the racial supremacy of the "Aryan" people. A Nazi spokesman, Bruno Malitz, condemned modern sports because they were international, "in-the 10,000-meter run as well as the German women who placed first and second in the javelin throw. By the time the German entrants in the high jump were eliminated it was dark and so he was not there to shake hands with the three American winners, two of whom were black.

This led the President of the International Olympic Committee to inform the Führer that, as guest of honor, he should henceforth congratulate all victors or none. Hitler

---

fested" with "Frenchmen, Belgians, Pollacks, and Jew-Niggers" who had been allowed "to start on the tracks, to play on the soccer fields, and to swim in the pools." On August 19, 1932, *Der Völkische Beobachter* demanded that the Olympic Games be restricted to white athletes. . . .

Among the most worried were the president and the secretary of the Organisationskomitee, Theodor Lewald and Carl Diem. . . .

Given . . . the shrill hostility of many Nazis to sports in general and the Olympics in particular, neither Lewald nor Diem was optimistic about the 1936 Games and both were apprehensive when they were summoned, on March 16, 1933, to meet with Hitler at the chancellory. To their astonishment and relief, Hitler did not order an immediate cessation of preparations but instead gave the two men his tentative approval. He had not suddenly changed his mind and become a convert to Olympism; rather, his propaganda minister, Josef Goebbels, had realized that the games were a splendid opportunity to demonstrate German vitality and organizational expertise. . . . On October 5, 1933, Hitler toured the site of the games, inspected the progress of the construction, and became positively lyrical about the prospects for the grandest Olympics ever. Five days later, at the chancellory, he promised the startled Lewald the full financial support of his regime, a sum later set at 20,000,000 Reichsmarks. Lewald and Diem were stunned by their unexpected good fortune.

Alan Guttmann, *The Olympics: A History of the Modern Games.* Chicago: University of Illinois Press, 1992, pp. 53–55.

chose the latter course and so did not meet Jesse Owens, who won four gold medals. That the Führer publicly turned his back on the great black athlete was denied by Owens himself, who further claimed that Hitler did pay him a tribute. "When I passed the Chancellor he arose, waved his hand at me, and I waved back at him. I think the writers showed bad taste in criticizing the man of the hour in Germany."

To the surprise of his entourage, the Führer attended almost every track and field event. Face contorted, he would watch the Germans perform with the passionate interest of a boy. (During the hockey game at the Winter Olympics in Garmisch-Partenkirchen he had been too nervous to stay till the end and had to have someone give him a brief account later.) The games ended on August 16 with Hitler on hand for the final ceremonies. As the orchestra played "The Games Are Ended," the crowd joined in the emotional farewell of the athletes, who rocked in time to the music. There were isolated shouts of "Sieg Heil!" for Hitler, who had been given no role at all in the final exercises. Others took up the cry and soon the stadium reverberated with the chant, "Sieg Heil! Unser Führer, Adolf Hitler, Sieg Heil!" [Hail to Our Great Leader, Adolf Hitler!]

The games had been an almost unqualified Nazi triumph. Germans had won the most gold medals (33), as well as the most silver and bronze; and, surprisingly, defeated the second-place Americans by 57 points. More important, many of the visitors left Germany pleased by their hosts' cordiality and impressed by what they had seen of Hitler's Reich. The success of the games was further enhanced by a two-part documentary filmed by Leni Riefenstahl [a film director whom Hitler admired and commissioned to produce documentary propaganda films] that won world-wide acclaim, despite [Joseph] Goebbels' attempted sabotage. He even tried to keep her from setting foot in the stadium.

In the paeans [hymns] of self-congratulation that followed there was a tragic note. Captain Fürstner, replaced at the last moment as commandant of the Olympic Village because he was Jewish, attended the banquet honoring his successor, then shot himself.

Chapter 5

Nazi Germany Threatens the World

Turning Points
IN WORLD HISTORY

Hitler and Mussolini Create the Berlin-Rome Axis

Mark Arnold-Forster

This essay by the noted English historian Mark Arnold-Forster outlines the events leading up to the so-called Berlin-Rome Axis, the 1936 alliance between Nazi Germany and Italy. Arnold-Forster begins with a brief overview of Benito Mussolini's acquisition of dictatorial power in Italy, which in some ways paralleled Hitler's rise to mastery over Germany. Then the author explains how Italy's 1935 invasion of Ethiopia (in northern Africa) created an international crisis. The inept way that the League of Nations and Allied leaders dealt with this crisis clearly revealed how weak, fearful, and ineffective they were. This reality was not lost on Hitler, who proceeded to ally himself with Mussolini in preparation for other such aggressions. As Arnold-Forster points out, from this time on, the risk of a major world war increased steadily until it "became a certainty."

Hitler had used apparently constitutional means [to gain power]. His Italian counterpart Benito Mussolini had seized power for himself. His Italian Fascist party had probably used more force and intimidation on the streets than Hitler's S.A. From 1919 until 1922, aided like Hitler by the general fear of Bolshevism [Russian communism], the Italian Fascists extended their political and physical power. In October 1922 they 'marched' on Rome and threatened in effect to start a civil war unless the king appointed them to govern Italy.

King Victor Emmanuel gave in. Mussolini consolidated his position quickly and skilfully. His 'corporate state' absorbed the trade unions into organizations which were virtually controlled by the Fascist party. Fascists took control of the Civil Service. Mussolini imprisoned any politician or trade unionist whom he suspected might resist. In 1924, the Italian Socialist Giacomo Matteotti was simply slain. Mussolini even sent assassins to France to kill two brothers, Carlo and Nello Rosselli, after Carlo had escaped from imprisonment on a Mediterranean island.

Mussolini was a tyrant and a dictator who did Italy a great deal of harm. At first, however, he gave the Italians at least some of the things that they wanted and needed. He restored order, which was not very difficult because the disorders which had preceded his march on Rome had been caused largely by his own followers. He also started a much needed public works programme. Part of it consisted of grandiose public buildings which Italy could not really afford, but it also included a quite large effort to restore prosperity to the poorer, southern parts of Italy which had been neglected by the central government. Grateful British tourists said that he had made the trains run on time.

Mussolini, like Hitler, was an opportunist. Like Hitler he preferred easy victories to difficult ones. Unlike Hitler, however, he did not pretend that the Italians were a master race. His philosophy did not tell him that he was destined to dominate Europe or anywhere else in particular. In foreign affairs Mussolini's chief motive was greed.

Mussolini's Initial View of Hitler

When Hitler came to power in 1933, and to absolute power in 1934, Mussolini was at first mistrustful of his intentions. Italy had been one of the victorious powers in 1918 and had signed the Treaty of Versailles. Mussolini was perhaps the first European statesman to comprehend that Hitler's immediate aim was to change the Versailles settlement in Germany's favour. In June 1933, when Hitler was Chancellor but not yet Führer, Mussolini tried to persuade France, Great Britain and Germany to agree that these four powers alone could alter the provisions of the Treaty. Formally they could only be changed by the League of Nations. Nothing much came of these negotiations. But nearly two years later, in April 1935 at Stresa, Italy, France and Britain undertook to resist jointly 'any unilateral repudiation of treaties, which may endanger the peace of Europe'. The so-called Stresa front was actually a sham. On 16 April 1935, two days after the Stresa conference ended, Hitler repudiated the Versailles Treaty by reintroducing conscription and launching a rearmament programme.

It is not clear whether Mussolini really wanted to restrain Hitler although at the time of the Stresa meeting he was certainly worried lest Hitler should annex Austria, and with reason. In any case Mussolini was planning transgressions of his own. He had his eyes on Ethiopia. In 1935 Ethiopia, governed by the Emperor Haile Selassie, was the only large independent African State. It was the only piece of Africa left for Europeans to colonize. It had a common frontier with Italian Somaliland. Mussolini picked quarrels with Ethiopia with the intention of causing 'incidents' which could lead to war and conquest. But he feared, needlessly, that the League would stop him.

On 3 October 1935, after a ritual quarrel about a well, Italian troops invaded Ethiopia. The Ethiopians resisted valiantly. On 7 October the Ethiopian delegate to the League Council asked that Italy's conduct should be condemned as aggression under Article 12 of the League covenant. On 11 October the Ethiopian complaint won the support of 50 of the League's 54 members. Only Italy, Albania, Austria and Hungary voted against. The question of sanctions, joint measures by all members of the League to deter Italy, was referred to a co-ordinating committee. The committee rejected the only sanction that would have been effective, the closure of the Suez Canal, then controlled by Britain, because it was likely to lead to war. Probably in France and certainly in Britain public opinion was on Ethiopia's side. The 'peace ballot', a referendum organised by the League of Nations Union and other organizations which supported the League and its principles, had just shown that at least 6.7 million British citizens favoured military sanctions by the League against aggressors and that 10 million favoured economic sanctions. The League of Nations Union and the 'peace ballot' enjoyed at least nominal support from all political parties in Britain. The Conservatives, returned to power in the general election of 14 November 1935 with a very large majority of 247 (in a House of Commons of rather more than 600 members), decided that Prime Minister Stanley Baldwin's new government ought to take account of this expression of popular feeling.

What the government did in collusion with the French was to attempt to carve up Ethiopia behind the Emperor's back. In December the then British Foreign Secretary, Sir Samuel Hoare, and the French one, Pierre Laval, meeting secretly in Paris (while Hoare was supposed to be skating in Switzerland), agreed that they would offer Mussolini very large parts of Ethiopia in return for his promise to stop the war. If Mussolini agreed they would put the same points to the Emperor. If the Emperor disagreed he would be seen— or could be made to appear—as the warmonger, the national leader who refused peace when it was offered to him. By this betrayal of the Ethiopians, Hoare and Laval hoped to assuage public opinion in their countries. In fact their plan had the opposite result.

Hoare had scarcely got his skates on in Switzerland before the news of the Hoare-Laval pact as it was called was leaked to the newspapers, perhaps by the French Foreign Office perhaps by the British one. There was public outcry in both countries. On 18 December Baldwin had to sack Hoare. In Paris the Government itself barely survived. Hoare was replaced by Sir Anthony Eden (later Lord Avon), a known supporter of the League and its principle of collective security. Diplomatically Mussolini had lost out. Militarily, he was not doing well either. The Italians had expected a walk-over [easy victory]. In fact they did not reach the Ethiopian capital, Addis Ababa, until May 1936; but no one except the Ethiopians themselves had tried to stop them.

In Ethiopia the League's collective resolve had foundered because its militarily effective members—Britain and France—

had shrunk from risking war when the risk was small. From then on—as Hitler and Mussolini provoked one new crisis after another—the risk of war increased until, in September 1939, it became a certainty.

Hitler had stated his intentions almost as soon as he came to power. He became Chancellor on 30 January 1933. On 3 February he told the army Chief of Staff, General von Hammerstein, and the other responsible military leaders, that he intended to restore German might and to use it to conquer new living space in the East which could be 'Germanized' regardless of the consequences. To make this possible the youth of Germany must be converted to the belief that only battle could save their country. The 'cancer' of democracy must be abolished. Rearmament was the essential pre-requisite for the achievement of these goals because without military power Germany could not exercise political power.

In August 1934, following [President Paul von] Hindenburg's death, Hitler made all German servicemen swear an oath of personal loyalty to him as Führer. In the spring of 1935 he reintroduced conscription and started to re-arm in earnest. A year later, while Mussolini was still trying to conquer Ethiopia, Hitler re-occupied the Rhineland which had been de-militarized under the Versailles Treaty. This was another direct breach of the Treaty. Neither Britain nor France lifted a finger to stop him. Rightly, perhaps, the two Governments surmised that public opinion in their countries would not endorse or support a war fought to keep German soldiers out of German territory. Italy, the third member of the now-hopeless Stresa front, was busy elsewhere. Later in the year—and after Mussolini had finally conquered Ethiopia—Hitler established the Rome-Berlin axis of Fascist States. In November he signed a similar pact—the Anti-Comintern Pact—with Japan. On paper, at any rate, the German-Italian-Japanese Alliance was in existence, already formidable, already preparing hard for war. . . . When the time came for war itself, Mussolini turned out to be a grave embarrassment to Hitler. Germany never helped Japan. Japan never helped Germany. But from 25 November 1936, the Alliance existed for all to see, and for all to judge.

Anschluss: The Reunification of Germany and Austria

F.L. Carsten

One of Hitler's major pre–World War II political triumphs was the *Anschluss*, his largely peaceful takeover of Austria in 1938 that fulfilled his dream of reuniting the two countries. The main reason the operation went so smoothly was that most of the führer's work in priming Austria for the *Anschluss* had already been done by Austrians. In this essay, F.L. Carsten, former professor of Central European history at the University of London, focuses on the political situation in Austria before the 1938 reunification. Carsten identifies Austria's "pan-German" groups, those who, like Hitler, viewed Germans and Austrians as a single people. These groups gained prominence in the years following the collapse of the Austro-Hungarian Empire (the monarchy ruled by the ancient, noble Habsburg family) in 1918. Like Hitler and his Nazis, the Austrian pan-Germans hated the Marxists (socialists), Bolsheviks (Russian communists) whom they referred to as "Reds," as well as advocates of democracy. Perceiving that these elements controlled the Austrian government, the pan-Germans staged a coup attempt that, like Hitler's 1923 beer hall *putsch*, failed. Also like Hitler, however, these pro-German Austrians prevailed, ultimately preparing their land for absorption into the führer's "greater German fatherland."

From *The Rise of Fascism*, by F.L. Carsten (Berkeley and Los Angeles: University of California Press), ©1967 by F.L. Carsten. Reprinted by permission of the publisher.

Austria, after the first world war, lost her Empire and became a small republic with far too large a capital, Vienna, which no longer served the needs of an Empire. Furthermore, Vienna was Red, dominated by left-wing workers' and soldiers' councils, while there was little industry in the other parts of the country and the prevailing political mood—in [the central and southern Austrian provinces of] Carinthia, Styria, the Tyrol—was conservative and anti-Marxist. Styria and Carinthia were threatened by claims of the new Yugoslav state to border areas with a mixed population, and as on the German eastern frontiers, guerilla warfare soon developed between irregular forces fighting over disputed areas. On the Austrian side these were defended by free corps similar to those which were founded in Germany—and they could equally well be used to fight Marxism or Bolshevism at home.

Austrian Groups with a Pan-German Agenda

On a local basis these pare-military associations continued to flourish long after the immediate danger of Yugoslav attacks had passed. The units were well supplied with funds by the industrialists as a counter-weight to the Marxist trade unions, but they also received help from abroad. Money and weapons for the Styrian units were sent by similar organizations from Bavaria [Germany's southernmost province]. . . . The local authorities, too, rendered every conceivable help . . . so that the Styrian *Heimatschutz* (Home Defence) possessed even guns and aeroplanes. Its leader was a local lawyer, Dr Walter Pfrimer . . . his ideas were pan-German. . . . His units wore the swastika and carried the German black, white and red flag in addition to the white-green of Styria. In the Tyrol another lawyer, Dr Richard Steidle, held a similar position; he was a native of the South Tyrol. . . . His forces too were supplied with weapons . . . from Bavaria. . . . He acquired an energetic chief of staff in the person of Major Waldemar Pabst, who had escaped from Germany and took up residence in Innsbruck, another link with the German counter-revolution.

The collapse of the Habsburg monarchy, the lost war, and

the inflation which resulted from it provided these units with many recruits: officials, ex-servicemen, small farmers, rentiers, members of the professions—groups which had been hit by the economic and social changes resulting from the first world war. They all hated Red Vienna, its strong working-class movement, its cosmopolitan culture, its parasites and profiteers. But for several years these pare-military units had only local importance, and no clear programme. In 1927, however, strong fear and hatred of the Marxists were aroused anew through the burning down of the Palace of Justice in Vienna by embittered crowds and the general strike proclaimed by the Socialists after the police had fired on the demonstrators. The *Heimwehren* (Home Defence Units) succeeded in defeating the strike everywhere and could welcome many new recruits eager to stem the Red tide. Their many local units for the first time acquired a centralized leadership and direction. Hitherto their programme had been merely anti-Marxist, but now it became anti-parliamentarian, aiming at the establishment of an authoritarian state based on corporations or estates, for which Italy provided the example. The government of Dr Ignaz Seipel saw in the *Heimwehren* welcome allies in its struggle against the Socialists. The *Heimwehr* organization was strengthened, and valuable connexions were established to officers of the police and of the army. But the units continued to wear local insignia, colours and costumes. Their politics, too, often were of a local colour, clerical or national, and national either in an Austrian or a pan-German sense. The local clergy often supported the movement and gave it their blessing. . . .

The Attempt to Make Austria a Fascist State

The ideology of the *Heimwehr* movement became increasingly pro-Fascist. When it submitted its programme to the Austrian chancellor in 1929 this included the erection of 'the authoritarian state based on estates and on Fascist foundations'. Its leaders began to dream of a march on Red Vienna. In May 1930 several hundred *Heimwehr* leaders at Korneuburg took an oath which betrayed strong Fascist influence. It sharply rejected 'western democratic parliamentari-

anism and the party state. In its place we want to put the self-government of estates and a strong leadership of the state.'
. . . On the same day Dr Pfrimer declared: 'On all sides the conviction was evident that here in Austria only Fascism can save us. We must make an attempt to seize power.' During

---

Mussolini Supports Hitler's Takeover of Austria

On March 11, 1938, with German troops pouring into Austria, Hitler received a phone call from the German aristocrat Philip of Hesse whom he had sent to Italy to consult with Germany's ally, Italian dictator Benito Mussolini. In this excerpt from a transcript of the call, Hesse informs the führer that Mussolini has given his blessing to the Anschluss, *thereby decreasing the already small chances of Allied interference.*

Hesse: I have just come back from the Palazzo Venezia. The Duce accepted the whole thing in a very friendly manner. He sends you his regards.

Hitler: Then please tell Mussolini I will never forget him for this.

Hesse: Yes.

Hitler: Never, never, never, whatever happens. As soon as the Austrian affair is settled, I shall be ready to go with him, through thick and thin, no matter what happens.

Hesse: Yes, my Führer.

Hitler: Listen, I shall make any agreement—I am no longer in fear of the terrible position which would have existed militarily in case we had got into a conflict. You may tell him that I thank him ever so much—never, never shall I forget.

Hesse: Yes, my Führer.

Hitler: I will never forget, whatever may happen. If he should ever need any help or be in any danger, he can be convinced that I shall stick to him, whatever may happen, even if the whole world were against him.

Hesse: Yes, my Führer.

Jeremy Noakes and Geoffrey Pridham, eds., *Documents on Nazism, 1919–1945.* New York: Viking Press, 1975, p. 536.

the following weeks the Korneuburg oath was taken by the *Heimwehr* units all over Austria. . . .

The long-awaited *Putsch* [coup] and deposition of the government were finally attempted by Pfrimer in September 1931. In Styria the attempt was at first entirely successful. The heavily armed *Heimwehr* units occupied many smaller places and surrounded the capital of Styria, Graz. But the other leaders did not support him, and the march on Vienna never started. The authorities reacted with unusual mildness, and the units with their weapons were permitted to disperse peacefully. Pfrimer and other local leaders were put on trial, but they were acquitted, the jurymen joining the accused in giving the Fascist salute. . . .

In January 1933 Hitler became the German chancellor, and the Austrian National Socialists were rapidly gaining ground. Already in January 1931 Major Pabst pointed out to a Hungarian visitor that their quick growth could partly be explained by the fact that they collected contributions from their members and thus were financially independent, while the *Heimwehr* relied too much on subsidies from industry and foreign countries. But it was the internal rivalry between its leaders, the ambiguity of its political programme, and its basic conservatism which militated against the *Heimwehr*. It was now faced by a much more extreme movement which was strongly supported from Germany and promised to fulfil the old dreams of the Pan-Germans, while a specifically 'Austrian' ideology had not struck root.

In August 1933 [Austrian] Chancellor [Engelbert] Dollfuss met Mussolini . . . [who] demanded an openly pro-Fascist course in Austrian internal policy, for which end he intended to use the *Heimwehr* as a pressure group. To prevent Austria from falling under German sway, all Austrian forces were to be united under the slogan of national independence. A few weeks after the meeting Dollfuss outlined to the so-called 'Fatherland Front' his own programme for a political reconstruction on the basis of corporations or estates. But this did not satisfy the *Heimwehr* leaders who—in accordance with Mussolini—wanted a Fascist Austria. Dollfuss, however, depended on *Heimwehr* support, for the Fatherland Front was too weak and too disunited to defend the government against the Socialists on the Left and the National Socialists on the Right. . . . Austria did not become a Fascist and totalitarian state, in spite of all Mussolini's efforts. . . .

Hitler Triumphs in Austria

In July 1934 Chancellor Dollfuss was murdered by National Socialists, and again it was Mussolini's support that saved Austria and the semi-authoritarian régime established there. Yet this régime was increasingly menaced by Germany and the Austrian National Socialists who received German support and could shelter there in case of need. . . . Meanwhile the *Heimwehren* disintegrated further, and many of their members joined the National Socialists who appealed to the same sentiments and were growing in strength. With this the Fatherland Front was unable to compete: it had no revolutionary fervour, it was too bourgeois and too conservative. In these circumstances the experiment to transplant Italian Fascism to Austria was bound to end in failure.

Not Mussolini, but Hitler triumphed in Austria, where he had grown up and where he had received his decisive political impulses. His policy of *Anschluss* was carried to success by a genuine Fascist party, the Austrian National Socialists, who continued to grow in spite of government persecution. Their mass appeal was based on Pan-Germanism which had been a strong current for decades, the ideal of generations of students—and Germany was now a strong power from which a magnetic influence emanated. In Austria, Pan-Germanism had been strongly reinforced by the peace settlement of 1919 which deprived Austria of her old provinces, but forbade her to join the new German Republic. Twenty years later the victorious western powers were willing to concede to the Austrian-born dictator what they had prohibited in 1919. Thus Fascism triumphed in Austria, but it was of the German, not the Italian variety, and it meant the subordination of everything Austrian to the new masters in Berlin. Berlin, not Vienna, was the capital of the 'Greater Germany' ruled by the Austrian lance-corporal [Hitler].

The Nazis Dismember Czechoslovakia

Gerrit P. Judd

After absorbing Austria into the German fold, Hitler turned next to the conquest of Czechoslovakia. The Sudetenland, the northern Czech region bordering Germany, had a large German population and Hitler reasoned that he could take advantage of this fact when dismembering the Czech state. In this lucid, informative essay, Gerrit P. Judd, former chairman of the Department of History at Hofstra University, explains how British, French, and other Allied leaders fatally underestimated the German führer. In a desperate attempt to avert a major European war, they met with him, believing that all parties could agree on a workable, honorable settlement of the Czech crisis. But they did not anticipate that Hitler secretly intended to absorb Czechoslovakia, no matter what any such agreement might say. In the end, the Allies gave in to the dictator, in what soon became known as a "policy of appeasement," and the democratic Czechs were doomed. Hitler's triumph boosted his popularity at home and helped pave the way for the very war the Allies had hoped to avoid.

After the annexation of Austria, Hitler turned, as many expected, to Czechoslovakia. The 15 million inhabitants of this little country enjoyed prosperity and a balanced economy. Czechoslovakia was the most democratic of the east Euro-

From *A History of Civilization*, by Gerrit P. Judd, ©1966. Adapted by permission of Prentice-Hall, Inc., Upper Saddle River, N.J.

pean states. Its constitution, copied from that of France, functioned well under the enlightened leadership of its first two presidents, Thomas G. Masaryk (1850–1937) and Eduard Benes (1884–1948). Czechoslovakia's population was mixed. Over half its citizens were Czechs, but it contained over three million Germans, over two million Slovaks, and lesser numbers of Magyars, Ruthenians, and Poles. The existence of these sizable minorities under Czech rule resulted directly from the Versailles Treaty. Nonetheless, like the other minority groups, the Germans in Czechoslovakia's Sudetenland were well treated and generally content.

Troops Mobilize on the Border

Hitler boldly plotted the conquest of Czechoslovakia. He began by encouraging the Sudeten German Party to demand autonomy. Under Hitler's direction, this puppet Nazi group created numerous disturbances. To increase tension in the growing war of nerves, even before the seizure of Austria Hitler pointedly promised to protect all German minorities abroad. In April, 1938, after the fall of Austria, the Sudeten Germans formally demanded their independence. When the Czech government refused, the Nazi-inspired disturbances increased. The Czechs replied by mobilizing 400 thousand men. The crisis deepened during the summer of 1938. Although the Czech government granted some of the Sudeten Party's demands, the Germans held extensive military maneuvers and stationed 30 divisions on the Czech border. At this time a situation developed which terrified the German generals. Czechoslovakia had 36 divisions under arms, together with strong border fortifications. Russia, France's ally, could use the Czech airfields to bomb Germany and invade Germany through both Poland and Rumania. In the west, the army of Czechoslovakia's ally, France, outnumbered the German forces eight to one. Besides, the British fleet was mobilizing. The German generals correctly believed that if Hitler provoked a war, as indeed he longed to do, Germany would be defeated in short order. Some of the leading generals had agreed to overthrow Hitler if he led Germany into such a suicidal conflict. Against this grave and uncertain background, with Nazi propaganda blaring over the radio and heavy black headlines appearing daily in the newspapers, international tension mounted steadily. Many dreaded that a major war was imminent. On September 7, the Sudeten Germans, at Hitler's orders, broke off negotiations with the Czech government. A few days later in a hysterical speech Hitler demanded self-determination for them. To check the increasing Sudeten disorder, the Czech government declared martial law.

Hitler's Demands

At this stage in the crisis Neville Chamberlain, Britain's prime minister, proposed, with French support, a personal conference with Hitler. Chamberlain, an honorable Conservative of the old school, represented, like [U.S. President] Woodrow Wilson, the conscience of the West. Above almost every consideration he wanted peace. He did not then know, as he later realized, that Hitler wanted war. On September 15, Chamberlain flew to Germany and at Berchtesgaden conferred with Hitler. Here Chamberlain learned that, under threat of war, Hitler insisted on the annexation of the Sudetenland. After talks with the French, Chamberlain persuaded the reluctant Czechs to agree. At that time many people believed, as they had in the case of Austria, that the German-speaking people had a right to national self-determination. Elated, Chamberlain flew back to Germany and met Hitler at Godesberg. Chamberlain was horrified to find that Hitler had further demands, among them plebiscites [national referenda in which the people express their support for a proposal] to be held to determine the political status of Czech areas with large German minorities. Again Chamberlain conferred with the French. Meanwhile, Russia continued to advise both Britain and France to take a firm stand. For a few days, as Britain and France contemplated helping Czechoslovakia, war seemed inevitable. In desperation, Chamberlain asked Hitler for a third conference. At [Italian dictator Benito] Mussolini's suggestion, Hitler replied by inviting Chamberlain, along with Mussolini and Premier [Édouard] Daladier of France, to meet him at Munich. The Czech crisis had reached its dramatic and shameful climax.

At Munich, Britain and France had to choose between sacrificing a sovereign democratic state to Hitler or risking a major war. They chose not to risk war. On September 29, the leaders of Germany, Britain, France, and Italy agreed on the German occupation of the Sudetenland and of Czechoslovakia's border forts. . . . In addition, Germany also received highway rights through central Czechoslovakia to Vienna. Czechoslovakia lost 16 thousand of its former 52 thousand square miles and five million of its former 15 million inhabitants. Of these, more than a million Czechs and Slovaks came under foreign rule. The four powers at the Munich Conference did not consult Czechoslovakia, which had no choice but to submit. Significantly, the powers did not invite Russia to the conference. As an indication of Hitler's characteristic duplicity, at Munich he secretly promised to let Mussolini participate in the planned German attack on Britain and France. Nonetheless, the democracies greeted the Munich settlement with wild rejoicing, mingled as it was with a genuine undercurrent of shame. Enthusiastic crowds cheered Chamberlain's return and his speech stating that he had brought back not only peace with honor but also, so he hoped, peace in our time. Equally enthusiastic members of Parliament protested loudly when [British statesman] Winston Churchill denounced the Munich Pact as a total defeat for the democracies.

At Munich Hitler eliminated Czechoslovakia as a hostile force, including its 36 magnificent divisions, air force, vast munitions works, and other resources, among them two-thirds of its coal and steel. Without the mountainous border fortifications, which fell into German hands, and with disrupted transportation and communications, the Czechs could not defend themselves. In addition, with Czechoslovakia all but helpless, Hitler had much easier access than before to southeast Europe. Within Germany, Hitler's popularity soared to new heights. The German masses hailed him as the Magic Man, who had added 10 million subjects and much new territory to the Third Reich within six months and without fighting a war. Hitler was also personally fortunate. His success at Munich discouraged the hostile German generals, who decided to wait until he suffered a military or diplomatic defeat before attempting to depose him.

The Final Extinction of the Czech State

The losses suffered by France and Britain at Munich were not only strategic in the material sense but also moral and diplomatic. Their policy of appeasement had lost them a valuable military ally. But Czechoslovakia's loss was also a moral disaster, since Czechoslovakia was a genuinely democratic state. The failure of France in particular to protect its eastern ally gave the impression that the democracies would not honor their treaty obligations. The Munich Pact also destroyed the French system of defensive alliances. France's ally, Poland, became isolated. France's ally, Russia, became even more suspicious of the democracies and tended to withdraw from the West. In long perspective, the western democracies lost prestige in eastern Europe, which they did not regain, even with American help, in the years after 1945. In short perspective they gained a year's respite before the actual outbreak of World War II. But in this interim Germany produced far more armaments than did the democracies. On the other hand, in at least one important respect the democracies salvaged something from their defeat at Munich. Britain had time to build an air force, without which the British Isles probably could not have survived the German air assaults during the dark summer months of 1940.

Those who expected Hitler to stop with his gains at Munich were soon disappointed. In November, 1938, after the murder of a German diplomat in Paris by a Jew, Hitler ordered a mass persecution of Germany's Jews. Many people asked if these atrocities represented "Peace in Our Time." In the middle of March, 1939, Hitler occupied Czechoslovakia and declared it under German protection. Here was the final extinction of the Czech state. The Nazi occupying forces behaved with characteristic ferocity. But despite their pledge at Munich Britain and France took no action. Hitler was jubilant. By this time he was fully convinced that the democracies would not stand in his way.

The Nazi-Soviet Pact and Outbreak of War

C.E. Black and E.C. Helmreich

With the fall of the city of Prague and the rest of Czechoslovakia to the Nazis in March 1939, both the Western Allies and the Soviets worried that Hitler would next turn on
Poland, on Germany's eastern front, and eventually on the
Soviet Union. Historians C.E. Black, formerly of Princeton University, and E.C. Helmreich, formerly of Bowdoin
College, here chronicle how, at first, the Soviets sought a
grand alliance with Britain, France, and other Western
powers. Soviet dictator Joseph Stalin and his foreign minister, Maksim Litvinov, hoped that such an alliance would
discourage Hitler from attacking the Soviet Union and
neighboring Baltic states, such as Estonia and Finland.
But Western leaders, including British prime minister
Neville Chamberlain and French premier Édouard Daladier, distrusted the Soviets and turned down the Soviet
offer. Frustrated, Stalin now worried that the Allies would
continue "appeasing" the Nazis, as they had at the 1938
Munich conference, in which they allowed Hitler to carve
up Czechoslovakia. After firing Litvinov and replacing
him with Vyacheslav Molotov, Stalin tried to buy time to
build up his own forces. To the surprise of many, Black
and Helmreich explain, Stalin's strategy was to conclude a
pact with Hitler and Nazi negotiator Joachim von
Ribbentrop on August 23, 1939, a move that led to the
outbreak of war only days later.

From *Twentieth-Century Europe*, by C.E. Black and E.C. Helmreich. Copyright
©1972 by Alfred A. Knopf Inc. Reprinted by permission of the publisher.

In the consultations which took place after the fall of Prague the Soviet Union promptly proposed, on March 18, that the situation be examined in a six-power conference of the Soviet Union, Great Britain, France, Poland, Rumania, and Turkey. This was a broader approach than the Western states were prepared for at the moment, and Chamberlain suggested instead that of the smaller states Poland alone be brought into the picture at this juncture. When Poland, which feared Russia as much as it hated Germany, refused to accept a guarantee with which the Soviet Union was associated, action was taken on a more restricted basis. On March 31 Britain pledged aid to Poland in case its independence was threatened by Germany. France had a treaty of mutual guarantee with Poland dating from 1925. Anglo-French pledges of aid were extended to Rumania and Greece on April 13, and Britain and France concluded separate mutual assistance agreements with Turkey in May. Moreover on April 27, the British government took the unprecedented peacetime step of introducing military conscription.

Western Worries About Soviet Aggression

It was thus in a somewhat friendlier atmosphere that negotiations between Russia and the Western states were resumed in April, 1939. When Great Britain suggested on April 15 that the Soviet Union make a unilateral guarantee of assistance to any neighboring state which expressed a desire for such a pledge, Litvinov replied with a proposal which made perfectly clear the price which the Western democracies would have to pay for their grand alliance. The Soviet proposal of April 17 stipulated that in addition to concluding a mutual assistance pact and a military convention, the Soviet Union, Great Britain, and France, should guarantee all the states between the Baltic and the Black Sea. For Russia this was not an illogical price to ask, since it would provide a defensive barrier against Nazi aggression not only in the immediately threatened states of Poland and Rumania, but also in Finland and the Baltic States to the north and in Bulgaria, Yugoslavia, and Greece, to the south. This was a price which such advocates of the grand alliance as [British statesman Winston] Churchill were prepared to pay, but Chamberlain and Daladier considered it to be more than the situation required. Not only were the smaller states of Eastern Europe opposed to receiving Soviet assistance, but the Western statesmen felt they would be placed in the position of granting to Russia in the extensive zone between the Baltic and the Black Sea a sphere of influence which they were convinced would soon be occupied by Soviet troops. To push these countries towards Russia against their will, under circumstances in which the Soviet Union might still in the end choose to remain inactive in case of Nazi aggression in the West, did not appeal to Chamberlain. On May 8 the Soviet proposals were rejected as being too comprehensive. In the meantime Litvinov, who was believed to favor a Western orientation, was dismissed on May 3, and Molotov was appointed in his place as Soviet foreign minister.

The Soviet-Western negotiations never proceeded much

Hitler's Decision to Attack Poland

On May 23, 1939, Adolf Hitler gathered together twelve of his senior commanders and outlined his plans for invading Poland. This is an excerpt from his statement, as recorded by one of his assistants.

After six years the present position is as follows:

With minor exceptions German national unification has been achieved. Further successes cannot be achieved without bloodshed.

Poland will always be on the side of our adversaries. Despite the friendship agreement Poland has always intended to exploit every opportunity against us.

Danzig is not the objective. It is a matter of expanding our living space in the east, of making our food supplies secure, and of solving the problem of the Baltic states. To provide sufficient food you must have sparsely settled areas. This is fertile soil, whose surpluses will be very much increased by German, thorough management.

No other such possibility can be seen in Europe. . . .

beyond the exchange of proposals which took place in the middle of April. Additional exchanges of views took place in May and in June. . . . Discussions continued throughout June and July, but the area of agreement did not widen perceptibly. The Russians insisted that the Baltic states should be included in the guarantee, and that under certain circumstances Soviet troops should be stationed in those countries, while the British and French were unwilling to extend the scope of joint assistance beyond Poland and Rumania. An Anglo-French military mission, which went to Moscow early in August to explore the possibilities of a three-power military convention, made equally slow progress. The Soviet statesmen were disconcerted not only by the persistent reluctance of the Western negotiators to meet their terms, but also by what appeared to them as distinct signs that the policy of appeasement had not really been abandoned. The Russian suspicions were particularly aroused by the visit to Lon-

The Polish regime will not resist pressure from Russia. Poland sees danger in a German victory over the west and will try and deprive us of our victory.

There is therefore no question of sparing Poland, and the decision remains *to attack Poland at the first suitable opportunity.*

We cannot expect a repetition of Czechoslovakia. There will be war. The task is to isolate Poland. Success in isolating her will be decisive. Therefore, the Führer must reserve to himself the final command to attack. There must be no simultaneous conflict with the West (France and England).

If it is not certain that a German-Polish conflict will not lead to war with the West, then the struggle will be directed in the first instance against England and France.

Basic principle: conflict with Poland, beginning with attack on Poland, will be successful only if the West keeps out. If that is impossible, then it is better to attack the West and finish off Poland at the same time.

Jeremy Noakes and Geoffrey Pridham, eds., *Documents on Nazism, 1919–1945.* New York: Viking Press, 1975, p. 559.

don in the middle of July of an impressive German economic mission, and by subsequent rumors of a large British loan to Germany. Convinced that the British and the French had no serious intentions of meeting their terms, Stalin and Molotov proceeded to bring to a head the negotiations with Germany which they had been secretly conducting since May.

The Soviets Turn to Germany

In turning to Germany rather than to the Western states for an agreement, the Soviet statesmen were doubtless making what was for them a second choice. While they had no great trust in Britain and France after Munich, the mutual assistance pact and military convention which Stalin proposed might have developed into a grand alliance which would have changed the course of European diplomacy. Combined as it was intended to be with guarantees to the states bordering on Russia, this alliance offered the maximum security which the Soviet regime could obtain against a Germany which it recognized as its principal enemy. The arrangement which it now negotiated with Germany, by contrast, was no more than a non-aggression pact which offered Russia a breathing spell before the inevitable conflict with Germany, and a security zone which increased the depth of Russia's defenses.

The agreement with Germany was more easy to negotiate, however, since the Nazis felt no inhibitions in paying the price which the Western states had considered to be too high. Where the latter refused in the end to associate themselves with guarantees which Russia's neighbors were unwilling to accept, Germany saw no difficulty in assigning to Russia the Baltic states and parts of Poland and Rumania. To Chamberlain and Daladier, it appeared to mean sacrificing the independence of the small states established after World War I, and with them the principles of sovereignty upon which the postwar European system had been founded. To Hitler, however, it was a concession which he expected to take back by force of arms within a few years. The Russian-German negotiations grew out of discussions concerning a trade agreement which started as early as May, 1939. It was not until July, however, that the possibilities of a political agreement were seriously explored, or until early August that the Germans were convinced of Russia's willingness to conclude a non-aggression pact. Once this willingness was ascertained events moved rapidly, since Hitler was concerned for his timetable with regard to Poland while Russia was apprehensive lest the Western states revert to a policy of appeasement.

The treaty of non-aggression which Molotov and [Nazi negotiator] Ribbentrop signed in Moscow on August 23, 1939, was essentially a simple document. The two parties pledged to refrain from aggression against each other, either individually or in alliance with other powers. Each party also pledged to remain neutral in case the other became the object of belligerent action by a third party. Issues arising between the two parties were to be settled by arbitration, and the treaty was concluded for a period of ten years. This much was immediately published to the world. The price paid by Germany was described in a "Secret Additional Protocol" signed on the same day. Under its terms, an assignment of spheres of influence was made "in the event of a territorial and political rearrangement" in Eastern Europe. Russia was to have Finland, Estonia, and Latvia, on the Baltic Sea, the eastern part of Poland with a population of some thirteen million, and the Rumanian province of Bessarabia. To Germany fell Lithuania and the rest of Poland.

Germany Attacks Poland

For Hitler, the pact with Russia was the last of a long series of measures which he had taken since March in preparation of the "territorial and political rearrangement" which he was planning for Poland. As early as March 21 he informed the Polish government that Germany must have the Free City of Danzig, and that the German minority in Poland must be given better treatment. The German occupation of Memel on the following day, which deprived Lithuania of most of its coastline, served notice that Hitler was now going to concentrate on the northern sector of his eastern front. Hitler replied to the Anglo-French guarantee of Poland by denouncing on April 28 the German-Polish non-aggression pact of 1934 and the Anglo-German naval treaty of 1935. On

May 22 he further strengthened his position by concluding the military alliance with Italy, which was christened the "Pact of Steel." A week later he concluded non-aggression pacts with Estonia and Latvia. All of these moves were part of a carefully prepared plan aimed at the destruction of Poland. The blueprints for the military campaign had been completed early in April, and on May 23 Hitler informed his chiefs of staff at a memorable meeting that they must not expect another Munich but should be prepared for war with France and Britain and perhaps with Russia as well.

The die was cast, and Hitler's task was now that of isolating Poland so that the war might be fought under the best possible circumstances. Within the framework of these plans the non-aggression pact with Russia of August 23 played a capital role, for it permitted Germany to proceed against Poland with no immediate concern for the Soviet army. Hitler even hoped in the last days of August that the Nazi-Soviet pact might induce Britain and France to renounce their guarantee of Poland, but in this he was disappointed. Chamberlain immediately wrote Hitler a letter which stated Britain's determination to fight in unmistakable terms, and on August 25 this stand was formally incorporated in a mutual assistance pact with Poland. This pact had reference to aggression by "a European Power," which in a secret protocol was defined as Germany. During the last days of peace, Hitler occupied his time with a series of conciliatory gestures towards Britain and France, and a mounting propaganda campaign against Poland. At dawn on September 1, 1939, the German army invaded Poland, thus starting the war which Hitler considered essential to his plans for a greater Germany and which proved to be its ruin.

The Fall of Nazi Germany

Koppel S. Pinson

The Nazi attack on Poland in September 1939 ignited World War II, the most destructive armed conflict in human history. In this brief but informative overview of the war, noted scholar of European history Koppel S. Pinson describes how, at first, the Nazis were successful on many fronts. As the Allies began mounting their own offensives, however, Germany found itself increasingly isolated and on the defensive. Pinson concludes with an account of Hitler's last days spent in an underground bunker in Berlin; then he describes the German dictator's death, which coincided with the Allies' total victory over the now-ruined Germany. To the end, says Pinson, Nazism remained the same as it had begun—irrational, brutal, and filled with hate and arrogance.

Hitler was absolutely certain that the Western democracies at the last moment would shrink from entering into a general war to defend Poland. "I witnessed the miserable worms [French premier] Daladier and [British prime minister] Chamberlain in Munich," he told his generals. "They will be too cowardly to attack.". . . He gave the signal on September 1, 1939, for the "invasion and extermination of Poland." The "propagandist cause" for starting this war was alleged atrocities by Poland against German minorities. "Never mind," Hitler had said, "whether the propagandist cause is plausible or not. The victor shall not be asked later on whether we told the truth or not. In starting and making a war, it is not the right that matters, but victory."

Reprinted from *Modern Germany*, by Koppel S. Pinson, 2nd ed. (New York: Macmillan, 1966), by permission of the author's estate.

Victory seemed to be all his. Although Britain and France, honoring their pledge to Poland, now declared war against Germany, they were in no position either geographically or militarily to come to Poland's aid. The Polish forces were annihilated in eighteen days, and Russian troops, on September 18, moved in from the east and joined with the Germans in destroying the Polish state. . . .

One Nazi Triumph to Another

A period of so-called "phony war" in the west was broken on April 9, 1940, with the Nazi invasion of Denmark and Norway and on May 10 with the lightning attack and conquest of Belgium, Holland, and Luxemburg. The way was now open for the final assault upon France . . . and on June 23 France laid down its arms and the Nazi . . . formations goose-stepped down the Champs Élysées in Paris. The entire civilized world was shaken to its depths as beautiful Paris, the heart of European civilization, lay at the feet of the new barbarians. A heart-rending photograph, circulated by the world news agencies, which showed the entry of the Germans into Paris with a Frenchman looking on and tears streaming down his agonized face, evoked the same tears and agony throughout the world. France, weakened by internal decay, defeatism, treason, and loss of nerve, became the Vichy satellite of the Third Reich. Britain was now left entirely alone to face the savage bombing of the Nazi air force and to brace itself for invasion. The British people, in the words of Winston Churchill, "held the fort alone till those who hitherto had been half-blind were half-ready."

For over three years Hitler went from one triumph to another and stood as the greatest conqueror of modern times. invading the Soviet Union on June 22, 1941, he was able to crush the completely unprepared Red Army. . . . From the Channel Islands eastward into the heart of the [Russian] Ukraine and close to the borders of the Caucasus, and from Narvik in northern Norway south to the Aegean Islands in the Mediterranean, the swastika fluttered proudly as the herald of Hitler's thousand-year Reich and of his new order in Europe. The Japanese attack on Pearl Harbor on December 7, 1941, brought the United States officially into the war, but it was still a long way from being prepared to test its strength against the Wehrmacht [German armed forces]. It was not until the end of 1942, with the American landing in North Africa . . . that the fortunes of the war finally turned to the side of the Allies. The [Allied] landings in Sicily, followed by the fall of Mussolini on July 25, 1943, and the final storming of "Fortress Europe," begun on the beaches of Normandy on June 6, 1944, coinciding with the continued offensive of the Red Army in the east, at long last brought the war in Europe to an end on May 8, 1945, with the utter collapse of the entire Nazi structure.

The Brutalities of Nazi Occupation

Hitler's plans, like all previous German war plans, had called for a short war. The unexpected reaction of the Western democracies to his aggression in Poland and the stubborn resistance of Britain threw off his timetable. But the Nazi leaders were full of confidence for at least the first four years of the war. The new gospel presented to the conquered peoples of Europe was that of a "new European order" with Hitler as the spokesman of the new Europe. The small nations, they said, could have their nationality guaranteed only by the leadership state of Europe under the new messiah Adolf Hitler. In every nation he conquered, Hitler found not only avowed fifth-column groups made up of native or ethnic German Nazis but also large elements of the population who were willing to give ear to this "new gospel." The extent of moral decadence in European countries was never so clearly revealed as in the widespread collaboration with the Nazis by large groups in the conquered states. Only the heroism and shining nobility of the various resistance movements in the occupied countries were able to provide partial atonement for the widespread collaboration.

In Russia the invading Nazi armies were hailed at first by the native peasantry as the long-hoped-for liberators who would free them from the tyrannical slave state of Stalin. It was the ruthless racialist doctrine of the "master race" and the policy of brutal terrorization by the invading German armies that finally sobered the enthusiasm of the Russian and Ukrainian masses and aroused them to the patriotic defense of their own fatherland. Even at that there were thousands of Russian deserters who were organized into a special army under the command of General Vlassov for service with the Germans. . . .

The record of Nazi brutalities is too long and too painful to list here. They were fully described and documented in the war crimes trials. A policy of complete physical destruction of land and people was carried out in Greece and in the eastern countries. All conquered areas served primarily to supply the needs of the master race. The most effective way of protecting themselves against possible resistance was to decimate the élite groups of the population. This too was carried out with special ruthlessness in Greece, Poland, and Russia. Priests, ministers, teachers, and intellectuals were subjected to extermination or torture. All the rest of the population became a huge reservoir of slave-labor supply for the armament industries of the Greater Reich. Resistance was punished unmercifully by execution of hostages or extermination of entire communities. . . .

A special object of Nazi vandalism was the artistic and cultural treasures of Europe. With all their barbarism, the Nazi leaders had the typical jealous admiration and concealed envy of the upstart for the refined culture of his victims. All the Nazi leaders from Hitler . . . down to the more lowly S.S. leaders engaged in a titanic policy of cultural looting to fill their private as well as public collections with the gems of the art galleries, museums, and libraries of the conquered peoples. . . .

The most gruesome and most tragic fate of all was reserved for the Jews of Europe. According to an estimate attributed to Adolph Eichmann, the chief of the Gestapo Jewish section, at least 6 million Jews were murdered by the Nazis between 1941 and 1944. When the war was over in May, 1945, the Allied armies found only approximately 100,000 Jews left in all of Europe outside the U.S.S.R. Hitler's promise to exterminate the Jews in the event of war was carried out, and the Nazi goal of ridding Europe of the "Jewish pest" was practically realized, despite their own final defeat. . . .

By the end of 1941 the decision was taken to carry out the "final solution" of the Jewish problem. "Final solution" always meant extermination. Directives for the action were almost always verbally transmitted from Hitler and [leading Nazi Heinrich] Himmler . . . to the Gestapo chiefs . . . and down the line to the local officials. The extermination of the Jews was a subject usually not discussed by Nazi leaders in public. In a secret session with S.S. generals on October 4, 1943, Himmler reviewed the "clearing out of the Jews." "This is a page of glory in our history," he said, "which has never been written and is never to be written. . . . It shall be said on this occasion, openly here among ourselves, but we shall never speak of it publicly. . . . But we have fulfilled this most difficult task out of love for our people."

Extermination of Jews was carried out first by special Einsatzgruppen [executioners] that would herd the Jews of a given area into a ditch and shoot them down. Then more refined techniques were devised in the form of death vans in which the victims were gassed while the vehicles were in motion. The capstone of this gruesome chapter of human depravity came with the establishment of specially constructed crematoria and gas chambers that were able to engage in mass slaughter with efficiency and dispatch. According to the testimony of Rudolf Hoess, commandant of the Auschwitz camp, at least 3,000,000 persons were exterminated at Auschwitz alone, of which all but 20,000 Russian prisoners of war were Jews gathered from all the conquered countries of Europe.

German industry co-operated with the Gestapo in running the camps to utilize the slave labor there, to collect the clothing and shoes of the victims, and to utilize their bones for fertilizer. German bankers received the jewelry and gold fillings of the victims and deposited them in the vaults of the Reichsbank. German scientists carried out gruesome medical experiments upon the victims, and toward the end of the war, when the German war economy was hard-pressed, Himmler and Eichmann offered for sale to Jewish leaders in Switzerland Jewish lives in return for ransom money and vehicles, which they badly needed. . . .

The Tide Turns Against Germany

As the war continued and German losses on the front as a result of Allied bombings increased, a contradiction developed between the policy of ruthless extermination of Jews and other conquered peoples and the mounting needs of labor supply. Manpower shortage in World War II as in World War I, became the most crucial problem for the German war machine. . . . Arms factories and farms required millions of additional workers. Voluntary recruitment and forced labor in labor and concentration camps were resorted to, to meet the needs. By the end of the war there were about 4,795,000 foreign workers in the Reich, and with war prisoners and political prisoners used to fill the gap in labor supply the amount reached 6,691,000. Whereas economic need asserted itself more in the treatment of most foreign workers, in the case of the Jews the antisemitic goal of extermination usually won out over economic necessity. Regular army circles frequently sought to halt deportation and liquidation of Jews, not so much because of their sympathy and humaneness but because these Jews were helping produce some essential materials necessary for the army. Those Jews who remained alive within the conquered areas owed their survival almost entirely to their continued usefulness to the German war machine.

The attitude of the German people toward the war gradually changed from pride in the great triumphs of the Wehrmacht to a dogged and patient fight for the preservation of the Fatherland. . . . There was no German resistance or opposition to speak of while German arms were being carried to victory. Not one of the [German] generals or political leaders . . . dared stand up to Hitler when he unfolded before them his vast plans of world conquest. It was only as the tide turned against Germany and the prospect of defeat seemed not out of the question that the whole tenor of opinion at home began to change. . . .

The defeat [of German forces] at Stalingrad in February, 1943, served even more to sober German opinion, since for most Germans, military leaders as well as civilian population, the war against Russia loomed largest in the picture. [Joseph]

Goebbels' propaganda machine began to turn from the motif of master race and world dominion to that of a battle for survival. The effect of the heavy Allied bombings on German morale was tremendous. Their earlier sense of pride in the fact that all the horrors of modern warfare were being carried out on enemy soil was rudely shattered. In a speech to a group of air-force engineers on March 25, 1944, Field Marshal Erhard Milch told his hearers to go out and look at the bombed districts in Berlin, Frankfurt, or Dusseldorf. "Not that there is any danger of revolution or any such thing as we know it from 1918," he said. "But at a certain point a human being just cannot endure any more. . . . The war of nerves has reached a point which causes us in the leadership group to worry. The people cannot endure that forever."

At no point in the war, up to the very end, was there any evidence of any diminution in the will to fight. True, there was an increased use of terror against the civilian population as the war dragged on, and Heinrich Himmler, head of the S.S., Gestapo and all the police forces of the Reich, became the most powerful figure in the Reich next to Hitler. But Himmler, who more than any other man in Germany had his hand on the pulse of popular opinion, was able to assure his S.S. commanders on October 14, 1943, "Our people, our workers are on the whole so remarkably decent and are so filled with a sense of faithful execution of their obligations in this war that they create no difficulties for us." It is exceedingly doubtful, however, that the Allied call for "unconditional surrender" had much to do with hardening the resistance of the German armies. Hitler and his henchmen knew that for them there was no half way between total victory or destruction, and they were determined, quite apart from Allied demands, to fight to the end. "I shall stand or fall in this struggle," Hitler told his generals at the start of the war, "and I shall never survive the defeat of my people." This remained his attitude all through the war up to the very end. Right after the attack on Russia he told a group of ministers that he would never give up any of the lands he occupied and that "even if it means war for a hundred years there must never be a military power west of the Urals except Germany.". . .

Nazi Germany in Ruins

Until the very end Hitler treated anyone who dared suggest that the war was lost as a traitor. [Chief Nazi architect] Albert Speer braved this policy on March 18, 1945, to write to Hitler that the war was lost and that some measures should be taken to preserve the subsistence level of the population. Hitler's reply to Speer was as follows:

> If the war is to be lost, the nation also will perish. . . . There is no need to consider the basis even of a most primitive existence any longer. On the contrary it is better to destroy even that, and to destroy it ourselves. The nation has proved itself weak, and the future belongs solely to the stronger eastern nations. Besides, those who remain after the battle are of little value; for the good have fallen.

The last weeks of the war revealed even more than ever before the bizarre and pathological character of the Nazi leaders. As the Allied armies of [U.S. general Dwight] Eisenhower and [British commander Bernard] Montgomery swept across Central Germany and deep into Thuringia, Czechoslovakia, and Austria, the Red Army under [Georgy] Zhukov drew a noose around Berlin. One by one the chief Nazi ringleaders realized that the end was near, and left Berlin to seek safety in less conspicuous places. Hitler spurned all pleas to retire to the Bavarian mountains and decided to stay in Berlin. With him remained the ever ambitious [Nazi ringleaders] Martin Bormann and Dr. Goebbels and his family. They entrenched themselves in the elaborately constructed underground bunker under the Reich chancellery, and from there the Führer continued to play the role of the war lord of a conquering army.

Life in the underground bunker during these last weeks, as described by surviving witnesses, was a weird and fantastic alternation of supreme confidence and abject despair, infused with recourse to astrology, horoscopes, and drugs. Almost to the last day Hitler and Goebbels hoped for a division in the Allied ranks between East and West that would play into their hands. On April 19, on the eve of Hitler's fifty-sixth birthday, the Führer declared, "We are now starting a battle as fanatical as that we had to fight for our ascent to power years ago." And Dr. Goebbels, on the same day, broadcast a speech in which he asked Germany never to forget Hitler. "We are witnessing the last acts of a tremendous tragedy," said Goebbels. "The decision is very near. Let us stake our hopes on our lucky star.". . .

More isolated from reality than ever before, Hitler continued to issue orders to attack to his vanishing army units and his depleted air force. The last conference he held with his war leaders was on April 22. He raged and shrieked wildly at everyone how all had betrayed him, how all was over and there was nothing left for him but to die. . . . Himmler, in the north, spurred on by his aide, Schellenberg, began negotiations with the Western Allies through the Swedish Count [Folke] Bernadotte. Himmler's offer was rejected by the Allies, but as the news of these negotiations came over the radio in the Berlin bunker Hitler was thrown into mad convulsions of rage and despair. . . .

Bombs were now falling in the yard of the chancellery. Communication with the outside world was completely cut off. By the 28th of April Hitler was convinced at last that the end had come. He proceeded to make his will, a political testament for the nation and a private will, and he decided finally to legalize his liaison with Eva Braun, who had remained loyally by his side to the end. There, in the underground bunker, to the musical accompaniment of shells and bombs and witnessed by Goebbels and Martin Bormann, Adolf Hitler took Eva Braun as his lawful wedded wife. . . . His final message to the German people was:

> Above all I impose on the leadership and following of the nation the obligation to hold fast to the racial laws and to carry on unmerciful resistance to the world poisoner of all nations—international Jewry.

Thus the Nazi movement ended, as it began, with a call to make war on the Jews.

On April 30 the final immolation rites were carried out. Eva took poison and Adolf shot himself. The bodies of both were then carried out to the courtyard of the chancellery and placed upon the funeral pyre. . . . Their bones most probably became mixed in with the remains of others who also perished in the same way and in the same place.

Goebbels and Bormann attempted a last desperate offer to negotiate with General Zhukov. The Russians replied with the demand for unconditional surrender. Goebbels thereupon followed the example of his Führer. He first gave poison to his six children, then he and his wife shot themselves and all the bodies were burned. As for Bormann, [he was long suspected of living in hiding in South America, however, in 1972 a skeleton was found in Berlin that most experts believe is his]. . . .

The entire civilized world was jubilant both at the end of the European war and at the final destruction of the Nazi tyranny. From all corners of Europe the oppressed and the tortured came out into the open sunshine of liberation and freedom. The idealism and self-sacrifice of the heroes of the Allied armies and of the resistance movements seemed at last to be rewarded, and while Nazi Germany lay a shambles of ruins, destruction, and dazed disintegration, the free world looked forward to the dawn of a new era of world peace and prosperity.

Appendix

Excerpts from Original Documents Pertaining to the Rise of Nazi Germany

Editor's Note: The documents that follow are listed in the approximate chronological order of their composition or publication. The amount of primary source material concerning Hitler and Nazi Germany—including books, essays, speeches, official documents, newspaper articles, diaries, and so forth—is so enormous that it could easily fill hundreds of volumes this size. Therefore the following excerpts (along with those quoted in my introductory essay) should be viewed as representative and illuminating highlights only. Those interested in locating more such original documents should begin with the sources listed in the first section of the For Further Research list at the back of this book.

Document 1: Hitler Compares the Jews with the Aryans

This is an excerpt from one of Adolf Hitler's earliest known political speeches, delivered on July 22, 1922. It establishes the core of his racist philosophy, in which the German Aryans are vastly superior to the supposedly subhuman Jews, a view he continued to express both privately and publicly the rest of his life.

Destroying the hostile national intelligentsia. That is the inevitable ultimate goal of the Jew in his revolution. And this aim he must pursue; he knows well enough his economics brings no blessing: his is no master-people: he is an exploiter: the Jews are a people of robbers. He has never founded any civilization, though he has destroyed civilizations by the hundred. He possesses nothing of his own creation to which he can point. Everything that he has is stolen. Foreign peoples, foreign workmen build him his temples, it is foreigners who create and work for him: it is foreigners who shed their blood for him. He knows no 'people's army': he has only hired mercenaries who are ready to go to death on his behalf. He has no art of his own: bit by bit he has stolen it all from the other peoples or has watched them at work and then made his copy. He does not even know how merely to preserve the precious things which others have created: as he turns the treasures over in his hand they are transformed into dirt and dung. He knows that he cannot maintain any State for long. That is one of the differences between him and the Aryan. True, the Aryan also has dominated other peoples. But how? He entered on the land, he cleared the forests; out of wildernesses he has created civilizations, and he has not used the others for his own interests, he has, so far as their capacities permitted, incorporated them into his State and through him art and science were brought to flower. In the last resort it was the Aryan and the Aryan alone who could form States and could set them on their path to future greatness.

All that the Jew cannot do. And because he cannot do it, therefore all his revolutions must be 'international'. They must spread as a pestilence spreads. He can build no State and say 'See here! Here stands the State, a model for all. Now copy us!' He must take care that the plague does not die, that it is not limited to one place, or else in a short time this plague-hearth would burn itself out. So he is forced to bring every mortal thing to an international expansion. For how long? Until the whole world sinks in ruins and brings him down with it in the midst of the ruins.

Norman H. Baynes, ed., *The Speeches of Adolf Hitler, April 1922–August 1939*. 2 vols. New York: Howard Fertig, 1969, vol. 1, pp. 30–31.

Document 2: An Acquaintance Describes Hitler as a Young Man

The noted German historian Karl von Müller here recalls meeting the youthful Adolf Hitler at a gathering at a friend's house early in 1923. At this time, the Nazi Party, which Hitler headed, was still a relatively small and unimportant political organization.

My foreboding about Hitler grew only slowly and uncertainly. The second time I met him was peaceful enough: it was for coffee at Erna Hanfstaengl's at the request of Abbot Alban Schachleiter who wanted to meet him; my wife and I were domestic decoration. The four of us had already sat down round the polished mahogany table by the window when the bell rang; through the open door we could see him greeting his hostess in the narrow passage with almost obsequious politeness, putting down his riding whip, taking off his velour hat and trenchcoat and finally unbuckling a belt with a revolver and hanging it on a peg. It looked comic and reminded me of Karl May [a popular German writer of adventure stories, particularly about the Wild West]. None of us knew then how minutely all these little details in dress and manner were calculated for their effect, just like his striking short trimmed moustache which was narrower than his unattractive broad nose. The man who entered was no longer the stubborn and gauche instructor in a badly fitting uniform who had stood before me in 1919. His look expressed awareness of public success; but a peculiar gaucherie [crudeness] still remained, and one had the uncomfortable feeling that he was conscious of it and resented its being noticed. His face was still thin and pale with an expression almost of suffering. But his protruding pale blue eyes stared at times with a ruthless severity and above his nose between the eyebrows was concentrated a fanatical willpower. On this occasion too he spoke little and for most of the time listened with great attention.

Jeremy Noakes and Geoffrey Pridham, eds., *Documents on Nazism, 1919–1945.* New York: Viking Press, 1975, pp. 51–52.

Documents 3-6: Hitler Summarizes His Early Life and Ideas in *Mein Kampf*

Following are four crucial selections from Hitler's Mein Kampf *("My Struggle"), written in 1924–1925, which became the Nazi Bible.*

Document 3: As long as my father's intention of making me a civil servant encountered only my theoretical distaste for the profession, the conflict was bearable. Thus far, I had to some extent been able to keep my private opinions to myself; I did not always have to contradict him immediately. My own firm determination never to become a civil servant sufficed to give me complete inner peace. And this decision in me was immutable. The problem became more difficult when I developed a plan of my own in opposition to my father's. And this occurred at the early age of twelve. How it happened, I myself do not know, but one day it became clear to me that I would become a painter, an artist. There was no doubt as to my talent for drawing; it had been one of my father's reasons for sending me to the *Realschule*, but never in all the world would it have occurred to him to give me professional training in this direction. On the contrary. When for the first time, after once again rejecting my father's favorite notion, I was asked what I myself wanted to be, and I rather abruptly blurted out the decision I had meanwhile made, my father for the moment was struck speechless.

'Painter? Artist?'

He doubted my sanity, or perhaps he thought he had heard wrong or misunderstood me. But when he was clear on the subject, and particularly after he felt the seriousness of my intention, he opposed it with all the determination of his nature. His decision was extremely simple, for any consideration of what abilities I might really have was simply out of the question. 'Artist, no, never as long as I live!' But since his son, among various other qualities, had apparently inherited his father's stubbornness, the same answer came back at him. Except, of course, that it was in the opposite sense.

Document 4: Today it is difficult, if not impossible, for me to say when the word 'Jew' first gave me ground for special thoughts. At home I do not remember having heard the word during my father's lifetime. I believe that the old gentleman would have regarded any special emphasis on this term as cultural backwardness. In the course of his life he had arrived at more or less cosmopolitan views which, despite his pronounced national sentiments, not only remained intact, but also affected me to some extent.

Likewise at school I found no occasion which could have led me to change this inherited picture.

At the *Realschule*, to be sure, I did meet one Jewish boy who was treated by all of us with caution, but only because various experiences had led us to doubt his discretion and we did not particularly trust him; but neither I nor the others had any thoughts on the matter.

Not until my fourteenth or fifteenth year did I begin to come across the word 'Jew,' with any frequency, partly in connection with political discussions. This filled me with a mild distaste, and I could not rid myself of an unpleasant feeling that always came over me whenever religious quarrels occurred in my presence.

At that time I did not think anything else of the question.

There were few Jews in Linz. In the course of the centuries their outward appearance had become Europeanized and had taken on a human look; in fact, I even took them for Germans. The absurdity of this idea did not dawn on me because I saw no distinguishing feature but the strange religion. The fact that they had, as I believed, been persecuted on this account sometimes almost turned my distaste at unfavorable remarks about them into horror.

Thus far I did not so much as suspect the existence of an organized opposition to the Jews.

Then I came to Vienna.

Preoccupied by the abundance of my impressions in the architectural field, oppressed by the hardship of my own lot, I gained at first no insight into the inner stratification of the people in this gigantic city. Notwithstanding that Vienna in those days counted nearly two hundred thousand Jews among its two million inhabitants, I did not see them. In the first few weeks my eyes and my senses were not equal to the flood of values and ideas. Not until calm gradually returned and the agitated picture began to clear did I look around me more carefully in my new world, and then among other things I encountered the Jewish question. . . .

Once, as I was strolling through the Inner City, I suddenly encountered an apparition in a black caftan and black hair locks. Is this a Jew? was my first thought.

For, to be sure, they had not looked like that in Linz. I observed the man furtively and cautiously, but the longer I stared at this foreign face, scrutinizing feature for feature, the more my first question assumed a new form:

Is this a German?

As always in such cases, I now began to try to relieve my doubts by books. For a few hellers I bought the first anti-Semitic pamphlets of my life. Unfortunately, they all proceeded from the supposition that in principle the reader knew or even understood the Jewish question to a certain degree. Besides, the tone for the most part was such that doubts again arose in me, due in part to the dull and amazingly unscientific arguments favoring the thesis.

I relapsed for weeks at a time, once even for months.

The whole thing seemed to me so monstrous, the accusations so boundless, that, tormented by the fear of doing injustice, I again became anxious and uncertain.

Yet I could no longer very well doubt that the objects of my study were not Germans of a special religion, but a people in themselves; for since I had begun to concern myself with this question and to take cognizance of the Jews, Vienna appeared to me in a different light than before. Wherever I went, I began to see Jews, and the more I saw, the more sharply they became distinguished in my eyes from the rest of humanity. Particularly the Inner City and the districts north of the Danube Canal swarmed with a people which even outwardly had lost all resemblance to Germans. . . .

The cleanliness of this people, moral and otherwise, I must say, is a point in itself. By their very exterior you could tell that these were no lovers of water, and, to your distress, you often knew it with your eyes closed. Later I often grew sick to my stomach from the smell of these caftan-wearers. Added to this, there was their unclean dress and their generally unheroic appearance.

All this could scarcely be called very attractive; but it became positively repulsive when, in addition to their physical uncleanliness, you discovered the moral stains on this 'chosen people.'. . . .

What had to be reckoned heavily against the Jews in my eyes was when I became acquainted with their activity in the press, art, literature, and the theater. All the unctuous reassurances helped little or nothing. It sufficed to look at a billboard, to study the names of the men behind the horrible trash they advertised, to make you hard for a long time to come. This was pestilence, spiritual pestilence, worse than the Black Death of olden times, and the people was being infected with it! It goes without saying that the lower the intellectual level of one of these art manufacturers, the more unlimited his fertility will be, and the scoundrel ends up like a garbage separator, splashing his filth in the face of humanity. And bear in mind that there is no limit to their number; bear in mind that for one Goethe [a great eighteenth-century German writer] Nature easily can foist on the world ten thousand of these scribblers who poison men's souls like germ-carriers of the worse sort, on their fellow men.

Document 5: The following theorem may be established as an eternally valid truth:

Never yet has a state been founded by peaceful economic means, but always and exclusively by the instincts of preservation of the species regardless whether these are found in the province of heroic virtue or of cunning craftiness; the one results in Aryan states based on work and culture, the other in Jewish colonies of parasites. As soon as economics as such begins to choke out these instincts in a people or in a state, it becomes the seductive cause of subjugation and oppression.

The belief of pre-war days that the world could be peacefully opened up to, let alone conquered for, the German people by a commercial and colonial policy was a classic sign of the loss of real state-forming and state-preserving virtues and of all the insight, will power, and active determination which follow from them; the penalty for this, inevitable as the law of nature, was the World War with its consequences.

For those who do not look more deeply into the matter, this attitude of the German nation—for it was really as good as general—could only represent an insoluble riddle: for was not Germany above all other countries a marvelous example of an empire which had risen from foundations of pure political power? Prussia, the germ-cell of the Empire, came into being through resplendent heroism and not through financial operations or commercial deals, and the Reich itself in turn was only the glorious reward of aggressive political leadership and the death-defying courage of its soldiers. How could this very German people have succumbed to such a sickening of its political instinct? For here we face, not an isolated phenomenon, but forces of decay which in truly terrifying number soon began to flare up like will-o'-the-wisps, brushing up and down the body politic, or eating like poisonous abscesses into the nation, now here and now there. It seemed as though a continuous stream of poison was being driven into the outermost blood-vessels of this once heroic body by a mysterious power, and was inducing progressively greater paralysis of sound reason and the simple instinct of self-preservation.

Document 6. The next few days came and with them the most terrible certainty of my life. The rumors became more and more oppressive. What I had taken for a local affair was now said to be a general revolution. To this was added the disgraceful news from the front. They [the German generals] wanted to capitulate. Was such a thing really possible?

On November 10, the pastor came to the hospital for a short address: now we learned everything.

In extreme agitation, I, too, was present at the short speech. The dignified old gentleman seemed all a-tremble as he informed us that . . . we must now end the long War, yes, that now that it was lost and we were throwing ourselves upon the mercy of the victors, our fatherland would for the future be exposed to dire oppression, that the armistice should be accepted with confidence in the magnanimity of our previous enemies—I could stand it no longer. It became impossible for me to sit still one minute more. Again everything went black before my eyes; I tottered and groped my way back to the dormitory, threw myself on my bunk, and dug my burning head into my blanket and pillow.

Since the day when I had stood at my mother's grave, I had not wept. When in my youth Fate seized me with merciless hardness, my defiance mounted. When in the long war years Death snatched so many a dear comrade and friend from our ranks, it would have seemed to me almost a sin to complain—after all, were they not dying for Germany? And when at length the creeping gas—in the last days of the dreadful struggle—attacked me, too, and began to gnaw at my eyes, and beneath the fear of going blind forever, I nearly lost heart for a moment, the voice of my conscience thundered at me: Miserable wretch, are you going to cry when thousands are a hundred times worse off than you! And so I bore my lot in dull silence. But now I could not help it. Only now did I see how all personal suffering vanishes in comparison with the misfortune of the fatherland.

And so it had all been in vain. In vain all the sacrifices and privations; in vain the hunger and thirst of months which were often endless; in vain the hours in which, with mortal fear clutching at our hearts, we nevertheless did our duty; and in vain the death of two millions who died. . . . Was it for this that these boys of seventeen sank into the earth of Flanders? Was this the meaning of the sacrifice which the German mother made to the fatherland when with sore heart she let her best-loved boys march off, never to see them again? Did all this happen only so that a gang of wretched criminals could lay hands on the fatherland? . . .

Miserable and degenerate criminals!

The more I tried to achieve clarity on the monstrous event in this hour, the more the shame of indignation and disgrace burned my brow. What was all the pain in my eyes compared to this misery?

There followed terrible days and even worse nights—I knew that all was lost. Only fools, liars, and criminals could hope in the mercy of the enemy. In these nights hatred grew in me, hatred for those responsible for this deed.

In the days that followed, my own fate became known to me.

I could not help but laugh at the thought of my own future which only a short time before had given me such bitter concern. Was it not ridiculous to expect to build houses on such ground? At last it became clear to me that what had happened was what I had so often feared but had never been able to believe with my emotions. . . .

I, for my part, decided to go into politics.

Adolf Hitler, *Mein Kampf.* Trans. Ralph Manheim. Boston: Houghton Mifflin, 1971, pp. 9, 51–58, 153–54, 203–206.

Document 7: Hitler Declares Himself Guiltless in God's Eyes

This is the arrogant closing speech Hitler delivered at his 1924 trial, in which he was sentenced to jail for organizing the infamous "Beer Hall Putsch" the preceding year. The accused warns that his prosecution will not stop the growth of his Nazi movement, which God and history will supposedly ultimately vindicate.

The army which we have formed grows from day to day; from hour to hour it grows more rapidly. Even now I have the proud hope that one day the hour is coming when these untrained bands will become battalions, when the battalions will become regiments and the regiments divisions, when the old cockade [revolutionary badge, often worn on a hat] will be raised from the mire, when the old banners will once again wave before us: and then reconciliation will come in that eternal last Court of Judgement—the Court of God—before which we are ready to take our stand. Then from our bones, from our graves will sound the voice of that tribunal which alone has the right to sit in judgement upon us. For, gentlemen, it is not you who pronounce judgement upon us, it is the eternal Court of History which will make its pronouncement upon the charge which is brought against us. The judgement that you will pass, that I know. But that Court will not ask of us 'Have you committed high treason or not?' That Court will judge us . . . who as Germans have wished the best for their people and their Fatherland, who wished to fight and to die. You may declare us guilty a thousand times, but the Goddess who presides over the Eternal Court of History will with a smile tear in pieces the charge of the Public Prosecutor and the judgement of the Court: for she declares us guiltless.

Norman H. Baynes, ed., *The Speeches of Adolf Hitler, April 1922–August 1939.* 2 vols. New York: Howard Fertig, 1969, vol. 1, pp. 86–87.

Document 8: The "Cult" of the Führer Gains Strength

This tract from the January 9, 1927, issue of a National Socialist newspaper proclaims the superiority and correctness of Nazi ideals and proudly vows loyalty "unto death" to the movement's "heroic" leader, Adolf Hitler—the führer (supreme leader). Though the Nazis were still a relatively minor political force in Weimar Germany at this time, it is plain that Hitler had already molded the party into a cohesive and effective political army fanatically devoted to him and his beliefs.

How could a National Socialist start this new year in any other way than with a salute to our honoured leader, a salute which expresses not only a personal devotion which is proof against any attempt to dim its flame but also the loyal pledge: To fight the battle for National Socialism with our life and soul this year like last year. For this is the great secret of our movement: an utter devotion to the idea of National Socialism, a glowing faith in the victorious strength of this doctrine of liberation and deliverance, is combined with a deep love of the person of our leader who is the shining hero of the new freedom-fighters. The tremendous superiority which the NSDAP [Nazi Party] has as a fighting instrument compared with all the other formations which instinctively pursue the same aim of German liberty and the rebirth of the German people, is due to the fact that we have the outstanding leader, who holds not only supreme power but also the love of his followers—a much stronger binding force.

'Duke and vassal!' In this ancient German relationship of leader and follower, fully comprehensible only to the German mentality and spirit, lies the essence of the structure of the NSDAP, the driving force of this aggressive power, the conviction of victory!

Heil Hitler! This is our first salute in the new year as it was the last one in the old year: Heil Hitler! In this salute lies the pride in the success of the past year which . . . saw the powerful, irresistible progress of the National Socialist ideal! In thousands of public meetings, members' evenings, in many hundreds of mass meetings the idea of National Socialism, the name of Adolf Hitler, was hurled among the masses of the German people and a hush fell on the ranks of this enslaved, exploited, starved people. An awareness of this glowing will for the struggle, the struggle to preserve the German people, the struggle for that people's freedom, freedom both within and without—for the one is worthless and impossible without the other—an awareness of those metallic accents of a brutal harshness which call things by their real names and challenges those things to a struggle, a relentless struggle giving no quarter. . . .

Friends, a new year lies before us. Let us join hands in a silent vow to struggle in the new year with redoubled, with threefold vigour, each one at his post, for the victory of National Socialism, this is for the inward and outward freeing of the German people, to struggle without wavering, without flinching, in selfless devotion and true comradeship. And then, friends, raise your right arm and cry out with me proudly, eager for the struggle, and loyal unto death, 'Heil Hitler'.

Jeremy Noakes and Geoffrey Pridham, eds., *Documents on Nazism, 1919–1945*. New York: Viking Press, 1975, pp. 84–85.

Document 9: The Nazis Promise Working Germans a Fair Deal

While many well-educated, upper-class Germans still did not take the growing Nazi movement seriously in the late 1920s, increasing numbers of factory workers, farmers, and other laborers began to listen to National Socialist propaganda. This Nazi leaflet, distributed in the Munich region in 1927, was directed at German farmers, many of whom were still struggling financially despite the Weimar Republic's improving economy

in this period. Note the appeals to the farmers' pocketbooks, respect for
God and country, and, of course, distrust of Jews.

GERMAN FARMERS!
Farmers, it is a matter of your house and home!

We told you years ago but you didn't listen, just like the rest of
the German people. The middle classes should have listened during the years of the insane inflation. Now they have been annihilated: their possessions and savings have been stolen—expropriated!

The German worker expected the revolution to bring honour
and beauty into his life. Now he is (to the extent that he can find
work) the starving wage-slave of the Bank-Jews.

AND NOW IT'S YOUR TURN GERMAN FARMERS!

Factories, forests, railways, taxes and the state's finances have all
been robbed by the Jew. Now he's stretching his greedy fingers towards the last German possession—the German countryside.

You farmer, will be chased from your plot of earth, which you
have inherited from your forefathers since time immemorial.

Insatiable Jewish race-lust and fanaticism are the driving forces
behind this devilish attempt to break Germany's backbone through
the annihilation of the German farming community.

Wake up! Listen to something other than the daily twaddle
printed in your local rags, which have hidden the truth from you
for years.

Doesn't it open your eyes when you see the economy of the
countryside being crippled by unnaturally high taxes, while you
have no commensurate income to set off against this because of
low prices for livestock and grain?

Don't you see the vile plan?! The same Jews who control the
monopoly on sales of nitrogen, calcium and phosphorus, thereby
dictating to you the high price of essential fertilizers, never give
you a just price for your produce on the *Stock Exchange*.

Huge imports of frozen meat and foreign grain, at lowest
prices, undercut you and push down your earnings.

The protective tariffs which the state has imposed are insufficient—not to say worthless. That same state is totally Jew-ridden
in all its organs, and today can be called Germany in name only.

Nevertheless the prices of groceries are rising sharply in the
towns day by day, driving your hungry German brothers to despair. Under the eyes of the so-called authorities the Jew is running a lucrative middle-man Stock Exchange.

And one thing more which is ruining you. You cannot obtain
credit to tide you over these hard times. If you want money the

usurious interest rates will wring your neck. Under the protection of the state it won't be long before the greater part of the land-owning farmers will be driven from their farms and homes by Jew-ish money lenders.

The plight of the German farmer is desperate.

Think it all over in your last few hours, and remember—we have been telling you the same thing for years!

Once again we're coming to you. This time you won't laugh at us!

BUT IT'S NEVER TOO LATE!

A people that has the will to live and struggle will survive. Don't stand on the sidelines. Join our struggle against the Jews and loan capital!

Help us build a new Germany that will be
NATIONALIST AND SOCIALIST
Nationalist because it is free and held in respect.

Socialist because any German who works and creates, will be guaranteed not just a slave's ration of bread, but an honourable life, decent earnings and the sanctity of his hard-earned property.

Farmers, it is a matter of the most holy possession of a people,
THE LAND AND THE FIELDS
WHICH GOD HAS GIVEN US
Farmers, it is a matter of house and home,
Of life and death,
Of our people and our fatherland!
THEREFORE FARMER—WAKE UP!
Join the ranks of our defence force.　　　　Fight with us in the
NATIONAL SOCIALIST GERMAN WORKERS PARTY

Quoted in Simon Taylor, *The Rise of Hitler: Revolution and Counter-Revolution in Germany, 1918–1933.* New York: Universe Books, 1983, pp. 83–84.

Document 10: Hitler Captivates His Audience

All who personally witnessed Hitler's lectures and speeches agreed that he was a clever and powerful orator who knew how to manipulate an audience. In this excerpt from his well-known memoir, Inside the Third Reich, *Albert Speer, the Nazis' chief architect, recalls the first time he saw the man who would later become his boss. Speer, then a teaching as-sistant at Berlin's Institute of Technology, heard Hitler speak at a local beer hall one late night in 1930 and was duly impressed.*

The students were chiefly turning to the extremists for their be-liefs, and Hitler's party appealed directly to the idealism of this generation. And after all, was not a man like [professor of architecture Heinrich] Tessenow also fanning these flames? About 1931 he had declared: "Someone will have to come along who thinks very simply. Thinking today has become too complicated. An uncultured man, a peasant as it were, would solve everything much more easily merely because he would still be unspoiled. He would also have the strength to carry out his simple ideas." To us this oracular remark seemed to herald Hitler.

Hitler was delivering an address to the students of Berlin University and the Institute of Technology. My students urged me to attend. Not yet convinced, but already uncertain of my ground, I went along. The site of the meeting was a beer hall called the Hasenheide. Dirty walls, narrow stairs, and an ill-kept interior created a poverty-stricken atmosphere. This was a place where workmen ordinarily held beer parties. The room was overcrowded. It seemed as if nearly all the students in Berlin wanted to see and hear this man whom his adherents so much admired and his opponents so much detested. A large number of professors sat in favored places in the middle of a bare platform. Their presence gave the meeting an importance and a social acceptability that it would not otherwise have had. Our group had also secured good seats on the platform, not far from the lectern.

Hitler entered and was tempestuously hailed by his numerous followers among the students. This enthusiasm in itself made a great impression upon me. But his appearance also surprised me. On posters and in caricatures I had seen him in military tunic, with shoulder straps, swastika armband, and hair flapping over his forehead. But here he was wearing a well-fitted blue suit and looking markedly respectable. Everything about him bore out the note of reasonable modesty. Later I learned that he had a great gift for adjusting—consciously or intuitively—to his surroundings.

As the ovation went on for minutes he tried, as if slightly pained, to check it. Then, in a low voice, hesitantly and somewhat shyly, he began a kind of historical lecture rather than a speech. To me there was something engaging about it—all the more so since it ran counter to everything the propaganda of his opponents had led me to expect: a hysterical demagogue, a shrieking and gesticulating fanatic in uniform. He did not allow the bursts of applause to tempt him away from his sober tone.

It seemed as if he were candidly presenting his anxieties about the future. His irony was softened by a somewhat self-conscious humor; his South German charm reminded me agreeably of my native region. A cool Prussian could never have captivated me that way. Hitler's initial shyness soon disappeared; at times now his pitch rose. He spoke urgently and with hypnotic persuasiveness. The mood he cast was much deeper than the speech itself, most of which I did not remember for long.

Moreover, I was carried on the wave of the enthusiasm which, one could almost feel this physically, bore the speaker along from sentence to sentence. It swept away any skepticism, any reservations. Opponents were given no chance to speak. This furthered the illusion, at least momentarily, of unanimity. Finally, Hitler no longer seemed to be speaking to convince; rather, he seemed to feel that he was expressing what the audience, by now transformed into a single mass, expected of him. It was as if it were the most natural thing in the world to lead students and part of the faculty of the two greatest academics in Germany submissively by a leash.

Albert Speer, *Inside the Third Reich*. New York: Macmillan, 1970, pp. 15–16.

Document 11: Instructions for Rural Propaganda

This excerpt from the July 1931 issue of the Nazi Party's official propaganda publication, Willie and Weg, *advises party operatives on the most effective methods of winning over rural Germans. Using such methods, the Nazis continued to increase their membership and electoral support in the early 1930s.*

The first meeting in a village must be prepared in such a way that it is well attended. A prerequisite is that the speaker should be fairly well informed about specifically rural questions. Then, it is most advisable to go to a neighbouring village some time after, but to advertise the meeting in the first village as well, then many people will certainly come over for it. After this, one holds a big German Evening in a central hall for a number of villages with the cooperation of the SA and the SA band. . . . The German Evening, provided it is skilfully and generously geared to producing a big public impact, has the primary task of making the audience enthusiastic for our cause; secondly, it is intended to raise the money necessary for the further build-up of propaganda. The preparation of the village meetings is best carried out in the following way: most effectively through written personal invitations to every farmer or inhabitant; in the bigger villages through a circular carried from farm to farm by Party comrades. For the meeting itself the question of finance has to be considered. Our movement is so poor that every penny counts. Collections must therefore be held during all discussion evenings and also in the big mass meetings if permitted by the police, either in the interval or at the end, even when an entrance fee has been taken at the beginning of the meeting. In this way, especially when plates and not caps are used, surprising amounts can sometimes be got out of a meeting.

Jeremy Noakes and Geoffrey Pridham, eds., *Documents on Nazism, 1919–1945*. New York: Viking Press, 1975, p. 105.

Document 12: The Myth of Hitler's Fearlessness

Hitler effectively used airplanes to ferry himself across Germany from one campaign rally to another during the 1932 election period. With equal effectiveness, his chief publicist, Otto Dietrich, transformed one of these routine flights into a journey of epic proportions in the following press release, which portrays the führer as a superior human facing and mastering nature's fury. Later, after Hitler came to power, Dietrich's tract became an obligatory addition to all reading texts used in German schools.

On April 8, 1932, a severe storm, beyond all imagining, raged over Germany. Hail rattled down from dark clouds. Flash floods devastated fields and gardens. Muddy foam washed over streets and railroad tracks, and the hurricane uprooted even the oldest and biggest trees.

We are driving to the Mannheim Airport. Today no one would dare expose an airplane to the fury of the elements. The German Lufthansa [Airline] has suspended all air traffic.

In the teeming rain stands the solid mass of the most undaunted of our followers. They want to be present, they want to see for themselves when the Führer entrusts himself to an airplane in this raging storm.

Without a moment's hesitation the Führer orders that we take off at once. We have an itinerary to keep, for in western Germany hundreds of thousands are waiting.

It is only with the greatest difficulty that the ground crew and the SA troopers, with long poles in their strong fists, manage to hold on to the wings of the plane, so that the gale does not hurl it into the air and wreck it. The giant motors begin to turn over. Impatient with its fetters, the plane begins to buck and shake, eager for the takeoff on the open runway.

One more short rearing up and our wild steed sweeps across the greensward. A few perilous jumps, one last short touch with earth, and presto we are riding through the air straight into the witches' broth.

This is no longer flying, this is a whirling dance which today we remember only as a faraway dream. Now we jump across the aerial downdrafts, now we whip our way through tattered clouds, again a whirlpool threatens to drag us down, and then it seems that a giant catapult hurls us into steep heights. And yet, what a feeling of security is in us in the face of this fury of the elements! The Führer's absolute serenity transmits itself to all of us. In every hour of danger he is ruled by his granite-like faith in his world-historical mission, the unshakable certainty that Providence will keep him from danger for the accomplishment of his great task.

Even here he remained the pre-eminent man, who masters danger because in his innermost being he has risen far above it. In this ruthless contest between man and machine the Führer attentively follows the heroic battle of our Master Pilot Bauer as he steers straight through the gale, or quickly jumps across a whole storm field, and then again narrowly avoids a threatening cloud wall, while the radio operator on board zealously catches the signals sent by the airfields.

George L. Mosse, *Nazi Culture: Intellectual, Cultural, and Social Life in the Third Reich*. New York: Grosset and Dunlap, 1966, pp. 291–93.

Document 13: An Anti-Nazi Warns the German People

During the controversial national elections of the early 1930s, a number of responsible German politicians became worried about the Nazis' growing appeal with the voters. This is an excerpt from a 1932 pamphlet titled The Menace *of* National Socialism *by a conservative but decidedly anti-Nazi politician named Ewald von Kleist-Schmenzin, who calls Nazism a "disease" and warns that Hitler is both a deceiver and an anti-Christian.*

The flow of followers to Hitler is largely a movement of fear and desperation. In fear of what may yet come, people flock to the National Socialist Party in senseless despair because they hope that the mass of voters, by casting like ballots, can avert the troubles threatening us and can above all spare the individual from personal involvement. Many of them put all their hopes in Hitler and do not want to see the shortcomings of National Socialism. Those who stick with the German National Party only do so because they believe that a counterbalance is still somehow necessary. No wonder there is such confusion of thought. If political action is to be successful for Germany's future, . . . our struggle against the aberrations of National Socialism must be waged promptly, with dignity and earnestness, but with rigorous determination.

Religious attitudes are crucial in separating conservative thinking from National Socialism. The foundation of conservative policy is that obedience to God, and faith in Him, must determine the whole of public life. National Socialism is based on a fundamentally different point of view in which questions of faith must, of course, be dropped as irrelevant. Hitler actually recognizes race and its demands as the highest law of governmental action; if at times he says otherwise, that does not make any difference. His materialism cannot be reconciled with Christianity. According to Hitler, the state does not have the responsibility to foster creativity, but only to guard the racial heritage! . . . Hitler is primarily interested in breeding healthy bodies; he stresses emphatically that building character is only of secondary importance. This conviction is unacceptable. . . . Inseparably connected with National Socialism are a superficial search for happiness and a streak of liberal rationalism that is expressed in its motto, group welfare has priority over individual desire. National Socialism leans increasingly toward the liberal conception of the greatest good of the greatest number. For us, the nation *per se* is not the ultimate measure, but rather the will of God which obligates us to live for the nation. That is a fundamental difference. . . .

Hitler has declared to a foreign correspondent that the Versailles Treaty cannot simply be torn up but must be replaced at a conference by a new one. Where does that leave the campaign he as hitherto fought against our foreign policy? Where does that put the slogan of a struggle for freedom? Hitler stated publicly in Lauenburg that he was not prepared to defend our borders against a Polish invasion as long as the present government was in power. This statement has been repeated and confirmed in writing by other National Socialists who were present. This declaration openly means abandonment of the German nation and actually encourages the Poles to invade. *Hitler and the party have publicly set themselves above the fatherland.* Given such an attitude, can one expect them to join a coalition government and conduct foreign policy in the national interest?

A glance at National Socialist newspapers, pamphlets, and other propaganda should convince anyone (who is still willing to look) of the unscrupulous dishonesty of the movement and its leaders. Their arguments can be cited both for and against almost any position. Since people are not aware of this duplicity, it is no wonder that they succumb to National Socialism in their ignorance. We can no longer tolerate the pretence that National Socialism is the one movement that can save the nation. This delusion must be destroyed together with the totally false image that the people have of Hitler. . . . A National Socialist government will inevitably end in chaos. Their rulers would soon be swept away by the unmanageable tide of upheaval they created. We conservative nationalists should no longer abet the destruction caused by Nazi slogans of national interest and by Hitler's romantic image. . . .

We conservatives are united in our common determination to supplant the present democratic leaders. We only seek this change so that a different policy can be pursued, one which will save the nation. The National Socialists, however, want to overthrow the present governmental system in order to assume power themselves. Once arrived, they will do all they can to dissolve the coalition and would ally with any other faction if necessary. Considering their numerical strength, the National Socialists would certainly not leave the important offices to administration experts. . . .

To summarize: it is the task of all conservative forces, like the German National Peoples Party and other patriotic organizations, resolutely to renounce cooperation with the politically fashionable Nazi disease; for the sake of Germany's future, we cannot tolerate the destruction of the remaining genuine conservative principles that are a necessary part of the foundations of the new state. . . .

We must redouble our political action and bring it elsewhere to bear on the political process. The thought and action of the people must be focused on crucial matters. It is always just a few individuals who institute crucial and favorable political change. But behind them must stand dedicated men whose every thought and action is determined by unselfish patriotism, who are united by a deep inner communion and whose whole posture is determined by unshakeable faith.

Henry C. Meyer, ed., *The Long Generation: Germany from Empire to Ruin, 1913–1945.* New York: Walker and Company, 1973, pp. 194–97.

Document 14: The New Nazi Regime Appeals for German Unity

On January 31, 1933, the day after Hitler was appointed chancellor of Germany, the new regime issued an "Appeal to the German People," excerpted here. Referring to the acquisition of power by the Nazis as a beneficial "National Uprising," the document attempts to project an image of national unity and assures the people that the patriotic new government will repair all that is broken in German society.

Over fourteen years have passed since that unhappy day when the German people, blinded by promises made by those at home and abroad, forgot the highest values of our past, of the Reich, of its honour and its freedom, and thereby lost everything. Since those days of treason, the Almighty has withdrawn his blessing from our nation. Discord and hatred have moved in. Filled with the deepest distress, millions of the best German men and women from all walks of life see the unity of the nation disintegrating in a welter of egoistical political opinions, economic interests, and ideological conflicts.

As so often in our history, Germany, since the day the [democratic Weimar] revolution broke out, presents a picture of heartbreaking disunity. We did not receive the equality and fraternity which was promised us; instead we lost our freedom. The breakdown of the unity of mind and will of our nation at home was followed by the collapse of its political position abroad.

We have a burning conviction that the German people in 1914 went into the great battle without any thought of personal guilt and weighed down only by the burden of having to defend the Reich from attack, to defend the freedom and material existence of the German people. In the appalling fate that has dogged us since November 1918 we see only the consequence of our inward collapse. But the rest of the world is no less shaken by great crises. The historical balance of power, which at one time contributed not a little to the understanding of the necessity for solidarity among the nations, with all the economic advantages resulting therefrom, has been destroyed.

The delusion that some are the conquerors and others the conquered destroys the trust between nations and thereby also destroys the world economy. But the misery of our people is terrible! The starving industrial proletariat have become unemployed in their millions, while the whole middle and artisan class have been made paupers. If the German farmer also is involved in this collapse we shall be faced with a catastrophe of vast proportions. For in that case, there will collapse not only a Reich, but also a 2000-year-old inheritance of the highest works of human culture and civilization.

All around us are symptoms portending this breakdown. With an unparalleled effort of will and of brute force the Communist method of madness is trying as a last resort to poison and undermine an inwardly shaken and uprooted nation. They seek to drive it towards an epoch which would correspond even less to the promises of the Communist speakers of today than did the epoch now drawing to a close to the promises of the same emissaries in November 1918. . . .

In these hours of overwhelming concern for the existence and the future of the German nation, the venerable World War leader [Hindenburg] appealed to us men of the nationalist parties and associations to fight under him again as once we did at the front, but now loyally united for the salvation of the Reich at home. The revered President of the Reich having with such generosity joined hands with us in a common pledge, we nationalist leaders would vow before God, our conscience and our people that we shall doggedly and with determination fulfil the mission entrusted to us as the National Government.

It is an appalling inheritance which we are taking over.

The task before us is the most difficult which has faced German statesmen in living memory. But we all have unbounded confidence, for we believe in our nation and in its eternal values. Farmers, workers, and the middle class must unite to contribute the bricks wherewith to build the new Reich.

The National Government will therefore regard it as its first and supreme task to restore to the German people unity of mind and will. It will preserve and defend the foundations on which the strength of our nation rests. It will take under its firm protection Christianity as the basis of our morality, and the family as the nucleus of our nation and our state. Standing above estates and classes, it will bring back to our people the consciousness of its racial and political unity and the obligations arising therefrom. It wishes to base the education of German youth on respect for our great past and pride in our old traditions. It will therefore declare merciless war on spiritual, political and cultural nihilism. Germany must not and will not sink into Communist anarchy. . . .

The National Government will combine this gigantic project of restoring our economy with the task of putting the administration and the finances of the Reich, the states, and the communes on a sound basis.

Only by doing this can the idea of preserving the Reich as a federation acquire flesh and blood.

The idea of labour service and of settlement policy are among the main pillars of this programme.

Our concern to provide daily bread will be equally a concern for the fulfilment of the responsibilities of society to those who are old and sick.

The best safeguard against any experiment which might endanger the currency lies in economical administration, the promotion of work, and the preservation of agriculture, as well as in the use of individual initiative.

In foreign policy, the National Government will see its highest mission in the preservation of our people's right to an independent life and in the regaining thereby of their freedom. The determination of this Government to put an end to the chaotic conditions in Germany is a step towards the integration into the community of nations of a state having equal status and therefore equal rights with the rest. In so doing, the Government is aware of its great obligation to support, as the Government of a free and equal nation, that maintenance and consolidation of peace which the world needs today more than ever before. . . .

With resolution and fidelity to our oath, seeing the powerlessness of the present Reichstag to shoulder the task we advocate, we wish to commit it to the whole German people.

We therefore appeal now to the German people to sign this act of mutual reconciliation.

The Government of the National Uprising wishes to set to work, and it will work.

It has not for fourteen years brought ruin to the German nation; it wants to lead it to the summit.

It is determined to make amends in four years for the liabilities of fourteen years.

But it cannot subject the work of reconstruction to the will of those who were responsible for the breakdown.

The Marxist parties and their followers had fourteen years to prove their abilities.

The result is a heap of ruins.

Now, German people, give us four years and then judge us.

Let us begin, loyal to the command of the Field-Marshal. May Almighty God favour our work, shape our will in the right way, bless our vision and bless us with the trust of our people. We have no desire to fight for ourselves; only for Germany.

Jeremy Noakes and Geoffrey Pridham, eds., *Documents on Nazism, 1919–1945*. New York: Viking Press, 1975, pp. 162–65.

Document 15: Nazi Women Pledge Support for God and the Third Reich

Early in 1933, shortly after Hitler came to power, the National Socialist Womanhood, an elite group of female Nazi activists, issued the following statement of basic principles. Like so many other Nazi documents, it is vague, rambling, and repetitive. Its essential point is that motherhood is now to be considered women's "most immediate service" to the fatherland.

I Basic Principles.

1. We desire the awakening, the training, and the renewal of women's role as the preservers of the nation's springs: the nation's love life, marriage, motherhood and the family, blood and race, youth and nationhood. The whole education, training, careers and position of women within the nation and state must be organized in terms of their physical and mental tasks as mothers.

2. We recognize the great transformation which has taken place in women's lives over the past 50 years as a necessity produced by the machine age, and approve of the education and official integration of women for the good of the nation in so far as they are not performing their most immediate service for society in the form of marriage, the family and motherhood.

3. We regret, however, the false paths of the democratic-liberal-international women's movement because it has not found new paths for the female soul rooted in GOD and his nation, but, on the basis of maintaining the ability to compete with men, has raised temporary expedients to the level of basic demands and has thereby created a womanhood which has lost its deepest sources of female strength and which has not understood its female task in the German crisis.

4. We desire a women's movement of renewal which reawakens those deepest sources of female strength and strengthens women for their particular tasks in the freedom movement and in the future Germany.

5. We demand and therefore carry out the fight against the planned denigration and destruction of women's honour and women's dignity and against the moral corruption of youth.

6. We erect against it the will of German women which is rooted in GOD, nature, the family, the nation and fatherland, and our own *Women's Cultural Programme*, which will be organized in the 3. Reich.

7. We participate, therefore, with all our strength in the struggle of the freedom movement for the transformation of the domestic political situation and the establishment of the 3. Reich through the strongest possible propaganda on a small scale.

Jeremy Noakes and Geoffrey Pridham, eds., *Nazism, 1919–1945, Vol. 2: State, Economy and Society, 1933–1939, A Documentary Reader.* Exeter, Eng.: University of Exeter, 1984, p. 461.

Document 16: Hitler Lays the Blame for the Reichstag Fire

On February 27, 1933, a young Dutch communist named Marinus van der Lubbe set the German Reichstag (parliament building) on fire. Apparently, it was a random act and not part of a greater conspiracy, as

Rudolf Diels, the police official in charge of the investigation, believed at the time. However, as Diels later told it in a statement excerpted here, Hitler and his cronies seized on the incident as a convenient way to discredit and purge the communists and other political opponents of the Nazis.

On that rainy evening in early spring, I was called away from a cosy and highly unofficial rendezvous in the Café Krantzler . . . by my old colleague, Schneider, with the cry, 'The Reichstag is on fire!' When I pushed my way into the burning building with Schneider, we had to climb over the bulging hoses of the Berlin fire brigade, although, as yet, there were few onlookers. A few officers of my department were already engaged in interrogating Marinus van der Lubbe. Naked from the waist upwards, smeared with dirt and sweating, he sat in front of them, breathing heavily. He panted as if he had completed a tremendous task. There was a wild triumphant gleam in the burning eyes of his pale, haggard young face. I sat opposite him in the police headquarters several times that night and listened to his confused stories. I read the Communist pamphlets he carried in his trouser pockets. They were of the kind which in those days were publicly distributed everywhere. And from the primitive hieroglyphics of his diary I tried to follow his trips down to the Balkans.

The voluntary confessions of Marinus van der Lubbe prevented me from thinking that an arsonist who was such an expert in his folly needed any helpers. Why should not a single match be enough to set fire to the cold yet inflammable splendour of the Chamber, the old upholstered furniture, the heavy curtains, and the bone-dry wooden panelling! But this specialist had used a whole knapsack full of inflammable material. He had been so active that he had laid several dozen fires. . . .

He also confessed to several smaller arson attacks in Berlin, the mysterious cause of which had aroused the attention of the Criminal Investigation Department. Several details suggested that Communist arsonists who had helped him in Neukölln and the Berlin Town Hall might have helped him with the Reichstag. The interrogating officers had pointed their investigations in this direction. But meanwhile things of a quite different nature had happened.

Shortly after my arrival in the burning Reichstag, the National Socialist elite had arrived. Hitler and Goebbels had driven up in their large cars; Göring . . . and Helldorf [the Berlin SA commander] arrived. . . .

One of Hitler's chief adjutants came to look for me in the maze of corridors, now alive with the fire brigade and the police. He passed me Göring's order to appear in the select circle. On a balcony jutting out into the Chamber, Hitler and his trusty followers were assembled. Hitler stood leaning his arms on the stone parapet of the balcony and stared silently into the red sea of flames. The first hysterics were already over. As I entered, Göring came towards me. His voice was heavy with the emotion of the dramatic moment: 'This is the beginning of the Communist revolt, they will start their attack now! Not a moment must be lost!'

Göring could not continue. Hitler turned to the assembled company. Now I saw that his face was purple with agitation and with the heat gathering in the dome. He shouted uncontrollably, as I had never seen him do before, as if he was going to burst: 'There will be no mercy now. Anyone who stands in our way will be cut down. The German people will not tolerate leniency. Every Communist official will be shot where he is found. The Communist deputies must be hanged this very night. Everybody in league with the Communists must be arrested. There will no longer be any leniency for Social Democrats either.'

I reported on the results of the first interrogations of Marinus van der Lubbe—that in my opinion he was a maniac. But with this opinion I had come to the wrong man; Hitler ridiculed my childish view: 'That is something really cunning, prepared a long time ago. The criminals have thought all this out beautifully; but they've miscalculated, haven't they, Comrades! These gangsters have no idea to what extent the people are on our side. They don't hear the rejoicing of the crowds in their rat holes, from which they now want to emerge', and so it went on.

Jeremy Noakes and Geoffrey Pridham, eds., *Documents on Nazism, 1919–1945*. New York: Viking Press, 1975, pp. 171–72.

Document 17: The Attempted National Boycott of the Jews

Hitler's first major move against the Jews occurred less than two months after he became chancellor. Using the trumped up excuse that "international Jewry" had made false accusations against the "virtuous" Nazis, he and his rabidly anti-Semitic henchman, Julius Streicher, plotted a national boycott against Jewish shops, businesses, and professional people. Streicher's official order for implementing the boycott, dated March 29, 1933, is presented here. To the Nazis' dismay, however, the move was unpopular with many Germans, who insisted on shopping wherever they pleased; disputes arose over whether certain shops were actually Jewish-owned. The boycott, which went into effect on April 1, was a dismal failure, and the government had to rescind the order the next day.

1. Action committees in every local branch and subdivision of the NSDAP [Nazi Party] organization are to be formed for putting into effect the planned boycott of Jewish shops, Jewish goods, Jewish doctors and Jewish lawyers. The action committees are responsible for making sure that the boycott affects those who are guilty and not those who are innocent.

2. The action committees are responsible for the maximum protection of all foreigners without regard to confession, background or race. The boycott is purely a defensive measure aimed exclusively against German Jewry.

3. The action committees must at once popularize the boycott by means of propaganda and enlightenment. The principle is: No German must any longer buy from a Jew or let him and his backers promote their goods. The boycott must be general. It must be supported by the whole German people and must hit Jewry in its most sensitive place. . . .

8. The boycott must be coordinated and set in motion everywhere at the same time, so that all preparations must be carried out immediately. Orders are being sent to the SA and SS so that from the moment of the boycott the population will be warned by guards not to enter Jewish shops. The start of the boycott is to be announced by posters, through the press and leaflets, etc. The boycott will commence on Saturday, 1 April on the stroke of 10 o'clock. It will be continued until an order comes from the Party leadership for it to stop.

9. The action committees are to organize tens of thousands of mass meetings, which are to extend to the smallest villages for the purpose of demanding that in all professions the number of Jews shall correspond respectively to their proportion of the whole German population. To increase the impact made by this action, this demand is limited first of all to three fields: (a) attendance at German schools and universities; (b) the medical profession; (c) the legal profession.

Jeremy Noakes and Geoffrey Pridham, eds., *Nazism, 1919–1945, Vol. 2: State, Economy and Society, 1933–1939, A Documentary Reader.* Exeter, Eng.: University of Exeter, 1984, p. 524.

Document 18: Hitler Justifies the Enabling Act

This is an excerpt from a speech Hitler gave on April 5, 1933, in which he attempted to justify passage of the Enabling Act on March 23. That act transferred all legislative powers from the Reichstag to the Nazi regime, thereby expanding and solidifying Hitler's power. Here, he assures the German people that they will continue to have a voice in decid-

ing their own destiny, a pledge that history would quickly prove as false as other Nazi promises of justice and fair play.

Owing to the Enabling Law the work of the deliverance of the German people has been freed and released for the first time from the party views and considerations of our former representative assembly. With its assistance we shall now be able to do what, after clear-sighted examination and dispassionate consideration, appears necessary for the future of the nation. The purely legislative previous conditions necessary for this have been provided. But it is also necessary that the people itself should take an active part in this action. The nation must not imagine that, because the Reichstag can no more restrict our decisions, the nation itself no longer needs to take part in the shaping of our destiny. On the contrary, we wish that the German people at this very time should concentrate once more and co-operate actively in support of the Government. The result must be that when we appeal to the nation once more, in four years' time, we shall not appeal to men who have been asleep, but will find ourselves faced by a nation that has finally awakened in the course of these years from its parliamentary trance and has realized the knowledge necessary to understand the eternal conditions of human existence.

Norman H. Baynes, ed., *The Speeches of Adolf Hitler, April 1922–August 1939.* 2 vols. New York: Howard Fertig, 1969, vol. 1, p. 427.

Document 19: A German Aristocrat Bemoans the Nazification of the Upper Classes

Erich Ebermayer, a German aristocrat who opposed all that the Nazis stood for, composed this part of his memoirs on May 9, 1933, a few months after Hitler came to power. Unlike many upper-class Germans who supported Hitler because they thought he might restore the old monarchy, Ebermayer saw the führer for the power-hungry dictator that he was. This melancholy tract reveals how dismayed Ebermayer, his mother, and other like-minded aristocrats were at the loss of old friendships and the breakdown of traditional German society in the wake of the growing popularity of the Nazi regime.

One becomes ever more lonely.

Everywhere friends declare their faith in Adolf Hitler. It is as if an airless stratum surrounds us few who remain unable to make such avowals.

Of my young friends it is the best who now radically proclaim their allegiance to National Socialism. This is not to be denied.

The two sons of the Leipzig art historian Wilhelm Pinder, two excellent young men of the first-class breed—the younger one had closely attached himself to me for a long time—are downright possessed Nazis. One can't even discuss things with them, because they believe. And there are no rational arguments against faith. They run around in the plain Hitler Youth uniform, radiant with happiness and pride. When today . . . I made an attempt to have a talk with Eberhard Pinder, daring to express—how weak and powerless one already is vis-à-vis this triumphant youth!—the idea that perhaps our whole ancient culture, the patrimony of the intellectual and artistic values of the last four hundred years, would go under in the vortex of our time. And the triumphant little gentleman, naïvely and a little bit shamelessly, said: "And what if it does, my dear friend! This culture is really not so important! According to the word of the Führer, the Thousand-Year Reich is already arising. And it will create a new culture for itself!"

My mother experienced something similar. She already had a radical falling out over politics with Baroness Richthofen, one of her closest friends. It was over the new flag. Frau von Richthofen demanded that she should now at last get a swastika flag made for herself. Mother indignantly rejected the idea, saying she would never think of such a thing, and if anybody forced her she would hang out "this rag from the toilet window." A beautiful, clear, and German language . . . otherwise not customary among the ladies of high society. . . . The Baroness then took offense with an audible noise, and the old friendship broke up. Mother suffers from it more than she admits.

George L. Mosse, *Nazi Culture: Intellectual, Cultural, and Social Life in the Third Reich*. New York: Grosset and Dunlap, 1966, pp. 385–86.

Document 20: The Nazis Burn "Un-German" Books

One of the chief methods the Nazis employed in reshaping German culture to fit the mold approved by Hitler and his assistants was the banning and burning of "dangerous," "decadent" literature. This article from the May 12, 1933, issue of a German newspaper describes the large-scale book-burning ceremonies staged the night before by students of the University of Berlin and other German universities.

Berlin, May 11, 1933. On Wednesday night the Student Activist Committee, "Against the un-German Spirit," staged a rally with the slogan "The German spirit awakes!" It culminated at midnight with the symbolic act of burning some 20,000 politically and morally un-German books. . . .

The burning of seditious writings was the focal point of these midnight ceremonies in all German university communities. The books were committed to the flames with the following incantations:

1st Crier: Down with class struggle and materialism! In the name of national cohesiveness and idealistic life, I commit the writings of [Karl] Marx and [Karl] Kautsky to the flames.

2d Crier: Down with decadence and moral decay! In the name of discipline and morality in family and state, I commit the writings of Heinrich Mann, Ernst Gläser, and Erich Kästner to the flames. [All were writers critical of superpatriotism.]

3d Crier: Down with turncoats and political traitors! In the name of dedication to the people and the state, I commit the writings of Friedrich Wilhelm Förster to the flames. [An anti-Prussian pacifist.]

4th Crier: Down with corruptive overemphasis of baser impulses! In the name of the nobility of the human soul, I commit the writings of Sigmund Freud [the famous psychoanalyst] to the flames.

5th Crier: Down with the falsification of our history and the degradation of its great personalities! In the name of reverence for our great past, I commit the works of Emil Ludwig and Werner Hegemann to the flames. [Both were writers of popularized pseudo-psychological history.]

6th Crier: Down with antipopular journalism in the democratic-Jewish style! In the name of responsible cooperation of the press in the work of national reconstruction, I commit the writings of Theodor Wolff and Georg Bernhard to the flames. [Editors of the liberal *Berliner Tageblatt* and *Vossische Zeitung*.]

7th Crier: Down with literary betrayal of the soldiers of the World War! In the name of educating our people in the spirit of valor, I commit the writings of Erich Maria Remarque to the flames. [Author of *All Quiet on the Western Front*.]

8th Crier: Down with degradation of the German language! In the name of fostering this precious possession of our people, I commit the writings of Alfred Kerr to the flames. [An expressionist literary critic.]

9th Crier: Down with impudence and pretension! In the name of honor and reverence for the immortal spirit of the German people may the flames also devour the writings of [Kurt] Tucholsky and [Carl von] Ossietzky! [Both were editors of the pacifist *Weltbühne*. Ossietzky received the Nobel Peace Prize in 1935 while a prisoner at Dachau concentration camp; later he was murdered there.]

Henry C. Meyer, ed., *The Long Generation: Germany from Empire to Ruin, 1913–1945*. New York: Walker and Company, 1973, pp. 220–21.

Document 21: Forced Sterilization of "Inferior" Persons

Hitler and other leading Nazis were intent on ridding German society of Minderwertigen, *or "inferiors." In their view, these included not only Jews and other supposedly worthless races, but also handicapped people, those suffering from depression, alcoholics, prostitutes, and many others that did not fit the Nazi Aryan ideal. On July 14, 1933, the regime passed the Law for the Prevention of Hereditarily Diseased Offspring, authorizing the forced sterilization of anyone the government deemed inferior. Some of the law's key provisions are listed here.*

1. (i) Anyone who has a hereditary illness can be rendered sterile by a surgical operation if, according to the experience of medical science, there is a strong probability that his/her offspring will suffer from serious hereditary defects of a physical or mental nature. (ii) Anyone is hereditarily ill within the meaning of this law who suffers from one of the following illnesses: (*a*) Congenital feeble-mindedness. (*b*) Schizophrenia. (*c*) Manic depression. (*d*) Hereditary epilepsy. (*e*) Huntington's chorea. (*f*) Hereditary blindness. (*g*) Hereditary deafness. (*h*) Serious physical deformities. (iii) In addition, anyone who suffers from chronic alcoholism can be sterilized.

2. An application for sterilization can legitimately be made by the person to be sterilized. In the case of persons who are either not legally responsible or have been certified because of mental deficiency or have not yet reached their nineteenth birthday, the legal guardian is so entitled.

3. Sterilization can also be requested by (i) The Medical Officer. (ii) In the case of inmates of hospitals, or institutions of the incurably ill or penal institutions, the director. . . .

5. The responsibility for the decision lies with the Hereditary Health Court which has jurisdiction over the district where the person to be sterilized officially resides.

6. The Hereditary Health Court is to be connected administratively to the Magistrates Court (*Amtsgericht*). It consists of a magistrate as chairman, a medical officer, and a further physician qualified to practise within the German Reich who is particularly familiar with the theory of hereditary health. . . .

12. If the Court had decided finally in favour of sterilization, the sterilization must be carried out even against the wishes of the person to be sterilized unless that person was solely responsible for the application. The medical officer is responsible for requesting the necessary measures to be taken by the police authority. In so far as other measures prove insufficient the use of force is permissible.

Reasons for the Law: Since the National Uprising [Nazi assump-

tion of power] public opinion has become increasingly preoccupied with questions of population policy and the continuing decline in the birthrate. However, it is not only the decline in population which is the cause of serious concern but equally the
increasingly evident genetic make-up of our people. Whereas the
hereditarily healthy families have for the most part adopted a policy of having only one or two children, countless numbers of inferiors and those suffering from hereditary ailments are reproducing
unrestrainedly while their sick and asocial offspring are a burden
on the community.

Jeremy Noakes and Geoffrey Pridham, eds., *Nazism, 1919–1945, Vol. 2: State, Economy and Society, 1933–1939, A Documentary Reader.* Exeter, Eng.: University of Exeter, 1984, pp. 457–58.

Document 22: An American Ponders Hitler's Success

William L. Shirer, author of the renowned Rise and Fall of the Third
Reich, *was an American news correspondent assigned to Berlin in 1934.
On September 5 of that year, he witnessed one of Hitler's colorful mass
rallies and made the following entry in his journal, which was later published (in 1941) to great acclaim as* Berlin Diary. *According to Shirer,
one of the reasons Hitler was so successful in swaying the German people
was his ability to stage a thrilling public spectacle.*

I'm beginning to comprehend, I think, some of the reasons for
Hitler's astounding success. Borrowing a chapter from the Roman
church, he is restoring pageantry and colour and mysticism to the
drab lives of twentieth-century Germans. This morning's opening
meeting in the Luitpold Hall on the outskirts of Nuremberg was
more than a gorgeous show; it also had something of the mysticism and religious fervour of an Easter or Christmas Mass in a
great Gothic cathedral. The hall was a sea of brightly coloured
flags. Even Hitler's arrival was made dramatic. The band stopped
playing. There was a hush over the thirty thousand people packed
in the hall. Then the band struck up the *Badenweiler March*, a very
catchy tune, and used only, I'm told, when Hitler makes his big entries. Hitler appeared in the back of the auditorium, and followed
by his aides, Göring, Goebbels, Hess, Himmler, and the others, he
strode slowly down the long centre aisle while thirty thousand
hands were raised in salute. It is a ritual, the old-timers say, which
is always followed. Then an immense symphony orchestra played
Beethoven's *Egmont* Overture. Great Klieg lights played on the
stage, where Hitler sat surrounded by a hundred party officials and
officers of the army and navy. Behind them the "blood flag," the

one carried down the streets of Munich in the ill-fated putsch [of 1923]. Behind this, four or five hundred S.A. standards. When the music was over, Rudolf Hess, Hitler's closest confidant, rose and slowly read the names of the Nazi "martyrs"—brown-shirts who had been killed in the struggle for power—a roll-call of the dead, and the thirty thousand seemed very moved.

In such an atmosphere no wonder, then, that every word dropped by Hitler seemed like an inspired Word from on high. Man's—or at least the German's—critical faculty is swept away at such moments, and every lie pronounced is accepted as high truth itself. It was while the crowd—all Nazi officials—were in this mood that the Führer's proclamation was sprung on them. He did not read it himself. It was read by *Gauleiter* Wagner of Bavaria, who, curiously, has a voice and manner of speaking so like Hitler's that some of the correspondents who were listening back at the hotel on the radio thought it was Hitler.

As to the proclamation, it contained such statements as these, all wildly applauded as if they were new truths: "The German form of life is definitely determined for the next thousand years. For us, the nervous nineteenth century has finally ended. There will be no revolution in Germany for the next one thousand years!"

Or: "Germany has done everything possible to assure world peace. If war comes to Europe it will come only because of Communist chaos." Later . . . he added: "Only brainless dwarfs cannot realize that Germany has been the breakwater against Communist floods which would have drowned Europe and its culture."

Hitler also referred to the fight now going on against his attempt to Nazify the Protestant church. "I am striving to unify it. I am convinced that [Protestant religious reformer Martin] Luther would have done the same and would have thought of unified Germany first and last."

William L. Shirer, *Berlin Diary: The Journal of a Foreign Correspondent, 1934–1941*. New York: Knopf, 1941, pp. 18–20.

Document 23: Hitler's Four-Year Economic Plan

Following are excerpts from Hitler's August 1936 memorandum outlining the economic goals he expected the country to meet in the succeeding four years. Note that he focuses mainly on three broad areas: military rearmament, which will give Germany the capacity to wage war; stepped-up production of raw materials, an essential contribution to that capacity; and an effort to keep Jewish "criminals" from sinking the nation any further into debt.

Germany's defensive capacity is based upon several factors. I would give pride of place to the intrinsic value of the German people *per se*. A German people with an impeccable political leadership, a firm ideology and a thorough military organization certainly constitutes the most valuable factor of resistance which the world of today can possess. Political leadership is ensured by the National Socialist Party; ideological solidarity has since the victory of National Socialism, been introduced to a degree that had never previously been attained. It must be constantly deepened and hardened on the basis of this concept. This is the aim of the National Socialist education of our people.

Military development is to be effected through the new Army. *The extent and pace of the military development of our resources cannot be made too large or too rapid!* It is a capital error to think that there can be any argument on these points or any comparison with other vital necessities. However much the general pattern of life of a people ought to be a balanced one, it is nonetheless imperative that at particular times certain disturbances of the balance, to the detriment of other, less vital, tasks, must be adopted. *If we do not succeed in developing the German Wehrmacht* [armed forces] *within the shortest possible time into the first Army in the world, in training, in the raising of units, in armaments, and, above all, in spiritual education as well, Germany will be lost!* The principle applies here that the omissions of peacetime months cannot be made good in centuries. . . .

We are overpopulated and cannot feed ourselves from our own resources. . . .

The final solution lies in extending the living space of our people and/or the sources of its raw materials and foodstuffs. It is the task of the political leadership one day to solve this problem.

The temporary easing can only be brought about within the framework of our present economy. In this connection, the following is to be noted: . . .

It is not sufficient merely to draw up, from time to time, raw material or foreign exchange balances, or to talk about the preparation of a war economy in time of peace; on the contrary, it is essential to ensure peacetime food supplies and above all those means for the conduct of a war which it is possible to make sure of by human energy and activity. And I therefore draw up the following programme for a final solution of our vital needs:

1. Like the military and political rearmament and mobilization of our people, there must also be an economic one, and this must be effected in the same tempo, with the same determination, and,

if need be, with the same ruthlessness as well. . . .

2. For this purpose, in every sphere where it is possible to satisfy our needs through German production, foreign exchange must be saved in order that it can be applied to those requirements which can under no circumstances be supplied *except* by imports.

3. Accordingly, German fuel production must now be stepped up with the utmost speed and be brought to final completion within eighteen months. This task must be attacked and carried out with the same determination as the waging of war; for on its solution depends the conduct of the future war and not on the laying in of stocks of petroleum.

4. It is equally urgent that the mass production of synthetic rubber should be organized and secured. . . .

5. The question of the cost of these raw materials is quite irrelevant, since it is in any case better for us to produce in Germany dearer tires which we can use, than for us to sell theoretically cheap tires for which, however, the Ministry of Economics can allocate no foreign exchange and which, consequently, cannot be produced for lack of raw materials and consequently cannot be used at all. . . .

It is further necessary to increase the German production of iron to the utmost. . . .

It is further necessary to prohibit forthwith the distillation of alcohol from potatoes. Fuel must be obtained from the ground and not from potatoes. Instead, it is our duty to use any arable land that may become available, either for human or animal foodstuffs or for the cultivation of fibrous products. . . .

It is further necessary to increase Germany's output of other ores, *regardless of cost*, and in particular to increase the production of light metals to the utmost in order thereby to produce a substitute for certain other metals. . . .

In short: I consider it necessary that now, with iron determination, 100 percent self-sufficiency should be attained in all those spheres where it is feasible, and not only should the national requirements in these most important raw materials be made independent of other countries but that we should also thus save the foreign exchange which in peacetime we require for our imports of foodstuffs. *Here I would emphasize that in these tasks I see the only true economic mobilization and not in the throttling of armament industries in peacetime in order to save and stockpile raw materials for war.*

But I further consider it necessary to make an immediate investigation into the outstanding debts in foreign exchange owed to

German business abroad. There is no doubt that the outstanding claims of German business are today quite enormous. Nor is there any doubt that behind this in some cases there lies concealed the contemptible desire to possess, whatever happens, certain reserves abroad which are thus withheld from the grasp of the domestic economy. I regard this as deliberate sabotage of our national self-assertion and of the defence of the Reich, and for this reason I consider it necessary for the Reichstag to pass the following two laws: (1) a law providing the death penalty for economic sabotage, and (2) a law making the whole of Jewry liable for all damage inflicted by individual specimens of this community of criminals upon the German economy, and thus upon the German people. . . .

I thus set the following tasks: (1) The German army must be operational within four years; and (2) the German economy must be fit for war within four years.

Henry C. Meyer, ed., *The Long Generation: Germany from Empire to Ruin, 1913–1945.* New York: Walker and Company, 1973, pp. 246–50.

Document 24: Art Criticism Banned

In the years immediately following the Nazi takeover of Germany, Hitler's propaganda minister, Joseph Goebbels, became increasingly frustrated with art critics. He could not understand why they failed to grasp what was perfectly clear to Hitler and himself, namely that if an artistic work had already been approved by the government, it was thereafter no one's place to criticize it. Fed up, Goebbels issued the following directive banning such criticism on November 27, 1936. From that time on, critics had to be licensed by the government and must "describe" rather than judge art.

In the context of the reconstruction of German cultural life, criticism of the arts is one of the most pressing but also one of the most difficult questions to solve. Since assuming power, I have given German critics four years to conform to National Socialist principles. The increasing number of complaints about criticism, both from the ranks of artists themselves and from other sections of the population, prompted me to summon the critics to a conference. At this conference I gave the German critics the opportunity to discuss in depth with the most prominent German artists the problem of criticism, at the end of which I expounded my own views on criticism in unambiguous terms. . . .

Since the year 1936 did not bring any satisfactory improvement in criticism, I finally forbid from today the continuation of criticism of the arts as hitherto practised.

Criticism of the arts as hitherto practiced had been turned into art judgement in the days of Jewish cultural infiltration, and this was a complete distortion of the term 'criticism'. From today criticism of the arts will be replaced by commentary on the arts. The place of the critic will be taken by the arts editor. Articles on the arts will describe rather than evaluate. They will give the public the opportunity to make their judgement, encourage them to form an opinion about works of art on the basis of their own intellectual and emotional responses.

In taking such an incisive measure I base it on the point of view that only those who have a real understanding of the area they are criticising should criticise. Those who are themselves creatively gifted will be less occupied with criticising and will feel much more the urge towards their own creative achievement. . . . The great critics of the past wanted only to serve art. They were respectful of the achievements of others and did not set themselves up as infallible judges of someone else's work. This was the case up to the Jewish *literati* [intellectuals] from Heinrich Heine to Kerr.

Future art reports require respect for artistic creation and achievement. They demand culture, tact, a proper attitude to and respect of artistic temperament. In the future the only ones able to discuss artistic works will be editors who undertake such tasks with honesty and in the spirit of National Socialism. Therefore we demand, as by right, that the art reviews should not be anonymous.

Therefore I order:

In the future, all art discussion must be signed fully by the writer. The office of the arts editor will need special authorisation in the professional register of the press, and this will depend on evidence of a really extensive background in the area of the particular art form with which the editor in question will be dealing. Since involvement with artistic works needs a certain maturity and experience of life, art editors must be at least thirty years old before they can be authorised to enter this branch of the German press.

David Welch, *The Third Reich: Politics and Propaganda*. London: Routledge, 1993, pp. 168–69.

Document 25: Hitler Celebrates Exclusion of Jews from Cultural Life

After Hitler came to power, Jews were increasingly driven out of cultural endeavors such as book publishing, newspaper editing, the arts, theater, and filmmaking. In the excerpt from a January 30, 1937, speech, Hitler claims that this exclusionary policy has greatly benefited Germany.

Consider this fact alone: our entire German educational system, including the Press, the theatre, films, literature, &c., is to-day conducted and controlled exclusively by our German fellow-countrymen. How often were we not told in the past that the removal of Jews from these institutions must lead to their collapse or to sterilization! And what has actually happened? In all these spheres we are experiencing a vast flowering of cultural and artistic life. Our films are better than ever before. The productions in our leading theatres stand in lonely pre-eminence over those of the whole world. Our Press has become a mighty instrument in the service of our people's self-preservation and contributes to strengthen the nation. German Science pursues its successful activity, while in architecture mighty evidences of our creative purpose will in the future bear witness to the achievements of this new age. There has been effected an unexampled immunization of the German people against all the disintegrating tendencies from which another world is forced to suffer.

Norman H. Baynes, ed., *The Speeches of Adolf Hitler, April 1922–August 1939.* 2 vols. New York: Howard Fertig, 1969, vol. 1, p. 734.

Document 26: Hitler Youth: Nazism's Hope for the Future

Hitler fully appreciated the importance of indoctrinating young Germans into militant Nazism as a way of ensuring continuing support for his reich from one generation to the next. This excerpt comes from a pep talk he gave to a contingent of Hitler Youth on September 11, 1937, in which he told the enraptured young people that in following him they were fulfilling the grand "dream" of the German people.

The youth which to-day is growing up will be educated not as in the past for enjoyment, but for hardships and for sacrifices, and above all it will be trained to discipline the body. We believe that, if the body has not health and large capacities of resistance, in the long run even a healthy mind cannot control the destinies of the nation. . . .

Over and over again it is the same petition that we would make to Providence—we have only one prayer: that our people may be sound and true; we would that Providence should teach our people the meaning of true freedom, that Providence should keep alive in it its love of honour. We would not ask that we should receive freedom as a gift: we would ask only that we may be a people of character that we may be ready at any time to conquer for ourselves that position in the world which a free people needs.

We do not wish for any present, we want only the grace that we may be permitted to play our part in an honourable struggle. Then it may be left to Providence to determine from time to time whether this people has earned its life or not. And when I look on you I know the answer: this people will in the future, as in the past, earn its freedom and with freedom its honour and its life.

You are now the youth of the German State. But never shall there be any other leadership of this youth than that which has come from the National Socialist idea, the National Socialist Movement. To-day you have already become an inseparable part of this idea and of this Movement. The Movement has formed you, from the Movement you have received your uniform, and in the service of the Movement you will remain your whole life through. That is the wonderful thing: in you the first link in the chain of our people's education is forged: with you the chain begins, and it will reach its end only when the last German sinks into his grave!

Never in the history of Germany has there been so deep an inner unity in spirit, in the constraint of a single will and in leadership. Many generations that have gone before us have dreamed of such a unity: we are the happy witnesses of the fulfilment of their dream.

Norman H. Baynes, ed., *The Speeches of Adolf Hitler, April 1922–August 1939.* 2 vols. New York: Howard Fertig, 1969, vol. 1, pp. 550–51.

Document 27: Justice in the Third Reich

In 1938, Dr. Franz Gürtner, Hitler's reich minister of justice, composed an essay, excerpted here, which explained how the Nazi regime defined the concept of justice. Gürtner claims that the rule of law is one of the main pillars supporting Nazi Germany, but then admits that in National Socialism's brand of justice, the needs of the state must always come before the needs, and ultimately the rights, of the individual.

It is sometimes said, even by critics usually endeavouring to be objective in their judgments, that National Socialism has abolished law in Germany and has substituted arbitrariness in its place. Those who hold that view must be completely ignorant of the principles maintained by National Socialism and of the conditions actually existing in Germany. The new German State is based upon the axiom that law is one of the main pillars supporting the solidarity of the nation and the political structure representing it. More than that, a conception of law deeply rooted in the nation's life and recognised as binding by every citizen is the foundation of the country's entire civilisation.

Seeing that law and justice are at the root of every activity carried on in the new Germany, it follows that the National Socialist State is a constitutional State in the best sense of the term. That term, however, must not be interpreted in accordance with the doctrine which demands that the interests of the individual must be regarded as the principal subject-matter of all legislation and that a comprehensive system of controls must be established to protect the individual against an excess of interference on the part of the State. That doctrine is no longer upheld in Germany. National Socialism looks upon the community of the nation as an organisation which has its own rights and duties and whose interests come before those of the individual. When we speak of the nation, we do not confine ourselves to the generation to which we happen to belong, but extend that term so as to comprise the sum total of the generations that have preceded us and those that will succeed us. This view has found expression in the National Socialist doctrine asserting that "the needs of the commonwealth take precedence of those of the individual." It dominates National Socialist policy, and its natural corollary is that the rights of the individual must be subordinated to those of the community. The protection enjoyed by individuals is not based on the assumption that their particular rights are sacrosanct and inviolable, but rather on the fact that all of them are regarded as valuable members of the national community, and therefore deserve protection. The reason, therefore, why the National Socialist State can justly claim to be called a constitutional State is that its laws are intended to promote the interests of the community, that—in pursuance of the confidence that forms a connecting link between the rulers and the ruled—every citizen can rest assured that his claim to justice will be satisfied, and that everyone who loyally fulfils his duties towards the community can look forward to receiving an equal measure of loyalty from the organs of the State. The political and economic development of the past four years has convincingly shown that we are doing our utmost to provide a secure basis of existence for everyone. Everywhere, waste land is turned into productive soil. Millions of citizens who had been haunted by the spectre of unemployment for months and even years, have been supplied with work. Unceasing endeavours are made by the National Socialist Government to strengthen the defence forces of the country and thus to safeguard the life and work of every citizen.

Leading Members of Nazi Party and German State, *Germany Speaks*. London: Thornton Butterworth, 1938, pp. 79–81.

Document 28: The Munich Agreement Appeases Hitler

On September 29, 1938, the most powerful European leaders met in Munich and agreed to give in to Hitler's demand that Czechoslovakia's Sudetenland region be ceded to Germany. These diplomats included, in addition to Hitler himself, Italy's Benito Mussolini, British prime minister Neville Chamberlain, and French premier Édouard Daladier. The agreement, reproduced here, provided for the evacuation of Czech troops and personnel from the disputed area and the redrawing of Czechoslovakia's borders by an international commission. Because the Czechs had no real say in the matter and also because the Allies appeared to be "appeasing" the Nazi dictator, the agreement was later severely criticized.

Germany, the United Kingdom, France, and Italy, taking into consideration the agreement, which has been already reached in principle for the cession to Germany of the Sudeten German territory, have agreed on the following terms and conditions governing the said cession and the measures consequent thereon, and by this agreement they each hold themselves responsible for the steps necessary to secure its fulfillment.

1) The evacuation will begin on October 1st.

2) The United Kingdom, France, and Italy agree that the evacuation of the territory shall be completed by October 10th, without any existing installations having been destroyed, and that the Czechoslovak Government will be held responsible for carrying out the evacuation without damage to the said installations.

3) The conditions governing the evacuation will be laid down in detail by an international commission composed of representatives of Germany, the United Kingdom, France, Italy, and Czechoslovakia.

4) The occupation by stages of the predominantly German territory by German troops will begin on October 1st. The four territories marked on the attached map will be occupied by German troops in the following order: the territory marked number I on the 1st and 2d of October, the territory marked number II on the 2d and 3d of October, the territory marked number III on the 3d, 4th, and 5th of October, the territory marked number IV on the 6th and 7th of October. The remaining territory of preponderantly German character will be ascertained by the aforesaid international commission forthwith and be occupied by German troops by the 10th of October.

5) The international commission referred to in paragraph 3) will determine the territories in which a plebiscite is to be held.

These territories will be occupied by international bodies until the plebiscite has been completed. The same commission will fix the conditions in which the plebiscite is to be held, taking as a basis the conditions of the Saar plebiscite. The commission will also fix a date, not later than the end of November, on which the plebiscite will be held.

6) The final determination of the frontiers will be carried out by the international commission. This commission will also be entitled to recommend to the four Powers, Germany, the United Kingdom, France, and Italy, in certain exceptional cases, minor modifications in the strictly ethnographical determination of the zones which are to be transferred without plebiscite.

7) There will be a right of option into and out of the transferred territories, the option to be exercised within 6 months from the date of this agreement. A German-Czechoslovak commission shall determine the details of the option, consider ways of facilitating the transfer of population and settle questions of principle arising out of the said transfer.

8) The Czechoslovak Government will, within a period of 4 weeks from the date of this agreement, release from their military and police forces any Sudeten Germans who may wish to be released, and the Czechoslovak Government will within the same period release Sudeten German prisoners who are serving terms of imprisonment for political offenses.

ADOLF HITLER
ED. DALADIER
MUSSOLINI
MUNICH, September 29, 1938.   NEVILLE CHAMBERLAIN

Francis L. Loewenheim, ed., *Peace or Appeasement? Hitler, Chamberlain, and the Munich Crisis.* Boston: Houghton Mifflin, 1965, pp. 65–66.

Document 29: Hitler's Grand Plans for European Conquest

On November 23, 1939, shortly after the Nazis' successful conquest of Poland, Hitler summoned the high commanders of his armed forces to a meeting. There, he delivered the incredible speech excerpted below. Many German commanders had been skeptical about the idea of attacking France and other Allied nations on Germany's western front, feeling that widening the war might be too risky. But they now learned that the decision to expand the conflict had already been made. In his combined historical lecture, pep-talk, and egomaniacal tirade, the führer first summed up the arrogant theories and principles behind the rise of Nazism over two decades and then outlined his grand plans to continue that rise by bringing all of Europe under Nazi domination.

The purpose of this conference is to give you an idea of the thoughts which govern my view of future events, and to tell you my decisions. . . . When I started my political work in 1919, my strong belief in final success was based on thorough observation of the events of the day and on a study of the reasons for their occurrence. I never, therefore, lost my faith in the midst of setbacks which were not spared me during my period of struggle. . . . After fifteen years, I arrived at my goal, after hard struggles and many setbacks. When I came to power in 1933, a period of the most difficult struggle lay behind me. Everything existing before that had collapsed. I had to reorganize everything, beginning with the mass of the people and extending it to the armed forces. First internal reorganization, the removal of symptoms of decay and defeatist ideas, education for heroism. In the course of the internal reorganization, I undertook the second task: to release Germany from its international ties. I would like to mention two points in particular: secession from the League of Nations and denunciation of the disarmament conference. It was a hard decision. . . . After that came the order for rearmament. . . . In 1935, the introduction of compulsory military service. After that the militarization of the Rhineland . . . a development considered impossible at that time. . . .

One year later came Austria. . . . It brought about a considerable reinforcement of the Reich. The next step was Bohemia, Moravia and Poland. But this could not be accomplished in one campaign. First of all, the western fortification had to be finished. It was not possible to reach the goal in one go. It was clear to me from the first moment that I could not be satisfied with the Sudeten German territory. That was only a partial solution. The decision to march into Bohemia was made. Then . . . the action against Poland was laid. . . . The pressure of events imposed the decision to fight with Poland first. . . . If the Polish war was won so quickly, it was owing to the superiority of our armed forces. The most glorious event in our history. . . . Now the situation is as follows: Our opponent in the west lies behind his fortifications. There is no possibility of coming to grips with him. The decisive question is: how long can we endure this situation? Russia is at present not dangerous. It is now weakened by many developments. Moreover, we have a Treaty with Russia. Treaties, however, are only kept as long as they serve their purpose. Russia will hold herself to it only so long as Russia herself considers it to be to her benefit. . . .

As the last factor I must in all modesty name my own person: irreplaceable. Neither a military nor a civil person could replace me. Assassination attempts may be repeated. I am convinced of the powers of my intellect and of decision. Wars are always ended only by the destruction of the opponent. Everyone who believes differently is irresponsible. Time is working for our adversaries. Now there is a relationship of forces which can never be more propitious, but can only deteriorate. The enemy will not make peace when the relationship of forces is unfavourable for us. No compromise. Sternness towards ourselves. I shall strike and not capitulate. The fate of the Reich depends on me alone. I shall deal accordingly. . . .

Every hope of compromise is childish: Victory or defeat! The question is not the fate of National Socialist Germany, but who is to dominate Europe in the future.

I ask you to pass on the spirit of determination to the lower echelons.

1. The decision is irrevocable.

2. The only prospect for success lies in the determination of all the armed forces. The spirit of the great men of our history must hearten us all. Fate demands from us no more than from the great men of German history. As long as I live I shall think only of the victory of my people. I shall shrink from nothing and shall destroy everyone who is opposed to me. I have decided to live my life so that when I have to die I can stand unashamed. . . . Only he who struggles with destiny can have a good intuition. In the last years I have experienced many examples of intuition. Even in the present development I see the work of Providence.

If we come through this struggle victoriously—and we shall— our age will enter into the history of our people. I shall stand or fall in this struggle. I shall never survive the defeat of my people. No capitulation to the enemy, no revolution from within.

Jeremy Noakes and Geoffrey Pridham, eds., *Documents on Nazism, 1919–1945*. New York: Viking Press, 1975, pp. 572–75.

Chronology

1889
Adolf Hitler is born the son of a civil servant in the Austrian town of Braunau am Inn.

1908
Hitler journeys to Austria's capital of Vienna, hoping to enroll in the city's prestigious art school; his application is turned down.

1912
Hitler moves to Munich, the chief city of the southern German region of Bavaria; there, he forms the extreme nationalistic and anti-Semitic views that will guide his actions for the rest of his life.

1914
World War I breaks out and Hitler joins the German army.

1919
Having lost the war, Germany is forced to sign the Treaty of Versailles, which officially ends the conflict and imposes heavy reparations and territorial cessions on the Germans; Hitler, like many Germans, feels humiliated by the treaty and vows vengeance on the Allies, the victors of the war; that same year, he joins an obscure political group, the German Workers' Party.

1923
Hitler, who has gained dictatorial leadership of the group, now called the National Socialist, or "Nazi," Party, stages the so-called Beer Hall *Putsch*, an attempted coup of the government; the move fails and Hitler is arrested.

1924
At his trial, Hitler is sentenced to jail; in his cell, he begins writing *Mein Kampf* ("My Struggle"), a book that soon becomes the Nazi Bible.

1925–1926
Mein Kampf is published; Hitler, paroled from prison, resumes his political activities, this time choosing to work within the German electoral system.

1929

Germany, whose economy had been on the upswing in recent years, is beset by severe economic troubles in the wake of the worldwide Great Depression touched off by the collapse of the American stock market.

1930

The Nazis poll 18 percent of the vote in the national elections, giving them 107 seats in the Reichstag, Germany's parliament.

1932

The Nazis increase their presence in the Reichstag to 230 seats, making them the largest single political party in the nation.

1933

January—German president Paul von Hindenburg appoints Hitler chancellor of Germany.

February—A Dutch communist sets the Reichstag building on fire; fearing a larger conspiracy, Hindenburg suspends freedom of speech and press, thereby allowing the Nazis to consolidate dictatorial power more easily.

March—The Nazis ram the Enabling Act through the Reichstag, suspending the constitution and giving Hitler full dictatorial powers; this marks the birth of the so-called Third Reich, the German empire Hitler claims will last a thousand years.

1934

On the night of June 30, Hitler purges his own party of potential troublemakers by ordering the arrest and execution of the leaders of his SA, or storm troopers, in what becomes known as the "Night of the Long Knives"; the SA is largely superseded by another elite paramilitary group, the SS.

1936

Summer—Germany hosts the Olympic Games, and Hitler takes advantage of the opportunity to show the world the supposed superiority of his "Aryan" athletes.

August—Hitler orders implementation of a four-year economic plan that will give Germany the ability to wage a large-scale war.

October—Hitler and Italy's fascist dictator, Benito Mussolini, sign a pact, creating the so-called Berlin-Rome Axis.

1938

March—The Nazis march into and take control of Austria, fulfilling Hitler's longtime dream of *Anschluss*, the reunification of Germany and Austria.

September—As a result of "appeasement" policy by the Allies, Germany gains the Sudetenland, the northernmost region of Czechoslovakia.

November—The Nazis attack and pillage Jewish shops and businesses all over Germany in what comes to be known as the "Night of the Broken Glass."

1939

August—Hitler and Soviet leader Joseph Stalin sign a nonaggression pact, sealing Poland's fate.

September—Germany invades Poland, initiating World War II in Europe.

1945

On April 30, with Germany in ruins and the Soviets and Americans closing in on Berlin, Hitler takes his own life; German armies across Europe soon surrender, ending the most devastating armed conflict in human history.

For Further Research

Collections of Original Documents Pertaining to the Rise of Nazi Germany

Norman H. Baynes, ed., *The Speeches of Adolf Hitler, April 1922–August 1939*. 2 vols. New York: Howard Fertig, 1969.

Adolf Hitler, *Mein Kampf.* Trans. Ralph Manheim. Boston: Houghton Mifflin, 1971.

Leading Members of Nazi Party and German State, *Germany Speaks.* London: Thornton Butterworth, 1938.

Francis L. Loewenheim, ed., *Peace or Appeasement? Hitler, Chamberlain, and the Munich Crisis.* Boston: Houghton Mifflin, 1965.

Henry C. Meyer, ed., *The Long Generation: Germany from Empire to Ruin, 1913–1945.* New York: Walker and Company, 1973.

Jeremy Noakes and Geoffrey Pridham, eds., *Documents on Nazism, 1919–1945.* New York: Viking Press, 1975.

———, *Nazism, 1919–1945, Vol. 1: The Rise to Power, 1919–1934, A Documentary Reader.* Exeter, Eng.: University of Exeter, 1983.

———, *Nazism, 1919–1945, Vol. 2: State, Economy and Society, 1933–1939, A Documentary Reader.* Exeter, Eng.: University of Exeter, 1984.

Alison Owings, ed., *Frauen: German Women Recall the Third Reich.* New Brunswick, NJ: Rutgers University Press, 1993.

William L. Shirer, *Berlin Diary: The Journal of a Foreign Correspondent, 1934–1941.* New York: Knopf, 1941.

Albert Speer, *Inside the Third Reich.* New York: Macmillan, 1970.

General Histories of Germany

Marshall Dill Jr., *Germany: A Modern History.* Ann Arbor: University of Michigan Press, 1961.

Erich Kahler, *The Germans.* Princeton, NJ: Princeton University Press, 1974.

Koppel S. Pinson, *Modern Germany: Its History and Civilization.* New York: Macmillan, 1966.

A.J. Ryder, *Twentieth-Century Germany: From Bismarck to Brandt.* New York: Columbia University Press, 1973.

Robert-Hermann Tenbrock, *A History of Germany.* Trans. Paul J. Dine. London: Longmans, Green, 1969.

Hannah Vogt, *The Burden of Guilt: A Short History of Germany, 1914–1945.* Trans. Herbert Strauss. New York: Oxford University Press, 1964.

Biographies of Adolf Hitler

Elenor H. Ayer, *Adolf Hitler.* San Diego: Lucent Books, 1995.

Joachim C. Fest, *Hitler.* New York: Harcourt Brace Jovanovich, 1974.

Eberhard Jäckel, *Hitler in History.* Hanover, NH: Brandeis University Press, 1984.

William A. Jenks, *Vienna and the Young Hitler.* New York: Columbia University Press, 1960.

John Toland, *Adolf Hitler.* Garden City, NY: Doubleday, 1976.

Studies of Hitler's Rise to Power

William S. Allen, *The Nazi Seizure of Power: The Experience of a Single German Town, 1930–1935.* Chicago: Quadrangle Books, 1965.

Martin Broszat, *Hitler and the Collapse of Weimar Germany.* New York: Berg, 1984.

F.L. Carsten, *The Rise of Fascism.* Berkeley and Los Angeles: University of California Press, 1967.

Robert Cecil, *The Myth of the Master Race: Alfred Rosenberg and Nazi Ideology.* London: B.T. Batsford, 1972.

Eugene Davidson, *The Making of Adolf Hitler: The Birth and Rise of Nazism.* Columbia: University of Missouri Press, 1997.

E.J. Feuchtwanger, *From Weimar to Hitler: Germany, 1918–33.* New York: St. Martin's Press, 1993.

Otis C. Mitchell, *Hitler over Germany: The Establishment of the Nazi Dictatorship (1918–1934).* Philadelphia: Institute for the Study of Human Issues, 1983.

Hans Mommsen, *The Rise and Fall of Weimar Democracy.* Chapel Hill: University of North Carolina Press, 1996.

Stephen H. Roberts, *The House That Hitler Built.* New York: Harper and Brothers, 1938.

Simon Taylor, *The Rise of Hitler: Revolution and Counter-Revolution in Germany, 1918–1933.* New York: Universe Books, 1983.

General Overviews of the Third Reich

Michael Freeman, *Atlas of Nazi Germany*. New York: Macmillan, 1987.

Robert Edwin Herzstein, *Adolf Hitler and the German Trauma, 1913–1945: An Interpretation of the Nazi Phenomenon*. New York: G.P. Putnam's Sons, 1974.

Arnold P. Rubin, *The Evil That Men Do: The Story of the Nazis*. New York: Bantam Books, 1979.

William L. Shirer, *The Rise and Fall of the Third Reich: A History of Nazi Germany*. Greenwich, CT: Fawcett, 1960.

Jackson J. Spielvogel, *Hitler and Nazi Germany: A History*. Englewood Cliffs, NJ: Prentice-Hall, 1996.

Society, Culture, Racism, and Propaganda in the Third Reich

Richard Bessel, ed., *Life in the Third Reich*. New York: Oxford University Press, 1987.

Saul Friedlander, *Nazi Germany and the Jews: The Years of Persecution, 1933–1939, Vol. 1*. New York: HarperCollins, 1997.

Richard Grunberger, *The 12-Year Reich: A Social History of Nazi Germany, 1933–1945*. New York: Holt, Rinehart and Winston, 1971.

Alan Guttmann, *The Olympics: A History of the Modern Games*. Chicago: University of Illinois Press, 1992.

Eileen Hayes, *Children of the Swastika: The Hitler Youth*. Brookfield, CT: Millbrook Press, 1993.

Roger Manvell, *SS and Gestapo: Rule by Terror*. New York: Ballantine Books, 1969.

George L. Mosse, *Nazi Culture: Intellectual, Cultural, and Social Life in the Third Reich*. New York: Grosset and Dunlap, 1966.

Detlev J.K. Peukert, *Inside Nazi Germany: Conformity, Opposition, and Racism in Everyday Life*. New Haven, CT: Yale University Press, 1987.

Abraham Resnick, *The Holocaust*. San Diego: Lucent Books, 1991.

David Welch, *The Third Reich: Politics and Propaganda*. London: Routledge, 1993.

Nazi Germany in the Greater Framework of European and World History

Mark Arnold-Forster, *The World at War*. New York: Stein and Day, 1973.

Edward W. Bennet, *German Rearmament and the West.* Princeton, NJ: Princeton University Press, 1979.

C.E. Black and E.C. Helmreich, *Twentieth Century Europe: A History.* New York: Knopf, 1952.

Crane Brinton et al., *A History of Civilization, 1815 to the Present.* Englewood Cliffs, NJ: Prentice-Hall, 1976.

Winston S. Churchill, *The Gathering Storm.* Boston: Houghton Mifflin, 1948.

Alfons Heck, *The Burden of Hitler's Legacy.* Frederick, CO: Renaissance House, 1988.

John Hiden, *Germany and Europe, 1919–1939.* London: Longman Group, 1978.

Gerrit P. Judd, *A History of Civilization.* New York: Macmillan, 1966.

John L. Snell, *The Outbreak of the Second World War: Design or Blunder?* Boston: D.C. Heath, 1962.

Louis L. Snyder, *The War: A Concise History, 1939–1945.* New York: Dell, 1960.

Gerhard L. Weinberg, *Germany, Hitler, and World War II: Essays in Modern German and World History.* New York: Cambridge University Press, 1995.

Index